WON'T BACK DOWN

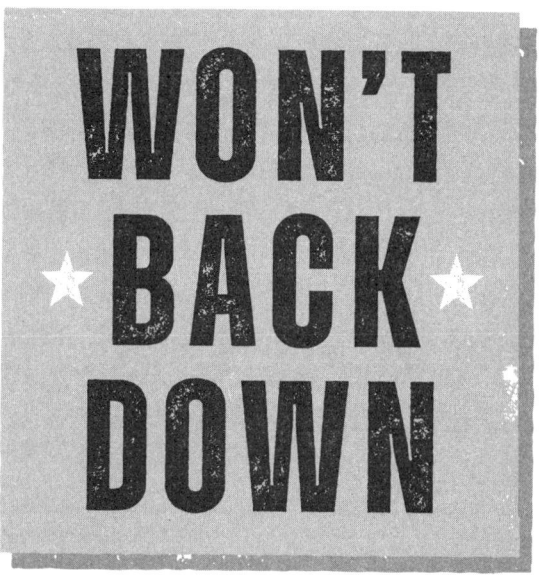

WON'T BACK DOWN

HEARTLAND ROCK AND THE FIGHT FOR AMERICA

ERIN OSMON

W. W. NORTON & COMPANY
Independent Publishers Since 1923

For information about permission to reproduce selections from this book, write to
Permissions, W. W. Norton & Company, Inc., 500 Fifth Avenue, New York, NY 10110

For information about special discounts for bulk purchases, please contact
W. W. Norton Special Sales at specialsales@wwnorton.com or 800-233-4830

Manufacturing by Lakeside Book Company
Book design by Daniel Lagin
Production manager: Lauren Abbate

ISBN 978-1-324-05137-4

W. W. Norton & Company, Inc., 500 Fifth Avenue, New York, NY 10110
www.wwnorton.com

W. W. Norton & Company Ltd., 15 Carlisle Street, London W1D 3BS

Authorized EU representative: EAS, Mustamäe tee 50, 10621 Tallinn, Estonia

10 9 8 7 6 5 4 3 2 1

To the woman I was when I began writing this book,
and to the woman I am today.

CONTENTS

INTRODUCTION

The term "heartland rock" dates to the 1970s when artists such as Bruce Springsteen, Bob Seger, and Jackson Browne crafted roots-driven rock music that spoke of small towns, the working class, the open road, and coming-of-age nostalgia. Songs such as "Factory," "Night Moves," and "Running on Empty" were an antidote to the bombast and individualism of the decade as they guided rock 'n' roll back to its simpler and more conscience-driven moments.

Heartland rock's songs were built with minimal chord changes and usually spare but powerful drumming. Its lyrics were often highly literate, earnest, and plain spoken. The music frequently featured sketches of common people and their trials and aspirations, especially as the recession, deindustrialization, and high inflation of the 1980s took hold. Choruses were anthemic and ripe for singalongs. Its artists didn't have to be from the American heartland, though many of them were. Instead, heartland rock musicians drew from the spirit, principles, and ideals of the heartland in their lyrical depictions of working people, and their families and lovers, stretching from small-town New Jersey to the farms of California's Central Valley. Heartland rock was populist music for the people.

The lyrics often focused on factory workers, farmers, the American dream, underdogs, childhood nostalgia, or a fondness for and dedication to a region that is overlooked and underestimated. The roots of heartland rock may be traced to singer-songwriters such as Woody Guthrie and Bob Dylan, and '60s rock songs such as "Fortunate Son" by Creedence Clearwater Revival, "The Weight" by the Band, and "Everybody Knows This Is Nowhere" by Neil Young—compositions with lyrics that detail the struggles of underdogs and the allure of home. Throughout the 1980s, when heartland rock rose to its commercial peak and then fell, most of its artists took anticorporate, anti-racist, or anti–Ronald Reagan political positions, even if they claimed to be nonpolitical.

Heartland rock as a genre was invented by media outside of the heartland. A generous person may view the term as a badge of honor—a way to commemorate a group of artists who worked outside of corporate pop music's trends and garnered acclaim. A more cynical person may say that the term was a product of college-educated metropolitan writers who couldn't tell the difference between Michigan and Florida. Most see it somewhere in between. Heartland rock musicians dislike the term—particularly John Mellencamp, who attributes it to lazy journalists—a sentiment similar to those musicians lumped into other made-up genres like alternative rock, yacht rock, and shoegaze.

In its infancy, some journalists and fans called this music "working-class rock." Most consider the two terms interchangeable. Early examples of these terms' use sprang up on the coasts. Writing for the *Los Angeles Times* in October 1977, the critic Richard Cromelin described the work of an up-and-coming songwriter named Don Harrison—leader of the five-piece Don Harrison Band, who worshipped at the altar of CCR—as "heartland rock 'n' roll" that, like Bob Seger and Bruce Springsteen, aimed to bring substance back to rock music. In an April 1978 issue of *New York Rocker*, Howie Klein described the Irish band Boomtown Rats as "working-class rock."

An early prerequisite of heartland rock was that it had to *rock*. Think the garage-rock rattlers of Bruce Springsteen's *The River*, Tom Petty and Mike Campbell's guitars on *Damn the Torpedoes* and *Hard*

Promises, and John Mellencamp's shotgun snare sound. It wasn't synth-driven pop-rock or wistful singer-songwriter music. As time passed, heartland rock morphed into a form in which synthesizers, introspection, folk instruments, Southern voices, and slower tempos were embraced. Artists such as Bruce Hornsby and Lucinda Williams emerged as its next-generation leaders. Heartland rock became so popular that it also lured its progenitors out from artistic slumps and semiretirement. Neil Young, Robbie Robertson, John Fogerty, and Bob Dylan released heartland rock songs and albums or worked with its younger artists throughout the decade.

Many point to Bruce Springsteen's 1975 album *Born to Run* as heartland rock's first big milestone. With it, a gifted songwriter from an unassuming area, who looked like a regular person and couldn't sing all that well, released a rock album rooted in historical sounds and the Everyman, to widespread acclaim. This may be true, but Bob Seger deserves far more recognition for being a cornerstone in the bridge between populist rock movements. His 1969 scorcher "Ramblin' Gamblin' Man," a song about a destitute loner who spends his life drifting, positioned him well within CCR's populist stratosphere; and Seger's late '70s albums *Stranger in Town* and *Night Moves* helped to carry that sentiment into the 1980s.

Though it was composed of some of the era's biggest rock stars, men whose individual characteristics interlocked to form larger-than-life American avatars, heartland rock also was a collective effort—an implicitly connected scene whose artists were inspired by one another, toured and recorded together, and played benefit concerts together in support of causes they believed in. The "core four" figures of Springsteen, Seger, Petty, and Mellencamp are familiar and important, but this book also examines the lives and work of musicians who never truly broke through to mainstream audiences. As heartland rock has long been considered the domain of white men, I've also sought to highlight the vital contributions of women and people of color.

The point of this book isn't to write biographies of every single artist whose work could possibly be considered heartland rock. The point also isn't to list the minute factual details of every recording or tour. Instead, I've tried to highlight key moments and figures in the heartland rock era to make sense of its development, its style, its social and political significance, and its legacy, and to frame it as an interconnected movement, which it was. In the half century since its rise, heartland rock has become the soundtrack of grocery stores, classic rock radio stations, bowling alleys, and your dad's midsize sedan. It signifies a time and a place in American culture that no longer exists, a fact that's most clear when it is held against the wreckage of President Donald Trump's administration.

Largely due to the reductive sirens of far-right political candidates such as Trump, and his allies and precursors, the left-leaning populist messaging of heartland rock, much like American populist sentiment at large, has experienced a kind of sabotage from which it has never really recovered. Minnesota governor Tim Walz gave a stellar effort to counter this misreading during his bid for the vice presidency in 2024, with his folksy catchphrases, photos of his VG–Bob Seger LPs, and use of Mellencamp's "Small Town" at campaign events. But his defeat seemed to echo what popular culture since 1990 has asked: In a climate of rampant anger, despair, and violence, can the earnestness and unifying sentiments of heartland rock be relevant?

In its day, heartland rock's solidarity with the working class, farmers, and servicemen, and its spirit of Everyman patriotism, continued the messages of Guthrie, Dylan, and CCR in less poetic and more commercial terms. Today, however, its themes have been so misinterpreted and misused that its roots have become a bit obscured. For many, heartland rock and the country musicians who cover it form the soundtrack of insidious white grievances rooted in prejudice, bigotry, and ignorance. This is a shame, but it is also understandable as the ruling class has masterfully driven wedges between populations who could once find common ground, and have made disenfranchised communities in Appalachia and beyond the fall guy for the wealth-obsessed fecklessness of billionaires and their enablers.

As a music journalist and critic who's also a daughter of the heartland—born and raised in Evansville, Indiana, and a longtime resident of Chicago—I have an intimate bond and complicated relationship with this music. It's no secret that us Hoosiers have love-hate responses to Mellencamp and his loud mouth, and there is the idea that heartland rock offers little more than a series of exaggerated caricatures of the Midwest's very real issues. Taken in context, however, there is no other musical movement before or since that has amplified my home and my people in such a relatable and earnest way. I've come to appreciate this as I've interviewed several artists in this book, and studied the details and arc of this movement, over the course of my nearly twenty-year career. I have come to appreciate that my family, my youth, and my American province will endure through heartland rock, and that Tom Petty's fighting spirit from 1989, which became the title of this book, remains a crucial rallying cry for us Americans born without silver spoons.

The Kentucky writer Silas House has posited the idea of "timesickness"—a "longing for the way things used to be in the place where I grew up." If there is anything that punctuates the cultural histories offered in these pages, it is this idea. As a child of the 1980s, I remember when my home state of Indiana was more purple, electing Democratic governors and mayors, and Republican presidents. I remember when Hoosiers could live in community with one another regardless of political affiliation. Heartland rock is the sound of a time when political disagreement didn't separate families and neighbors. It's a sonic reminder of more civil and cooperative days, free from the insidiousness of digital echo chambers, "alternative facts," and exhausting agenda-ridden commentary masquerading as news. Where I grew up, left and right water skis sped alongside one another across Ohio River waters, working together to reach the same destination. I hope this book can be a reminder of that time, a chance to crank up unifying proletarian rock, and turn down our collective existential dread and fear of the "other."

Heartland rock was born of the left end of American populism, and misappropriation of the music remains an anathema to those roots, but its artists didn't shun those who disagreed with them. Instead, they created Farm Aid, where Americans of all stripes could gather, and they rallied in support of veterans and factory workers, many of whom no doubt voted for Reagan. Today, Bruce Springsteen is one of the loudest voices ringing in opposition to Trump's open corruption, and John Mellencamp and Tom Petty's estate have spoken out against Trump as well. Unlike many Americans, Springsteen and Mellencamp have become more progressive and outspoken as septuagenarians. But they continue to live in places where plenty of people voted for Trump. As they did in the '80s, they frequent New Jersey and Indiana diners, bars, and ice cream stands, surrounding themselves with neighbors and kin. They survive as unifying figures for the 99 percent even as they rake in millions and speak out against the administration many working people voted for.

In its day, heartland rock was set against the dramatic developments of Reagan's two terms as president. The story of this music in the 1980s is also the story of Cold War paranoia, labor resistance, embattled farmers, Southern reckoning, technological advancements, national mourning, jingoism, generational change, and cultural appropriation. Heartland rock was as well-meaning and imperfect as the country it was founded in, and it marked both the rebirth and death of mainstream rock as we know it.

CHAPTER 1

1980

RUNNING AGAINST THE WIND

Let's make America great again.

—RONALD REAGAN,
1980 PRESIDENTIAL CAMPAIGN

A t the dawn of a new decade, three heartland rock albums became the soundtrack of America.

Bruce Springsteen's double album *The River*, released in October 1980, was his first to climb to No. 1 on the Billboard Top LPs & Tape chart (later the Billboard 200). It produced a string of enduring singles, including "Hungry Heart" and "Fade Away." Springsteen's tour in support of the album, which ran for 140 dates, crystallized Bruce Springsteen and the E Street Band's reputation as one of America's best live acts.

Tom Petty and the Heartbreakers' *Damn the Torpedoes* had arrived a year earlier, in October of 1979, and spent seven weeks at No. 2 on the same chart. Only Pink Floyd's rock opera *The Wall* performed better, staying at No. 1 for fifteen weeks, until another heartland rock act released an exceptional album.

In April 1980, Bob Seger & the Silver Bullet Band knocked Roger Waters and company out of the top spot with *Against the Wind* and remained at No. 1 for six weeks. They were the only group to reach No. 1 for the first time since the Knack with *Get the Knack* in June of 1979. Legacy bands such as Pink Floyd and Led Zeppelin had dominated in the months leading to Seger's triumph.

This made *Against the Wind* an extraordinary symbol. With the dawn of a new decade came a hunger for a new rock archetype, one that was more relatable and less showy than many bands of the 1970s. American listeners seemed to crave music that was clearsighted and down-to-earth. They were also feeling a bit tender. About 60 percent of *Against the Wind* was composed of mid-tempo ballads—what Seger called "mediums"—his most celebrated musical form.

Throughout 1980, Springsteen, Petty, and Seger's tuneful nostalgia towered in an atmosphere of American uncertainty. Unemployment was growing, nuclear power was ominous, fallout from the Vietnam War rippled, and unions across the country were on the precipice of a strike. Hit singles such as "Hungry Heart," "The River," "Even the Losers," "Refugee," "Fire Lake," and "Against the Wind" demonstrated the return of American greatness in rock music as the nation's collective confidence waned, and they did so without the pompous savior complex exuded by Reagan during his 1980 presidential campaign. In amplifying the struggles and desires of everyday Americans, heartland rock's songs and their writers and performers became unmistakable allies.

Petty and Springsteen didn't win anything, but Bob Seger & the Silver Bullet Band took home the Grammy Award for Best Rock Performance by a Duo or Group with Vocal for the song "Against the Wind" at the Recording Academy's twenty-third annual ceremony, beating Pink Floyd, Blondie, the Pretenders, and Queen. The win was a long time coming. Seger, by then thirty-five years old, had been at it for nearly two decades.

Despite its merits, the success of *Against the Wind* was met with suspicion by some of Seger's longtime fans, particularly those in and

Bob Seger performs in
1979, just before *Against
the Wind* was released.
PHOTO COURTESY
MEDIAPUNCH INC.

from Michigan. Many felt as if they'd spent much of their lives fostering his rise. Seger had played their high school sock hops in the '60s, had gotten his brakes fixed in their uncle's garage, and had stood behind them in line for ice cream. Fifty thousand people bought Seger's first big single "East Side Story," recorded with his second band, the Last Heard. They were the base of support that helped launch his first single for Capitol Records, "Rambin' Gamblin' Man," to No. 17 on the Billboard singles chart. This was another mark of heartland rock—regional loyalty, a sense of ownership, which was reciprocated through its artists' lyrical portraits of home and everyday life.

For some of those who had a vested interest in Seger as an authentic representative of Michigan rock, *Against the Wind*'s success was both a boon and cause for suspicion. The album's moments of mid-tempo tenderness seemed to some like an abrupt turn from the singer's hard-rocking bar-band origins, even though he'd already demonstrated it with "Night Moves" and other songs. As the rock critic Dave Marsh put it in 1980, "Seger spent the past year crafting failureproof songs that are utterly listenable and quite meaningless. His commercial tactics, I suppose, were a triumph. But as music, *Against the Wind* is heartless and mediocre—a lot worse than something like Billy Joel's *Glass Houses*, because at least Joel is trying to expand his identity, is risking something. All that Seger risks here is his credibility, and then accidentally."

Joel had released his own set of heartland-esque tunes in March 1980 with *Glass Houses*, which bore all the markings of a tourist waving at factories, poverty, and rural hardship from the comfort of a Mercedes Benz. Marsh no doubt knew this. If he was giving Joel too much credit—and he was—the writer was also conveying a well-trod cliché related to the rock vs. disco binary that arose in the 1970s and grew more acute when pop music exploded in the 1980s.

At issue, too, was that California soft-rock giants the Eagles loomed large over *Against the Wind*. Glenn Frey, a Michigan native and Seger's longtime friend, contributed backing vocals to the title track and "Fire Lake." Don Henley sang on the latter as well. For the first time, Seger and his manager Edward "Punch" Andrews called on Bill Szymczyk, yet another Michigander who was best known for his work with the Eagles. Regarded as one of the architects of album-oriented rock, Szymczyk helped push the California cowboys into a harder rock direction, but he also aimed for perfection, as heard on *Hotel California*, one of the best-selling rock albums of all time.

Bringing on Szymczyk was in part an act of self-preservation. "This is a true story, I told Springsteen this—I mixed 'Nine Tonight' 151 times, five days a week for three solid weeks. Punch had a real hard on for that song, he loved it, and made us go in and mix it over and over," Seger explained. "And now Szymczyk does all that. And when we cut 'Against the Wind,' 'Her Strut' and 'Betty Lou,' we just went in and cut it. And Szymczyk said, 'Goodbye, I'll call you when the mix is done.' And he mixed it about three or four times and it was perfect because the guy's got such good ears." The result was the cleanest-sounding of all Seger's albums, even *Night Moves* and *Stranger in Town*, the pair of LPs that helped raise his profile on the national stage; and it was a far cry from Seger's early works like *Back in '72*, which sounds as if it was recorded in a dive bar men's room.

As some diehard Seger fans bemoaned the success of *Against the Wind*, the majority embraced it for what it was: a grown-up work born of heartrending perseverance. *Against the Wind* was also ahead of its time. It demonstrated the highly commercial, accessible, slick recording and mixing qualities that would spur the rise and dominance of heartland rock throughout the decade.

The producer Jimmy Iovine demanded perfection of Tom Petty and the Heartbreakers, and John Mellencamp's producer Don Gehman insisted on take after take. Bruce Springsteen's *Born in the USA*, in all of its glorious gloss, redefined populism in music entirely. Bonnie Raitt helped establish the clean, hard-meets-soft mid-tempo yearning that Seger embraced, but when it comes to white male heartland rock artists, Seger made the crossover into burning mid-tempo ballad territory first. His lovelorn hit singles dominated before Springsteen's "I'm on Fire" and Petty's "Here Comes My Girl."

Seger's success with such ballads also foretold the widespread appeal of heartland rock. If the original sounds of the people— American folk music—connected with the everyday listener as imperfect regional field recordings captured by primitive technology, heartland rock was its inverse. Using cutting-edge recording techniques, Springsteen, Petty, and Seger helped reflect and contour the culture of the 1980s by sharing their memories of adolescence, home, and family, as well as the sounds and imagery of the 1950s and '60s. They were inspired by the places where they came of age, but not constricted by them.

Unlike American folk music, heartland rock was highly commercial, broadcast on nearly every radio station and sold in every shopping mall, truck stop, and local record store. Its blue-collar imagery was printed on album covers and broadcast on VH1 and MTV. Heartland rock seemed to reflect small towns and regular jobs across the country. Working people heard themselves in its lyrics, and saw themselves in its stories. It seemed to embody both the strength and vulnerability of America's heart.

As Seger and the genre at large rose, middle-class kids in the suburbs, and critics in metropolitan ivory towers, could be quick to judge heartland rock artists because they were blinded by their own safety nets. Unless one has lived a small-town life of poverty, hasn't gone to college, or failed to excel at anything other than music, it's impossible to understand the gravity of the choice between success and failure. For those without a parachute, there are much worse options than major labels and commercial radio. In a 1994 interview, Seger explained that growing up poor implanted a desire "to make sure I had that big stack of chips I could fall back on before I kicked back at all."

With *Against the Wind*, Seger's idea of a "good" song may have evolved, but "good" remained the enduring goal. "It's a matter of the best songs," he said. "If the best songs are medium, those are the ones I gotta use . . . as far as being good, whole-entity song from top to bottom and not sounding like anything I'd done before." He was also concerned about the live show. "I don't wanna be playing 10 songs that sound the same, you know what I mean?"

"You'll Accomp'ny Me," "No Man's Land," "Good for Me," "Fire Lake," "Shinin' Brightly," and "Against the Wind" were songs of love, nostalgia, and promise set against mid-tempo instrumentation played by the Silver Bullet Band or the Muscle Shoals Rhythm Section. Seger regularly worked with the latter on his records, in addition to his hometown group. The hard-rocking tracks threaded between the mediums were unabashedly horndog ("The Horizontal Bop," "Her Strut," "Betty Lou's Gettin' Out Tonight") or used transportation as an analog for strength, liberation, or both ("Long Twin Silver Line"). Each was familiar lyrical terrain for Seger.

The title track, built around the piano playing of Paul Harris, a session musician who also contributed to John Mellencamp's self-titled LP (released under the stage name John Cougar), among hundreds of others, was submerged in the same kind of pining nostalgia that made Seger's "Night Moves" and "Still the Same" moving and relatable to fans. Its lyrics, which were delivered via Seger's best singing to date, were specific enough to evoke a memoir-like quality but universal enough to transcend individual experience. They recalled a former love and the ease with which we drift from where we truly belong.

The song "Against the Wind," like Springsteen's "The River," Mellencamp's "Jack & Diane," and Petty's "American Girl," contained memories that confronted aging and doubled as an important kind of underclass representation. "Against the Wind" resonated with listeners, peaking at No. 5 on the Billboard Hot 100 singles chart. Today, if streaming numbers are to be believed, it's one of the singer's most-loved songs. On Seger's official YouTube channel, about four thousand people have written comments under the song's video, many of which place it in Seger's top three best tracks. "Bob wrote this song about my life whether he knew it or not," wrote one fan.

Seger, a regular guy writing about common people in a world that felt increasingly alien and uncertain, was real and approachable in his mediums. Such heartland rock became the music of the people by virtue of its accessibility and resulting ubiquity. Though its tales were of hard luck and hard lives, its sounds were anything but callous. "Against the Wind" struck a mightier spark than any of Seger's early hard rockers, reaching the greatest listenership of his career to that point.

★ ★ ★

By 1980, the elbow-grease anthems of Bob Seger, Bruce Springsteen, and Tom Petty were everywhere. In the wake of the genre's success—and particularly Springsteen's *Born to Run*—young men and women raised in humble American corners began writing of their own lives in earnest. The media began searching for the genre's next stars.

Speculation about who would be the "the next Springsteen" was rampant. John Mellencamp was known as Johnny Cougar, a persona and name orchestrated by David Bowie's former manager Tony Defries, and was perceived as a fraud by most critics. Some listeners were uncomfortable with his bratty, overly sexual lyrics. Others viewed him as a hayseed dope. Though the *Chicago Sun-Times* called him "a poet of the real world" in 1980, the rest of America had yet to catch on. After he finally broke through with *American Fool* in 1982, Mellencamp wasn't hailed as the next Springsteen. He was maligned as an imitator. "I had never even seen Springsteen perform live until last December in Indianapolis," he told *Rolling Stone* in 1986. "I remember saying to one magazine, 'I can't wait until I meet Bruce Springsteen so I can tell him what a problem he's been for me.' So when I met him at that show, I told him. He acted like he was my big brother, which was nice. He said he really liked 'Pink Houses.' And I said, 'Well, I stole it all from you.' We laughed and shook hands."

Jersey Shore darling John Lyon, who performed as Southside Johnny, was often summoned alongside Springsteen for his regional proximity and collaborations. Lyon and his band the Asbury Jukes found modest success with songs written by Springsteen and E Street Band guitarist Steven Van Zandt, including "I Don't Want to Go Home," which became a local favorite. But Lyon wasn't the next thing. He was Springsteen and the E Street Band's chosen brother. He and the Asbury Jukes had been working the same clubs as Springsteen for years, and had shared members, including Van Zandt, Clarence Clemons, Max Weinberg, and Springsteen's future wife Patti Scialfa.

New York by way of South Jersey songwriter D. L. Byron recorded his 1980 breakthrough album *This Day and Age* at The Record Plant (just like Springsteen) with Jimmy Iovine as producer (just like Petty). He embodied all the hardscrabble biographical bona fides of the working-class rock contingent, and even opened for Bob Seger on tour. But he was far too enmeshed in power pop and new wave, in line with British artists like Elvis Costello. His vibe was a bit too art-school wimp. Byron wrote the song "Shadows of the Night" for the mawkish rock-drama *Times Square*, whose cult-favorite soundtrack featured tunes by Talking Heads, Ramones, the Pretenders and others.

However, it was rejected and never made it onto the album. Luckily for him, Pat Benatar made it a Top 10 hit two years later.

After hearing Patti Smith's "Because the Night," cowritten with Bruce Springsteen, singer-songwriter Mark Knopfler hired Iovine to produce his band Dire Straits' third album, 1980's *Making Movies*. The producer brought on the E Street Band's keyboardist Roy Bittan, and the album marked the band's highest-ever chart positions in the US and UK. Its single "Romeo and Juliet" has the lyrical makings of a heartland rock tale: Two young lovers break up after one finds fame and ditches the humble neighborhood of their origins. But the group and Knopfler were still too British, and the singles didn't have a wide-enough appeal. Dire Straits would find its place within the canon in 1985 with its release of *Brothers in Arms*, when heartland rock began to shift from a principled form to a sonic mood.

Robin Lane & the Chartbusters were one of few early female-fronted contenders. The bandleader's raspy vocals had a force that landed somewhere between Patti Smith and Springsteen. Like Bonnie Raitt, Lane was raised in Southern California the daughter of a famous name in music—Ken Lane, a composer best known as Dean Martin's pianist. After a stalled launch there, she found her footing by moving east to work the Cambridge, Massachusetts, folk clubs (like Raitt) and then New York, where she signed with Private Stock Records (Blondie's first label) and then Warner Bros. "When Things Go Wrong" was an early favorite among a burgeoning MTV viewership, but Lane was too modern and hip to truly be blue-collar, nostalgic, or both. There was the sense that she was most interested in the future.

Rhode Island outfit John Cafferty & the Beaver Brown Band over-cooked the roast. Cafferty's participation in the 1983 film *Eddie and the Cruisers* didn't help. Its director reportedly tasked a gofer with finding a musician who could emulate Springsteen's style after he passed on the soundtrack. Cafferty climbed aboard, and Southside Johnny was hired as a technical advisor to help produce a convincing regional flare. It was a sensible choice for a Jersey bar band story set in the early '80s. But in this film, the Cruisers were supposed to be gigging two decades earlier. "Eddie's music sounds good, but it also sounds a lot like Bruce Springsteen's, and it would not have been the rage in 1963," wrote a *New York Times* critic.

Garland Jeffreys came up through the New York underground, and his urban sketches were often brilliant and innovative. His 1979 album *American Boy & Girl* was heartland rock in the same way that Lou Reed's *New York* would be: as a coastal ally, filled with stories of regular folks navigating the mean streets of Manhattan. Graham Parker worked with Iovine and Springsteen, but his lyrics were uneven and he was closely associated with the English pub-rock scene. Dave Edmunds was too retro. The Canadians of Red Rider were still relatively unknown south of the border. Steve Forbert was gifted and well on his way to being a songwriter's songwriter. Lucinda Williams was taken for a folkie. So was Rickie Lee Jones. Pittsburgh's Donnie Iris was closely connected to Wild Cherry's "Play That Funky Music."

Ian Hunter's 1979 crackerjack *You're Never Alone with a Schizophrenic*, featuring members of the E Street Band, was his best solo album, and its single "Cleveland Rocks" left him well positioned. But his time with Mott the Hoople loomed too large.

Ultimately, just three candidates fit heartland rock's salt-of-the-earth criteria. After drawing local praise during a residency at the Greenwich Village club Kenny's Castaways, Buffalo native Willie Nile was compared to both Dylan and Springsteen, and signed a deal with Clive Davis's Arista Records in 1978. Two years later, he released an excellent, self-titled debut album that featured Patti Smith Group's Jay Dee Daughtery on drums. Its Everyman poet-philosopher lyrics were served over unfussy arrangements that centered guitar or piano. His raspy voice seemed worn by the grit of New York streets, booze on stoops, hard living amid urban blight.

"Vagabond Moon," the album's standout, combined Petty's guitar jangle, Seger's lyrical tenderness, and Springsteen's feral might. Other songs like "Dear Lord" and "Old Men Sleeping on the Bowery" reflected the yearning conscience of the heartland rock movement, and a natural capability to subvert the meathead rock star image without being sappy, pretentious, or weak. Ads that ran in *Billboard* declared that "America is discovering a major new figure in rock & roll." *The New York Times* called the singer's self-titled work the "most exciting debut album by a singer-songwriter in some time."

Pete Townsend was a fan, and asked Nile to open a tour for the Who. It was all a whirlwind—flattering but burdensome. Nile cracked under the pressures of success. "My advice to people looking for record deals is to go bowling and forget it," he told the *Philadelphia Daily News* in 1980. "Now that I've finally got my album, and finally gotten a band together, I think I'm gonna quit, scrap it all. You know, there's a lot to be said for a simple existence."

Cleveland native Michael Stanley hit all the right thematic notes. His lyrics spotlighted Middle American nostalgia and proletarian merit. He conveyed solid Midwestern grit. He even received a symbolic key to the city after he sold-out Ohio's Richfield Coliseum faster than Led Zeppelin in its prime.

Statewide enthusiasm for the Michael Stanley Band's live shows was so great its leader garnered comparisons to Bob Seger's stronghold in Michigan. "MSB" is what Ohio natives called the group, a shorthand usually reserved for more popular acts like Average White Band (AWB) and Dave Matthews Band (DMB). An August 1980 review in the *Akron Beacon Journal* described the Michael Stanley Band's concert at the outdoor Blossom Music Center as "thunderous" and "explosive." "Even the heavy rain couldn't dampen the energy of the sold-out crowd," the writer noted.

Stanley was discovered by Bill Szymczyk. The Eagles' producer was impressed with Stanley's teenage garage band and signed on to produce his first two solo albums. *Friends and Legends* was issued by MCA, while *Michael Stanley* was an early title on Szymczyk's Tumbleweed Records. Each LP was released in 1973 and featured Joe Walsh on guitar and backing vocals. Both albums went nowhere.

After releasing six albums with his Michael Stanley Band, and being dropped by Epic and then Arista, the singer was finally ready to take a big swing with *Heartland*, the band's seventh album, released in 1980.

Stanley's coarse-ground vocals were a convincing vehicle for songs like "Lover," which heralded the Ohio Turnpike, workers who paint lines on highways, and the snow of a Midwestern winter. The E Street Band's Clarence Clemons even played sax on the album, which received little national press but managed to climb to No. 86 on the Billboard albums chart and was eventually certified Gold. In a 1980 preview of a MSB concert, a newspaper in Escondido, California, described the band as a "blend of the Bruce Springsteen and Bob Seger formulas."

Though Nile and Stanley were making gains, a band out of Pittsburgh was fast closing in on the heir-to-Springsteen finish line. In 1980, the critic Greil Marcus called the Iron City Houserockers' *Have a Good Time but Get Out Alive!* the "strongest album an American band has made this year, and when the year ends the word 'American' may come off."

The Pittsburgh sextet had all of the working-class credentials. Raised in Pennsylvania by auto mechanics, coal miners, and construction workers, the band had been grinding in local bars since high school before signing with industry veteran Steve Popovich's Cleveland International Records, a label founded in Willoughby, Ohio.

Popovich had helped spread the gospel of Springsteen in his former role as vice president of promotion for Columbia Records, and had signed Cheap Trick and Southside Johnny and the Asbury Jukes as vice president of A&R at Epic. He clinched a major win with Meatloaf's *Bat Out of Hell* in 1977. Popovich was a son of working-class lineage, born in rural Pennsylvania and raised in Cleveland. He saw a bit of himself in the Houserockers, who wrote their breakthrough album with the belief that they may never escape Pittsburgh alive, that they were staring down a dead end metaphorically but also literally. As a bar band, the Houserockers had witnessed their fair share of fistfights. In the new decade, amid unemployment and economic uncertainty, drunken quarrels could turn deadly. According to singer-songwriter-guitarist

Joe Grushecky, distressed young men in Pittsburgh were shooting, beating, and stabbing one another. "Everyone was laid off, and everyone was waiting in these gas lines, and everybody was pissed," he said. "We felt, Jesus Christ, we're gonna die here in one of these bars."

Such terror proved effective. With Popovich's help, the Houserockers landed a deal with MCA, a label that had recently struck gold with Lynyrd Skynyrd. Released in June 1980, *Have a Good Time but Get Out Alive!*, the band's second album, and first that truly embraced its working-class environs, propelled the Houserockers from local unknowns to critical darlings. It couldn't have hurt that five of its songs—"Junior's Bar," "Angela," "Running Scared," "Blondie," and "Don't Let Them Push You Around"—were produced by the E Street Band's Steven Van Zandt, who also played lead guitar on "Junior's Bar," the band's best song. Ian Hunter produced "Hypnotized."

The album is perhaps the most honest depiction of working-class life ever produced by the heartland rock movement. As Seger, Springsteen, and Petty elevated humble origins into a specific strain of tuneful mythology—something perhaps grander and more beautiful than its reality—the Houserockers opted for scarred reality. Two of the album's songs are about bars, and one toys with the image of "pumping iron." There are sad old men, unruly greaseballs, and a lusty ode to Blondie's Deborah Harry.

"Springsteen may have popularized the subject matter, but the Houserockers . . . attack with a relentless fury that the Sage of the Jersey Shore merely hints at," the *LA Weekly* declared of the group. In November of 1981, they even appeared on the popular Sunday evening music television show *Solid Gold*. The band was poised for something big, and was frequently mentioned in the same breath as heartland rock's biggest names.

"While you are waiting for Bob Seger's new release, this will do," a critic for the *Dayton Daily News* wrote of the band's 1981 album *Blood on the Bricks*. "Iron City House Rockers [*sic*] is a high quality group from Pittsburgh with just the right amount of rough edges."

As is the case with a lot of objectively great rock bands girded for the next level, the Iron City Houserockers' album sales weren't proportional to the press coverage the group received. By 1983, the group dropped "Iron City" from its name in an effort to transcend a regional pigeonhole and appeal to a national audience. Legend also has it that their van's tires had been slashed in Cleveland—Michael Stanley territory.

By the band's fourth and final album, *Cracking Under Pressure*, they were down two original members, and had turned to synthesizers in an attempt to keep up with the times. The writing was on the wall. MCA dropped the band two days after the album was released, and the Houserockers broke up six months later.

Much like a quest for the bard who would inherit Dylan's throne, the hunt for the next Springsteen was a fool's errand. Instead, 1980 saw an entire strain of worthy peers on the precipice of reaching the masses. While some of them did, more of them did not.

★ ★ ★

Amid the rise of the yuppie in the Reagan era, John Mellencamp exalted trash. "It's like a joke on America," he explained of his new album, titled *Nothin' Matters and What if It Did*, released under the name John Cougar. "It's the way some people in the United States live and it's not a bad attitude," he added, with palpable sarcasm, to a television interviewer in New York. "If you could have that attitude, if you didn't care about anything, that would be great."

Mellencamp's fourth studio album found the singer inching toward the musical geography that would inspire his most renowned work. By 1979, he'd split with manager Tony Defries, and had gone to London under new management and a new record label, Riva Records. He had a Top 10 hit with "I Need a Lover" in 1978, but he wasn't yet a household name. Back at home in Indiana, with an Indiana band, he had aimed for more.

Recorded in Bloomington with veteran musician and producer Steve Cropper—guitarist of Booker T. & the M.G.s, the Stax Records house band who backed Otis Redding, Sam & Dave, and many others—

Nothin' Matters and What if It Did hinted at some of the sounds and themes that would soon make Mellencamp a star.

The album's cover art spoke volumes. It was designed by Jimmy Wachtel, the artist who also created iconic covers for Bruce Springsteen's *The River*, Jackson Browne's *Running on Empty*, and Stevie Nicks and Lindsey Buckingham's cult-favorite debut *Buckingham Nicks*, among many others. It depicted Mellencamp in a white undershirt-style tank top, posing like a country bumpkin rebel. Behind him sat Edith Massey, the campy, snaggletoothed actress who regularly appeared in the work of Baltimore filmmaker John Waters, including his "Trash Trilogy" of *Pink Flamingos, Female Trouble*, and *Desperate Living*. The flipside of the album cover showed the pair outside an unkept trailer home. Near them, a dirty mop hung from a clothesline, like a rancid apparition.

It's unclear if Massey is meant to be Mellencamp's mother, lover, or friend. In the music video for the schmaltzy love song "This Time," the pair descend a staircase arm-in-arm, glancing at one another with put-on affection: Mellencamp a skanky peacock, Massey a gussied-up goof. It was a display that would be a cruel joke when placed in the right teenage coming-of-age film. Massey also appeared in print advertisements, a mascot for the first album Mellencamp had made largely of his own accord. Together, the pair projected an unapologetic image of America: a redneck and a trailer queen living their best lives, or more accurately, their worst ones.

According to a report by the US Census Bureau, 3.2 million more Americans lived below the poverty line between 1979 and 1980, one of the largest annual increases since the late '50s. By 1980, 13 percent of the US population was below that threshold—$8,414 for a nonfarm family of four (about $31,000 today). The poverty level for farm families was even lower at $5,889 (about $22,000 today). Mellencamp would set his sights on the latter issue soon. But first, he made sure Americans understood where he was coming from. The singer and his muse stood for the kind of white trash populace summoned in "scared straight" lectures, a visual rendering of what happens when you don't stay off drugs; when you fail at school; when you don't have a generational financial safety net. In this period, Mellencamp was still a shock-focused agitator. Making Massey so central to the album's visuals was no doubt an extension of that. For the King of Confrontation, only the Pope of Trash would do. "Someone once said, 'There's always a loudmouthed kid with a guitar ready to screw everything up. I thought, 'That's me,'" he once said.

In kicking against the self-absorption and greed that came to mark the decade, Mellencamp demonstrated his kinship with the underclasses, with those who did their best with the little they were handed. The album's low-grade visuals asked listeners to acknowledge the margins of American society; to see those who they may have otherwise ignored. It was the artsy smut of John Waters projected through the lens of a small-town Hoosier who'd taken his fighting spirit from the streets to the studio.

"There's a certain type of woman in the United States that really looks that way," Mellencamp explained. "You see them on front porches drinking beer and smoking cigarettes and beating the kids." His previous albums had hinted at these kinds of societal margins, from *Chestnut Street Incident*, which was named after a road in his Seymour, Indiana, hometown, to songs like "The Great Midwest," released in 1979, which recounted rural malaise. But here was an unmistakable call for the overlooked and down-and-out to be seen, whether Mellencamp intended it or not. The album cover was like American Gothic crudely refracted. It signaled Mellencamp's desire to "write about something that matters to people," as he told the *Los Angeles Herald Examiner*.

The album found Mellencamp's band the Zone, which consisted of piano, drums, bass, and guitar, and a few auxiliary sounds such as saxophone and pedal steel, in back-to-basics mode. His North Star was the soul and R&B music he loved as a teenager, songs from Detroit transmitted through Seymour's local AM radio signal. It was the same music he performed in an integrated covers band before he set out on his own. The amalgam yielded mixed results, but the album reached No. 37 on the Billboard 200, his highest charting work to date.

The single "Ain't Even Done with the Night" name-checked soul music icon Sam Cooke, and included a bassline reminiscent of the Temptations' classic "My Girl." Combined with threads of mandolin, it foretold a combination of genres that would come to define future Mellencamp albums. Its video also featured the band in an awkward tribute to the Temptations. In matching red-and-black suits, they performed a wobbly step-touch line dance as Mellencamp sang into a retro microphone.

"Cheap Shot" pointed at the trend-chasing and price-gouging of the record business, issues that would soon be raised by Tom Petty and Bob Seger. "To M.G. (Wherever She May Be)" was a reflective ode to a bygone teenage relationship steeped in the kind of nostalgia that became a staple of heartland rock. Taken together, the songs were inconsistent, but they bore many of the themes that would preoccupy Mellencamp for much of his career: racial inequality, the plight of the working class, the decline of the Midwest.

During a 1980 appearance on Dick Clark's long-running music show *American Bandstand*, Mellencamp explained that he and his ragtag band—Doc Rosser on piano, Kenny Aronoff on drums, Larry Crane on guitar, Mike Wanchic on guitar, and Robert Frank on bass— were traveling in a mobile home because the cost of airfare was outrageous and he wanted to keep his overhead low, particularly in the midst of broader economic decline. "In places like Youngstown, Ohio, and Detroit, Michigan, where people are out of work . . . they just can't afford to spend $7.99, $8.99, $9.99 for an album," he explained and added that, in an ideal world, he'd charge $2.50 a ticket for his concerts. "$8.50 to see me?" he exclaimed. "You could see me last year pouring concrete."

"White boys go Black!" Mellencamp later declared to Clark, before he and his band launched into "Ain't Even Done with the Night" and its step-touch line dance. For all of that statement's offensiveness, it was prescient. John Cougar was no wildcat. He was a slowly maturing

Bruce Springsteen and the E Street Band perform at the Arizona
State University Activity Center in Tempe on November 5, 1980.
PHOTO BY PETER HOWES

hellraiser who would soon elevate what he knew and loved in spite of
Reagan, yuppies, and squares. He was a simple, rough-and-ready guy
who longed to sing of what he knew. And with *Nothin' Matters and
What if It Did*, he was no longer out of his province.

★ ★ ★

On November 5, 1980, one night after the presidential election in
which Ronald Reagan beat the incumbent Jimmy Carter with 50.7 percent of the vote, Bruce Springsteen, then a fast-rising star on the most
successful tour of his life, pivoted his usual stage banter from personal
to topical. "I don't know what you guys think about what happened
last night, but I think it's pretty frightening," he told a packed stadium.
In Tempe, Arizona, on stage at the Arizona State University Activity
Center, he transformed into a populist leader.

The election results were scarcely a surprise. America's collective anxiety was surging amid the Cold War, a looming recession, the aftermath of the Vietnam War, and a general sense that New Deal America was losing its footing. The country's future felt touch-and-go for many. A smooth-talking former actor well versed in campaigning and commentary was hardly an answer, but perhaps his confidence could inspire a capable cabinet? Reagan's victory marked the launch of an ideological struggle for the heart of the country, and what it meant to be American. Were we a society whose virtue was molded by principles? Or had posturing displaced backbone? Could charisma save what work ethic had built?

By that night in November, Reagan had made so many conflicting points and promises that Americans had become inured to a kind of ideological whiplash. The country waited to find out which version of Reagan they had elected. Was it the man who called the Vietnam War a "noble cause," questioned biological evolution, and promised to cut taxes, eliminate welfare programs, and let US automakers marinate in their own failures? Or was it the man who promised to provide aid to keep auto workers on the job, protect Social Security, and negotiate an arms reduction treaty? That night, Springsteen, who'd just released his double album *The River* in October, was emboldened to weigh in.

He'd stayed up late the night before watching the election returns, and later worried, alone in his hotel home, about whether he should say something at the concert the next day. His remark that night was met with gasps, applause, and some murmurs. It's plausible that a large segment of the audience that night had voted for Reagan. The former president won Arizona by a mile that year. But it probably had more to do with the fact that Springsteen had never really expressed a political position. He'd never endorsed a candidate or spoken out against an administration. His only evident allegiance was with working Americans who made the country run.

Springsteen and Petty were probably the most neutral performers at the previous year's No Nukes concerts at Madison Square Garden, uttering nary a word about the cause at hand from the stage. Petty's participation in the event was in fact spurred by Springsteen. "Mike [Campbell] and I discussed playing one of those benefits because we thought we'd draw a completely different crowd to the people Jackson Browne and Graham Nash get, the Woodstock types. When Bruce phoned me to play with him—and he doesn't usually have other groups on his bill—we decided to do it," Petty told *New Musical Express* in March 1980. Petty explained that he wasn't a particularly political person, but that he was coming around on it due to current events. He'd read coverage in the *Los Angeles Times* that discussed the dangers of nuclear energy and radiation, for example. "I've changed my mind about a lot of things," he added. "I used to say 'Fuck the whales,' but now I think we ought to save them too. Why not?" Following his No Nukes performance, Springsteen dropped a few political breadcrumbs. Unlike Petty, he allowed his band's performance to be included in the concert film *No Nukes*, released in July 1980 at movie theaters across the country. The documentary wove live music footage with behind-the-scenes images, remarks by MUSE organizers, and man-on-the-street interviews related to nuclear power. It also included scenes from a MUSE-organized antinuclear rally held in New York's Battery Park, which featured speakers Jane Fonda, Ralph Nader, and others, and drew about two hundred thousand people. It was the first time Bruce Springsteen and the E Street Band's live show had been released on film. That this milestone was tied to such a progressive, pronounced form of activism was remarkable.

Springsteen also pondered the subject of nuclear power in the song "Roulette," which was partially about the meltdown at Three Mile Island in 1979, told through the lens of human anxiety. It was the first song recorded for *The River*, but Springsteen ultimately scrapped it from the double album's final sequence. It wasn't officially released until 1988, and it appeared again on the 1998 collection *Tracks*, as did other songs he'd cut during *The River* sessions that didn't make the album.

Springsteen's cleareyed assessments of the US, and its glories and failures, was something he usually reserved for his music, not his stage banter. After declaring Reagan's election "frightening" in Arizona, he launched into "Badlands," one of his most defiant compositions about haves and have-nots, and the cruelty of fate. That night in Arizona, he offered a scorching rendition that rang of a newfound force, elevating the song from tuneful poetry to a prognosis of the social and political rancor looming in the distance. It was a clairvoyant warning of the trouble that would course through the heartland and beyond.

"I was interested in what it meant to be an American, one small participant in current history at a time when the future seemed as hazy and shapeshifting as that thin line on the horizon," he explained in his 2016 autobiography *Born to Run*. "Can a rock 'n' roll artist help sculpt that line, shade its direction?"

The River, Springsteen's follow-up to *Darkness on the Edge of Town*, was similar to its antecedent in its themes of family, place, and conflict. It furthered that album's lyrical plunge into issues of work and identity. But *Darkness* was measured, pensive, and studious, a sort of thesis statement for an entire career to come. *The River*, on the other hand, would symbolize the places and people of his origins but also be imbued with chaos and fraternity. It would invoke the raw power of the E Street Band in its natural habitat—Jersey Shore bars—and would, as a byproduct, steer the group to its full potential. It would have more joy. It wouldn't take itself so seriously, even if it was at times a weighty pursuit. It would be big and bold in its assertions. It would present the full spectrum of human experience, from darkness to light. Its title track was heavily influenced by Springsteen's newfound interest in country music, and centered on the hard luck of workers amid the crash of the construction industry in New Jersey in the late '70s. "When I did *The River*, I tried to accept the fact that . . . the world is a paradox, and that's the way it is. And the only thing you can do with a paradox is live with it," he said.

The making of the album was rife with abundance and indecision. Springsteen was on a writing streak and decided to record everything pouring out of him at the Power Station, where bands like Blondie and David Bowie also recorded. Over the course of nearly two years, he wrote, recorded, and agonized. At one point, he sequenced a single album consisting of "The Ties That Bind," "Cindy," "Hungry Heart,"

"Stolen Car," "Be True," "The River," "You Can Look (But You Better Not Touch)," "The Price You Pay," "I Wanna Marry You," and "Loose Ends," in that order. He had it mixed and then shipped off to be pressed on vinyl. But in a moment of panic, he canceled the album, and then embarked on the double LP.

His new friend Seger, whose own *Against the Wind* had been a tortured process, was well aware of the singer's predicament and empathized. "You should see Springsteen," he told *Creem* magazine amid the making of *The River*. "He's going through the same movie right now. He's pulling his hair out."

Ultimately, six tunes from the scrapped single LP were included on *The River*, along with a spate of new ones. At a time when the American auto industry's future began to feel uncertain, Springsteen celebrated US-made vehicles ("Cadillac Ranch"). As humorlessness and puritanism began to shroud the country under the guise of "family values," he offered frat-party rockers and euphemistic anthems ("Ramrod," "Sherry Darling," "I'm a Rocker"). As a Hollywood actor became the leader of the free world, and performance began to outweigh substance in the dawn of the material age, he offered sturdy lyrical maxims and stirring ballads about home, family, love, honest work, and a loss of innocence ("Drive All Night," "Stolen Car," "The River," "The Ties That Bind").

By harnessing the sound of Bruce Springsteen and the E Street Band's live performances on an album, *The River* also had the effect of predicting the singer's personal crisis to come, manifested on 1982's *Nebraska*. The double album's sequence pings from extreme highs to the lowest lows. Among its turns of phrase and explosive solos, there's also the quiet desperation of the search for joy and satisfaction, and the loneliness that comes with being responsible for an entire bar's good time.

"Hungry Heart" distills these sentiments into the most palatable and infectious of throwback packages. That the song was originally written for New York pop punks the Ramones makes its subversive quality that much more salient. Springsteen counts "Ramrod," one of music's greatest libidinous double-entendres, among the saddest songs he's ever written.

The River went to No. 1 on album charts in the US and Canada, and rested near the top of year-end "best of" lists. In his supervisory role for the *Village Voice*'s annual Pazz & Jop critic's poll, Robert Christgau, the self-appointed "Dean of American Rock Critics," wrote that "by continuing to root his writing in the small victories and large compromises of ordinary joes and janies whose need to understand as well as celebrate is as restless as his own, he's grown into a bitter empathy."

"Hungry Heart" became the biggest single of Springsteen's career to date, broadcast on radio stations across the country to hearts in need of nourishment. By fall, arena audiences began singing its lyrics at the band in an evident display of enthusiasm that ignited a long-running tradition. America and its characters had long given voice to Springsteen's lyrics in an artistic sense. In a new decade rife with anxiety and doubt, Springsteen decided to make America's voice in his music literal, concrete, and audible. From now on, the band would play the first verse and chorus of "Hungry Heart" as an instrumental, and the audience would sing the lyrics. America would be the voice. After burning through his advance, and then draining his own bank account to finish *The River*, the popularity of the album and its tour was a financial and spiritual boon, a welcome form of exhaustion. Tickets to a Springsteen show became a hot commodity. Scalpers became a problem. Over the course of more than one hundred shows in the US, Canada, United Kingdom, and Europe, Springsteen rose from scrappy New Jersey buckshot to an epic arena rocker serving marathon gigs. The bard of New Jersey was suddenly an American symbol outside of himself, and that moment on stage in Tempe, Arizona, marked a turning point.

"It is an almost certain bet that the songs Springsteen will now be writing will have something to do with the events of November 4. Those songs likely will not comment on those events; they will, I think, reflect those events back to us, fixing moods and telling stories that are, at present, out of reach," Greil Marcus predicted in February 1981. And he was right. The Boss had become a star. He'd also become overtly and publicly political.

CHAPTER 2

UGLY TRUTHS AND HARD PROMISES

This land was made for you and me.

—WOODY GUTHRIE, 1940

W hen President Ronald Reagan was inaugurated on January 20, 1981, he placed his hand on a Bible opened to 2 Chronicles 7:14, a verse in which God promises to forgive and heal those who shun wickedness. Minutes later, Iran released fifty-two American hostages, ending a crisis that had gripped the nation for more than a year and effectively torpedoed former president Jimmy Carter's reelection campaign. For some, it was an auspicious beginning, and others, a man playing God. Gary Sick, an expert on the Middle East who helped with the crisis under the Carter administration, and other officials from both parties, maintained that Reagan's campaign offered quid pro quo deals with Iran in order to delay the release of the hostages.

As questions around the crisis swirled, a series of menacing events unfolded and metaphorical storm clouds gathered over the nation. In March, the Ku Klux Klan lynched a nineteen-year-old Black man named Michael Donald in Mobile, Alabama. June saw the first recognized cases of AIDS among five men in Los Angeles. Suspected serial killer Wayne Williams was arrested on June 21 after twenty-eight children and adults had been killed in Atlanta since 1979. Two skywalks at a hotel in Kansas City collapsed, killing more than one hundred people. There were arms negotiations amid the ongoing Cold War and growing fears about nuclear weapons; a severe recession continued to pummel the nation.

These events rattled the country, especially after a young man tried to assassinate President Reagan in March. John Hinckley Jr. was one of hundreds gathered outside a Hilton hotel in Washington, DC, as Reagan addressed a conference of the American Federation of Labor and Congress of Industrial Organizations. Obsessed with the actress Jodie Foster and Martin Scorsese's psychological drama *Taxi Driver*—a film about a Vietnam veteran in crisis—Hinckley Jr. fired six shots at Reagan from a Rohm RG revolver as he exited the hotel and walked toward a limo. The last bullet bounced off of the vehicle and hit the president in his left arm and rib before lodging into his lung just an inch away from his heart.

Given that Hinckley Jr. was once a Reagan supporter and had also schemed to assassinate President Carter, experts didn't view the act as political in nature. A note he'd written prior to the shooting indicated that it was a desperate attempt to get Ms. Foster's attention. Hinckley Jr. was found not guilty by reason of insanity and was institutionalized for the next sixteen years. Reagan survived the assassination attempt, capitalized on the public's emotional distress to appear invincible, and passed sweeping cuts to social spending as well as tax cuts for the wealthy.

Amid such conflicts and cruelties, heartland rock assumed its own battles on behalf of Americans who found themselves caught in cultural and political crosshairs. In the process, its figureheads seemed to transform into omniscient narrators evangelizing the plights of the marginalized and those who worked hard but had little.

★ ★ ★

During Bruce Springsteen and the E Street Band's tour in support of *The River*, the singer began covering Woody Guthrie's "This Land Is Your Land." After writing specific songs about the hardships of working Americans—like "Factory," "The River," and "Promised Land"—he was compelled to investigate the links between the country's past and present. He read *Woody Guthrie: A Life* by Joe Klein, *A Pocket History of the United States* by Henry Steele Commager, *Born on the Fourth of July* by Ron Kovic, and Howard Zinn's *A People's History of the United States*. He dove into musical genres he'd previously ignored, such as gospel, country, and blues. Hoping it would help shape his own perspective on what it meant, in 1981, to be American, he became a student of history.

In a recording from December 1980, Springsteen described Guthrie's opus as "just about one of the most beautiful songs ever written." Though his guitar was electric, and his audiences filled arenas, Springsteen's version of "This Land Is Your Land" summoned the original in its stark imperative: America didn't belong to the power elite. America belonged to the people.

Though he was becoming steadfast in his mission to "give voice to the stories that in Reagan's 1980s America, rock 'n' roll wasn't often telling," Springsteen's efforts had only manifested in his lyrics to this point. For many, his support of working people was an important poetic symbol, but something that was largely philosophical. He also hadn't spoken out about the Vietnam War in any meaningful way, though some of his peers had.

The Bob Seger System released "2+2=?" in 1969, a biting anti–Vietnam War song that paired garage rock's propulsion with fiery lyrics that critiqued the conscription of young American men. It was a cult-favorite tune in Seger's native Detroit that went largely unnoticed elsewhere, and so it is no wonder that fellow Motor City garage-rock icon Jack White has cited it as influential. The parallels between its haunted guitar line, primal drumming, and lyrical desperation, and the White Stripes' stadium-rock mainstay "Seven Nation Army," are difficult to miss.

Country music stars including Loretta Lynn had released songs in support of Vietnam veterans in the late '60s, amid a wave of antiwar protests they viewed as un-American. Creedence Clearwater Revival's "Fortunate Son" can be viewed as both an antiwar protest and a pro working-class veteran public service announcement. Johnny Cash had walked a similar line when he performed for troops in Vietnam while at the same time being vocal about his opposition to the war. But no major recording artist had taken such a nuanced view—one that separated the war and its warriors—since Vietnam fully ended and its veterans were cast aside.

Springsteen changed that on May 20, 1981, when he dedicated one of his concerts to the plight of Vietnam veterans. It was the result of a series of chance encounters that began at the Sunset Marquis hotel in West Hollywood in the late '70s. Outside by the swimming pool, Springsteen ran into Ron Kovic. The author, a Vietnam veteran who was paralyzed from the chest down due to injuries sustained in the war, had become a vocal antiwar and pro-veteran activist. During their encounter, Springsteen agreed to accompany Kovic on a visit to a local veterans' center in Los Angeles. There, the musician took in the stories of Vietnam veterans who were suffering from posttraumatic stress disorder, drug addiction, and homelessness. The exchange marked an irrevocable shift in the musician.

In July 1981, after a few encounters with Kovic, Springsteen invited another veteran to his concert in East Rutherford, New Jersey. Bobby Mueller was a former Marine who had fought in Vietnam and also returned paralyzed from the chest down. He cofounded the Vietnam Veterans of America. Between May 1975, when President Gerald Ford declared the end of American participation in the Vietnam War, and 1981, next to nothing had been done to aid or even recognize the difficulties Vietnam veterans faced. Their return had marked a complex reckoning in the nation's collective consciousness. Unlike the men who'd returned from previous wars and were received as heroes, Vietnam vets represented the country's failure in a crippling and widely disliked conflict. To many, it seemed that America, once a pinnacle of geopolitical influence and mythic exceptionalism, could no longer save the most vulnerable of humanity abroad or at home. This widespread sentiment became known as Vietnam Syndrome.

Due to widespread conflation of the "war" and its "warriors," Vietnam veterans were consigned to the shadows, and they were left with the unenviable work of self-advocating for their rights within the bloated bureaucracy that was the VA and its crude, understaffed, and overcrowded facilities. The protesters' demonstrations were often dramatic. In May 1981, Kovic led a hunger strike that lasted seventeen days in front of the Wadsworth Veterans Administration Hospital in Los Angeles. More than a dozen protesters also occupied the offices of California Senator Alan Cranston, forcing the head of the VA, Donald E. Johnson, to meet with them. At a hunger strike in Washington, DC, three vets held out for forty-five days. Such demonstrations would stretch into the new millennium.

Mueller was an early participant. In 1972 he, Kovic, double-amputee Bill Wieman, and another veteran, Mark Clevinger, became known as the quartet of men who disrupted the 1972 Republican Convention in Miami Beach, Florida. There, Mueller threw his medals on the ground and the foursome was reportedly spat upon, a scene depicted in Oliver Stone's film *Born on the Fourth of July*. Though such demonstrations drew attention via widespread media coverage, they did little to legitimize the men and their grievances to the US government. "[Mueller] was sort of viewed as un-American," an aide to Democratic Representative Thomas Daschle told a reporter for *Newsday* in November 1981. However, attitudes began to shift when a glaring disparity was brought to light just after Reagan was sworn into office. American hostages held captive in Iran for 444 days received a triumphant welcome after they were released on January 20, 1981. Meanwhile, Vietnam veterans who'd been conscripted to serve in far-away jungles received nary a handshake. Instead, their physical and psychological traumas had come to signify a cartoonish rendering of crazed outcasts relegated to the margins of society.

By 1981, the VVA organization was growing in membership and

had about thirty chapters scattered across the country. But its budgets were anemic and the organization was on the brink of collapse. After meeting with Mueller and taking in his concerns, Springsteen decided to dedicate the first night in a six-date run at the Los Angeles Memorial Coliseum to Mueller's cause, a show whose proceeds would go directly to the VVA. In doing so, he both advanced and subverted the grievances threaded through rock music of the 1960s.

Under Springsteen, what was once a forum for protesting the Vietnam War became a mechanism through which to support its survivors. In highlighting its veterans, Springsteen bucked against the polite society that had cast all notions of Vietnam aside, much as the hippies had protested LBJ's warmongering. Springsteen even opened the evening with an impassioned cover of Creedence Clearwater Revival's 1970 single "Who'll Stop the Rain," a thinly veiled protest against the Vietnam War. At the concert on May 20, Springsteen announced that the show would benefit Vietnam veterans and invited Mueller onstage to speak. Springsteen likened the government's negligence on the issue of Vietnam veterans to ignoring someone being assaulted in a dark alley. "Vietnam turned this whole country into that dark street," he said. "And unless we can walk down those alleys and look into the eyes of those men and women, we're never gonna get home." As an encore, he performed a cover of Roger McGuinn's "The Ballad of Easy Rider," a meditation on freedom and its costs, and a nod to veterans' expressed love of the song. The concert became one of the most heralded of Springsteen's career.

According to Mueller, Springsteen's concert raised $100,000 (about $350,000 today) for the VVA, which he considered a "staggering amount of money." It didn't cover all of the organization's bills, but it did provide a lifeline. "Had Bruce not come and put us in the public light, and got, as a result, other musicians that wanted to chip in and help us out the way that they did, we never would have made it, period," Mueller said in 2019.

In the wake of Springsteen's gesture, Charlie Daniels, Pat Benatar, and eventually John Fogerty performed benefit concerts in support of Vietnam veterans. Perhaps more importantly, Springsteen had finally made his allegiance to working and marginalized people of America material. He had long written about working people, but his financial support of veterans became a thematic link throughout his entire career. Since 2007, Springsteen has performed at all but one Stand Up for Heroes concert, which benefits the Bob Woodruff Foundation, an organization that supports charities and programs for veterans, as well as other organizations.

In 2023, after canceling a run of arena shows with the E Street Band due to peptic ulcer disease, Springsteen made a comeback on November 6 with his performance at Stand Up for Heroes. There, Springsteen joined John Mellencamp on stage at Lincoln Center's David Geffen Hall where the pair performed Mellencamp's "Wasted Days," and Springsteen told dirty jokes and performed four additional songs on acoustic guitar. "I'm going to bring out one of the best songwriters of our generation, and he's my big brother and I've looked up to him my whole life," Mellencamp said by way of introducing his friend. "Whole life" may have been an exaggeration, but without Springsteen, Mellencamp's success in music and in public support of farmers may have never happened. Springsteen had made his perspective clear.

* * *

By the release of the album *Hard Promises* in May of 1981, Tom Petty was a bona fide rock star. He was also, despite his slim frame, a heavyweight fighter. In the late '70s and early '80s, Petty's public battles were unprecedented and uniquely telling of his character. Fifty years later, they endure as a critical symbol of resistance.

Petty was riding high by the second year of the new decade. *Hard Promises* went to No. 5 on Billboard's album chart and featured guest vocals by Fleetwood Mac's Stevie Nicks, by then a pop culture icon, who'd taken note of Petty's place within the growing heartland rock movement. "I would laughingly say to anyone that if I ever got to know Tom Petty and could worm my way into his good graces, if he were

Stevie Nicks and Tom Petty perform in 1982.
PHOTO COURTESY MEDIAPUNCH INC.

ever to ask me to leave Fleetwood Mac and join Tom Petty and the Heartbreakers, I'd probably do it—and that was before I even met him!" she said.

With his crystal-blue eyes, shaggy blond hair, and svelte physique— like a working-class version of David Bowie—Petty was declared a fashion trendsetter in *People* magazine that fall, alongside celebs including Christopher Reeve and Princess Diana. The magazine's blurb, placed alongside a photo of the singer in a striped blazer, fitted black jeans, and Nike wrestling shoes, declared his aesthetic akin to Mick Jagger and Bowie, "just how a rock star should look."

Petty-as-style-influencer was so intense in 1981 that Nike invited him and the Heartbreakers to its store in the Westwood neighborhood of Los Angeles for freebies. Petty said in an interview that employees loaded the band up with so much gear that they had to pile it in several leather equipment bags to haul it home. The exchange was exciting, but also vexing to the formerly hard-up musician gigging at Gainesville frat parties. "You know, when you're broke, nobody gives you nothing,'" he said. "But as soon as you can afford it, it's 'Sure, go ahead, take whatever you want.' It's absolutely backwards." Petty's good looks and style had also made him an easy mark. "Tom Petty just wants to look cool all the time," said David Crosby, the former Byrds member, after Petty refused to be a part of the *No Nukes* concert film. "It's all he ever thinks about . . . he just didn't think he looked cool enough for the movie."

Crosby, a fellow flaxen-haired fighter, was partially correct. Petty cared about his personal style and image, as did every other rising musician; but his refusal to participate in the *No Nukes* film was a much different calculation. That night on stage at Madison Square Garden was the first time Tom Petty and the Heartbreakers had played a twenty-thousand-seat arena. The band was also performing with borrowed gear; Petty couldn't hear his voice in the monitors, and couldn't get anyone to turn up the volume. On top of it all, he was nervous.

Their September 23, 1979, performance coincided with Bruce Springsteen's thirtieth birthday, and Boss mania at the Garden was cranked to 11. As Petty and the Heartbreakers approached the stage for their performance, heartland rock progenitor Jackson Browne attempted to soothe the frontman. "If you think they're booing you, they're not. They're just saying 'Broooce,'" he explained. With superb comic timing, Petty responded: "Well, what the hell is the difference?"

Petty's choice to omit his band's performance from the 1980 concert film, to be shown in movie theaters across America, and sold on VHS, Betamax, and LaserDisc, was an act of self-preservation. "I'm just amazed that I finished the set that night," he later explained. "It wasn't my favorite show . . . the audience was very kind, I thought." From a wide-angle view, however, the move could be construed as Petty—once again—putting up his dukes.

He spent much of 1979 in a legal battle with MCA Records. Petty had originally contracted with Shelter Records, singer-songwriter Leon Russell's label with English producer Denny Cordell in 1975. Tulsa sound originator J. J. Cale and cult-favorite power-pop artist Dwight Tilly were also clients. Shelter's distribution arm was ABC Records.

According to Petty, Shelter took advantage of his youth and inexperience, and he'd signed away his publishing rights for just $10,000. Whether or not that was true, ABC upped Petty's income to a $50,000 advance for the band's second album, *You're Gonna Get It!*, released in 1978, and offered a $250,000 advance for a third album, with increases for future albums based on sales. Rumor has it that those increases materialized during a negotiation in which Petty pulled a switchblade out of his boot and proceeded to clean his fingernails with it. But with the success of *You're Gonna Get It!*, the band's first gold record, Petty began to see that even $250,000 was nowhere close to right. So, when MCA bought out ABC, Petty saw his chance to get out. He insisted that his contract with Shelter-ABC prohibited assignment to MCA and that he wouldn't allow himself to be sold without his permission like livestock at an auction. (MCA argued that his contract did permit assignment.)

"I could work my ass off for the rest of my life, and for every dime I saw, the people that set me up would've seen 10 times as much," he told *Rolling Stone* in 1980. "MCA's attitude was, 'We know your next album's going to be bigger than your last, and we got you, son: the deal's done.'" So, Petty refused to turn over a new album. MCA and Shelter Records sued him for breach of contract, asking the court to prohibit him from recording with anyone else, and his career all but stalled. *Billboard* reported that Al Bergamo, head of MCA Distributing, told attendees of an industry conference that Petty "originally wanted more money than Olivia Newton-John gets to re-sign."

The Heartbreakers laid all but fallow amid the litigation, yet another reason for the group's shaky performance at No Nukes. "We were pretty well beat up," Petty explained. The Floridian's fight with MCA embodied the same spirit of Bruce Springsteen's legal battle with his former manager Mike Appel, whom the singer had accused of fraud, breach of trust, and unreasonable influence. The dispute played out in the press in the late '70s, after the success of *Born to Run*, and ended in a settlement in which Appel received a handsome sum and

Springsteen could release his next album, *Darkness on the Edge of Town*, free from his original contract with Appel. Though born and raised on opposite sides of the Mason-Dixon line, the two musicians engaged in similar industry battles, and their childhood experiences were also closely aligned in their themes of poverty, difficult fathers, feelings of alienation, and ensuing rebellion.

Fearing that Petty's battle could kickstart a wave of dissent among musicians, MCA, according to the singer, pulled no punches. Petty then dealt a huge blow when he filed for bankruptcy in late July, citing $576,638 in debts and $56,845 in assets. His creditors were listed as Electrosound North Hollywood, Cherokee Recording, Sound City Studios, BMI, Shelter Records, and ABC Records. In a 2015 authorized biography by Warren Zanes, Petty said his management, led by Elliot Roberts, who also managed Neil Young, came up with the bankruptcy idea; it had the immediate effect of blocking any further legal action by MCA until the matter of Petty's finances was sorted.

There is conflicting information about who was paying for the ultra-secretive making of *Damn the Torpedoes* amid the litigation. In the book, Petty said Roberts had been fronting for the sessions with Jimmy Iovine—Bruce Springsteen's former engineer. Petty also stated in '80s-era interviews that the money was coming out of his own pocket. Either way, Petty and Roberts refused to admit that they were making a record for fear of it being stolen and released under his existing contract. MCA was effectively hamstrung.

In a 1980 interview with England's *New Musical Express*, Petty said that it "reached the stage where it was almost funny." "Me, the band and Jimmy Iovine were midway through [the sessions] and US Marshals were coming to the studio to steal the tapes, confiscate everything," he explained. "We had to hide all the boxes, smuggle things in and out. I had to go on the stand and evade issues like, 'Where are the tapes? What songs have you written? Recite the lyrics.'"

The industry waited to see who would fall first. Would Petty set a new precedent for musicians to get out of bad corporate record deals? Or would he crumble in the process?

Ultimately, there was a draw. MCA didn't want to risk a judge ruling in Petty's favor and retreated as the Floridian agreed to sign with an MCA subsidiary, Backstreet Records. Petty viewed the company, named after the Bruce Springsteen song "Backstreets," as more friendly to him and his goals. He also reportedly received a $3 million guarantee, and reclaimed his publishing rights.

Backstreet was founded by a young Petty ally, twenty-six-year-old Danny Bramson, whose goal was to bring to MCA what Asylum Records had brought to Atlantic: visionary songwriters. He and Petty were friendly. Bramson had even booked Petty and the Heartbreakers at Los Angeles' Universal Amphitheater in the summer of 1979, amid the drama with MCA.

In order to fulfill the dates, and a few others across California, Petty had to go to court. According to the singer, lawyers for MCA were seeking some form of "security" related to any more debt Petty might incur. They wanted assurance that it wouldn't be used against the company. In another feat of comic brilliance, Petty assessed the tone-deaf nature of the request, looked at the judge and declared, for all to hear, "There is no security in rock 'n' roll!"

By October of 1979, Petty had ostensibly won. *Damn the Torpedoes*, named for the historical navy battle cry "Damn the torpedoes, full speed ahead," a sentiment that encapsulated Petty amid the MCA warfare, went to No. 2 on the Billboard albums chart. But more importantly, like Bruce Springsteen before him, he'd drawn a line in the sand.

With that war and its hardship finally behind him, Petty chose his next battle. Hoping to capitalize on the success of *Damn the Torpedoes*, MCA sought to raise the price of Petty's new album *Hard Promises* from the industry standard of $8.98 to $9.98. In response to the proposal, Petty went on a media blitz. He encouraged fans to write letters decrying the price hike. He wouldn't hand over the *Hard Promises* masters until MCA capitulated.

Financial realities outside of Petty's new album and record label also drove his fight. The nation was suffering the longest recession and the highest rate of unemployment since the Great Depression. Reagan was sworn in as the fortieth president of the United States in January. His economic policies, dubbed Reaganomics, which relied on supply side theory and "trickle down" optimism, were poised to significantly benefit the rich, and not the working poor.

Such bias would reveal itself more clearly in August 1981, when the Reagan administration fired 11,345 striking air traffic controllers and banned them from federal service for life. Their union, the Professional Air Traffic Controllers Organization (PATCO), was also decertified by the Federal Labor Relations Authority. PATCO was composed of many Vietnam veterans who'd learned air traffic control in the military. It was also one of few unions that supported the Reagan presidency in 1980, which made the blow much more painful.

This series of events, and a high-pressure national environment more broadly, snowballed into one of the largest labor demonstrations in American history. On September 19, 1981, workers across unions, sectors, ages, races, and religions descended on Washington, DC, in an event known as the first Solidarity Day. Some estimates place attendance at nearly a half million Americans, with 250 organizations taking part, including 100 unions and a variety of civil rights, religious, and civic groups.

This isn't to say that all of these workers were Tom Petty fans, though a lot of them probably were. Tom Petty and the Heartbreakers had sold hundreds of thousands of records and were in heavy rotation on the radio. Hits like "Don't Do Me Like That," "Refugee," "Even the Losers," and "Here Comes My Girl," and album cuts like "Nightwatchman," which chronicles a nightshift security guard who trusts that he's worth more than minimum wage, demonstrated an intimate understanding of what it means to be a David against a Goliath. Petty himself had risen, against all odds, from a poor and abusive childhood in Gainesville, Florida, to become a national treasure. He and his band stood as a symbol of underclass solidarity even as Petty became a multimillionaire.

"I wanted to write anthems for underdogs, songs like 'Even the

Losers' and 'Refugee,'" he said of *Damn the Torpedoes*. "The theme of the album wasn't conscious, but when I put it together afterwards, I could see it was about standing up for your rights, the ones that everyone has which can't be fucked with or taken away."

Reagan's firing of the PATCO strikers who'd supported him was an implicit attack on Petty's mission statement, but it wasn't just cruel. This action may also be viewed as one of the first major events in the shrinking of the middle class that has taken place over the last fifty years. Republicans have praised Reagan's act as the fulcrum on which our current "flexible" labor market with widespread at-will employment rests. This is to say nothing of the current state of dysfunction in American commercial aviation and a dire shortage of air traffic controllers.

In a 2003 speech at the Reagan Presidential Library in Simi Val-

A farm worker participates in the Solidarity Day march in Washington, DC, on September 21, 1981.

PHOTO COURTESY WORLD HISTORY ARCHIVE

ley, California, Alan Greenspan, then the chair of the Federal Reserve, lauded Reagan's "firing of the air traffic controllers in August 1981." "The President invoked the law that striking government employees forfeit their jobs, an action that unsettled those who cynically believed no President would ever uphold that law," he said. "President Reagan prevailed . . . but far more importantly his action gave weight to the legal right of private employers, previously not fully exercised, to use their own discretion to both hire and discharge workers."

As the Reagan administration's policies reverberated through the middle class, heartland rock musicians took note. Bob Seger cited such struggles in his decision to continue to release his albums on eight-track cassette, a less expensive format, despite its general decrease in popularity. John Mellencamp took his *American Fool* tour to midsized stadiums in midsized markets in order to keep travel and ticket costs down for fans. With *Hard Promises*, Petty battled a major record company over its proposed $1 increase of the album's list price.

The monthlong conflict was printed in newspapers and magazines across the country. The kerfuffle prompted one writer to declare that "it's as easy to praise Tom Petty for what he doesn't do, as it is to celebrate the positive contributions he makes to both the idea and substance of rock and roll."

As was his way, Petty eventually won. MCA released *Hard Promises* at $8.98, his desired list price. "I think the press had a lot to do with winning that particular battle," he said a few months after the album's release. "Not because they intimidated MCA, but because they made the kids aware of what was going on. My hat's off to the press because there wasn't much I could do except speak out about it. I wasn't going to let it go for two reasons: one, $9.98 is just too much to pay for a record, and two, I didn't want MCA hanging a record price rise on me." His fight was memorialized on the cover of *Rolling Stone*'s October 1981 issue. In the photo, Petty rips a dollar bill in half.

"We got a lot of letters pledging support, people saying 'We'll wait a year for the new record if we have to. Don't give up your fight!' It's important to have that kind of support on the street," he added. "Kids can control entertainment prices: Just don't pay it! I think that fear hit MCA and that's why they changed."

Petty's next act of Everyman advocacy came in the form of a promotion. Rock radio station WLUP in Chicago offered to buy all fourteen thousand tickets to Tom Petty and the Heartbreakers' local gig on the *Hard Promises* tour and distribute them to listeners free of charge. But the ostensibly sweet deal had hidden costs. Due to perceived favoritism, and in retaliation, rival Chicago rock station WMET boycotted *Hard Promises*. Petty was naturally incredulous. "I'm getting paid and 14,000 kids are getting in for free? Fuck, yeah, I'll do that. For *anybody*," he insisted. At the height of his powers in the 1980s, Tom Petty was widely viewed as singularly lionhearted, particularly to his fans. A letter to the editor of *Rolling Stone*, in response to Petty's price war with MCA, spoke volumes. "After all," it concluded, "Tom Petty is on our side."

By 1981, most major players in heartland rock were beginning to take up a cause via their music, their charitable work, or their broader activism. Springsteen advocated for veterans, and Seger for Michigan auto workers. Bonnie Raitt concerned herself with nuclear safety, and John Mellencamp fought on behalf of farmers. Petty had raised his fist against predatory corporations, and he'd also become one of the movement's greatest champions of musical elders.

Working-class heroics aside, with *Hard Promises*, Petty and the Heartbreakers also achieved the kind of success they'd long desired— through chart positions and sales, but also their leader's actions. Petty's moral compass was so publicized that he was awarded the key to the city of Gainesville, Florida, his hometown, in October 1981. In a press conference held at a local Hilton hotel, the mayor touted the fact that Petty and his band regularly donated proceeds from his record sales to the local Ronald McDonald House.

Tom Petty and the Heartbreakers was also finally accepted as the truest version of itself, not a new wave act, a fashion brat, or a flash in the pan. "I . . . want people to realize that what we are is an American rock and roll band," Petty once declared. "We're an American rock band, and we never tried to have any other pretense."

★ ★ ★

When Neil Young's fourth studio album with Crazy Horse was released in November 1981, it was easy to assume that it signaled protest. In the wake of the accident at Three Mile Island Nuclear Generating Station in central Pennsylvania, its thematic breadcrumbs seemed obvious: how the title was styled with asterisks—jagged like the nation's cracked sense of security; how the second verse of "Rapid Transit," the album's seventh song, seemed to narrate the federal government's flippancy in the wake of near-nuclear disaster; how its red-and-black cover art channeled America's collective dread amid the Cold War with the Soviet Union.

But the heart of *Re*ac*tor* wasn't nuclear trepidation. In spite of the meltdown depicted in Young's first film *Human Highway*—released in 1982—the singer, in the early '80s, stated that he was actually a fan of nuclear energy. Though he worried how America would dispose of its waste, he was more excited about nuclear energy's potential to launch humans into outer realms. In a 1982 interview with *New Musical Express*, Young explained, "If anyone wants to take me to space I'm ready to go. I'd like to take my family too."

And nuclear arms? "I stand behind Reagan when it comes to buildup, to stand, be able to play hardball with other countries that are aggressive towards free countries. I don't think there's anything wrong with that," he told a reporter for *Melody Maker* in 1985. "I don't put down anybody who says we should stop building weapons and everything," he clarified. "I disagree with them, practically. Idealistically, I agree with them. It's like walking both sides of the fence . . . so that's why I have more of a sympathy for Reagan than other people would have—a lot of other people in my walk of life."

While Young was decidedly not part of the antinuclear movement that had become de rigueur among many popular musicians, *Re*ac*tor* did embrace an important sentiment burbling in American music. The album's B-side, composed of "Southern Pacific," "Motor City," "Rapid Transit," and "Shots," was emphatically proletariat-core.

With *Re*ac*tor*, Young became the first hippie-era elder—though he was nearly nine months younger than Bob Seger—to board the heartland rock express.

Like Bob Dylan and Creedence Clearwater Revival's John Fogerty, Young's spin on the movement was uniquely his own as it embraced heartland rock's lyrical motifs and back-to-basics spirit. Released in November of 1981, *Re*ac*tor* was also Young's most punk album to date; it was fierce and elemental, spare and repetitive, and at times imbued with twang, like Merle Haggard held against a bench grinder. When it wasn't squealing like a discordant opossum, Young's guitar produced sound effects—like the machinegun in "Shots" or the backfiring engine of "Motor City."

Influenced by an intense therapy program Young and his wife Pegi participated in to help with their communication with a nonverbal child—a program that involved a lot of verbal repetition—the album's lyrical tales were undeniably drawn from hardship and the way such trials cycle through one's mind. Paired with extremely loose production, its clear sense of adversity also seemed to embrace modern rock music's growing concern for everyday Americans.

The B-side of *Re*act*or* recounted an old man who was laid off from his longtime job on the railroad ("Southern Pacific") and offered a paean to American-made cars ("Motor City"). "Rapid Transit" signaled a simple man's grievances about new wave music, and "Shots" summoned images of manual and mechanical labor. Even the A-side's widely panned "T-Bone," with its refrain about having potatoes but not having steak, could be interpreted as an unconscious but entirely prescient commentary about class warfare looming on the horizon.

With *Re*ac*tor*, Young also celebrated the influence that heartland rock would have on country music. There is an evident inflection on the album. That sound signaled a future transformation of Young into a country music bandleader—one that happened in the near-succeeding years after *Re*ac*tor*'s release.

In 1983, the singer gathered a group of studio pros for sessions that produced the first version of Young's album *Old Ways*, which also had an alluring twang. But Young's new label Geffen Records rejected it, citing the album's lack of commercial potential. The event kickstarted an ideological war, and Young's five-album run of defiant releases: *Trans, Everybody's Rockin'*, the second version of *Old Ways, Landing on Water*, and *Life*.

For the original *Old Ways*, Young and his band—dubbed the International Harvesters, which included players such as Muscle Shoals great Spooner Oldham (piano), Young regulars Tim Drummond (bass), Karl T. Himmel (drums), and Anthony Crawford (guitar, banjo, vocals), and Cajun artist Rufus Thibodeaux (fiddle)—recorded a collection of country-rock songs. Then, in 1984 and 1985, Young took to the road, playing at least eighty-five shows, including a stop at Americana television darling *Austin City Limits*. The group would also bless the inaugural Farm Aid benefit concert.

In this period, the group performed countrified versions of "Motor City" and "Southern Pacific," which didn't see an official release until 2011 via the live album *A Treasure*. But their country-rock makeovers pointed to the ways future country stars would herald and adopt the sounds and message of '80s-era heartland rock.

According to several newspapers, Young's performance at the 1984 Louisiana World Exposition in New Orleans was riddled with pro-Reagan declarations. After deriding those critical of Reagan's "trigger-happy cowboy" image, he also disavowed the rose-colored glasses of his hippie origins. "This is not the age of idealism," he said. "I'm very pro-American, actually—very patriotic." He also spoke out in support of work. The bootstraps kind. "You can't always support the weak. You have to make the weak stand up on one leg or half a leg, whatever they've got."

Though he has since walked back these statements, claiming they were blown out of proportion by reporters and fans, they tender an eerie prophecy. Heartland rock originated as a practical evolution of leftist working-class solidarity and hippie idealism. It grew in service of underdogs and the overlooked. In drawing a line in the sand between optimism and patriotism, however, Young extolled the kind of white male grievance that would pervade America in the new millennium under President Donald Trump. With Re*ac*tor and his work with the International Harvesters, he harnessed the widespread appeal of heartland rock, and demonstrated how it would be mishandled by politicians, fans, and country music stars in succeeding years.

In August of 1985, ahead of a benefit concert in Cheyenne, Wyoming, Young expressed his support for local farmers whose land had been wrecked by five days of intense rainfall that killed eighteen people. Neil Young and the International Harvesters, and their glorious twang-fueled racket, were set to raise money in service of relief efforts. "We're having our equipment flown in on the same plane that carries troops," Young explained to a reporter. Though he was excited about the prospect of helping others, particularly those whose labor signaled a kind of patriotic authenticity, he was seemingly more thrilled about the source of the opportunity. Of the planes, he said, "that had to come right from Reagan."

★ ★ ★

MTV officially launched on August 1, 1981, broadcasting an English new wave band to homes in New Jersey. The Buggles' "Video Killed the Radio Star" music video became the first set of moving images associated with executive Robert Pittman's experiment in music television. But heartland rock became some of its most valuable imagery by the time MTV went national and moved toward a Top 40 format.

The heartland-heartthrob archetype popularized in the 1980s is inextricable from the advent of music videos, which animated John Mellencamp's Midwest rebel bona fides, Tom Petty's Southern eccentricity, Bonnie Raitt's salt-of-the-earth romance, and Bruce Springsteen's denim-clad ass. The Boss's austere black-and-white video for "Atlantic City" depicted the barren landscapes of his concern on the album Nebraska. The video for "Jack & Diane," one of Mellencamp's most beloved songs, romanticized the people and locales of rural small-town life. "You Got Lucky," Petty's cinematic take on Mad Max futurism, conveyed just how creative the Everyman could be.

The archetype, solidified via Springsteen's Brian De Palma–directed "Dancing in the Dark" video, lionized the imperishable sex appeal of a regular dude in a tight white shirt and broken-in jeans—even one who could not dance. MTV did what no regional radio station could: broadcast the same music video to millions of teenagers and young adults across America. In pairing musicians' images with their music, MTV promoted humans as brands long before the internet and influencers. It encouraged musicians and fans to choose a team by adhering to a prescribed look. In the process, it elevated denim-wearing heartland rockers to symbols of sex and solidarity, an antidote to new wave fantasy, pastel pop, and hair metal spandex. MTV made heartland rock's lowbrow interpretations of James Dean fashionable. Promoting music may have been the stated goal, but style and image became MTV's most powerful byproduct. Or, as Mellencamp put it in a "style diary" published in *Rolling Stone* in 1999: "Unlike style, which for me is a private accident that spills into a public place, music begins in a private space but moves on purpose into a public forum."

The TV channel's national reach was an astronomical leap from the regional radio stations attributed to heartland rock's rise. There may be no better example of this than Cleveland's 100.7 WMMS "The Buzzard," which promoted rock 'n roll as a form of heartland authenticity and a salve for the area's industrial decline. The station made its name by airing '70s and early '80s album-oriented rock, including beloved locals the Michael Stanley Band, Jersey's South Side Johnny and the Asbury Jukes, and Springsteen, Mellencamp, Seger, and Petty. It became so beloved and synonymous with the problematic anti–new wave, pro "real rock" sentiment coursing through the nation's working class that it was voted Radio Station of the Year in *Rolling's Stone*'s annual reader poll for seven years straight, from 1979–1986. It also helped solidify Cleveland's status as the "home of rock 'n' roll."

Throughout his career as a disc jockey, the station's DJ Kid Leo played Springsteen's "Born to Run" on Friday nights as a signal of the coming weekend, making it synonymous with the two-day sanctuary for area workers. The Cleveland native born Lawrence James Travagliante—who now serves as general manager and afternoon disc jockey on Steven Van Zandt's long-running Sirius XM channel Little Steven's Underground Garage—began spinning the "Born to Run" 45 in the '70s long before it was widely available. He is credited with helping make The Boss a household name beyond his New Jersey stomping ground early on. By the 1980s, WMMS was proving that the earnest songs of Mellencamp, Petty, Seger, and Springsteen, and the social and political messages they represented, rang true to large swathes of working people.

Stations such as WMMS primed heartland rock for its success on MTV, where its existing fanbase reveled in seeing heightened versions of themselves on national television. Such radio stations are also the reason regionally beloved rock groups such as the Michael Stanley Band, Robin Lane & the Chartbusters, and Illinois power-pop act Shoes were among the first groups with videos in regular rotations on MTV. Throughout much of the '70s and '80s, everyday working people from the Midwest were an exception to popular culture broadcast on television. Most sitcoms were set in California, big cities, and tony suburbs. With heartland rock, places like Bloomington, Indiana, became visible and even alluring.

Enthusiasm for heartland rock's blue jean dream boats culminated in an ill-conceived 1984 promotion tied to Mellencamp's single "Pink Houses," whose 45 and cassette sleeves depict the Hoosier in a denim jacket with the collar popped and a cigarette hanging from his lips. MTV's "Paint the Mutha Pink" contest, which had absolutely nothing to do with the song's themes of inequality and disenfranchisement, was a "Party House" promotion in which one lucky winner scored a house painted pink in Mellencamp's hometown, along with a pink Jeep CJ, a Pioneer stereo system, and a housewarming party in which Mellencamp would man the grill and perform with his band in the living room. Runners-up received a copy of Mellencamp's album *Uh-Huh*. Viewers entered the contest by mailing a postcard.

Though the contest's contrived premise seemed to counter the small-town genuineness it sought to give away, there was an even bigger problem with "Paint the Mutha Pink." The little one-story house in Monroe County that MTV purchased for $20,000 was located across the street from a forty-acre landfill, named one of the nation's most hazardous in a 1981 study by the Environmental Protection Agency.

"We had the well tested, and the water samples came out OK," said Priscilla Mellencamp, the singer's ex-wife who'd served as MTV's real estate agent on the deal. "Basically, John just did not feel right about it." The network put the house back on the market for $38,900, purchased a new one closer to Bloomington, and painted it Pepto Bismol pink. Journalists across the country soon caught wind of the snafu, and published stories with headlines such as "Little Stink Houses."

A college student from Washington was the lucky winner. Susan Miles of Seattle featured heavily in an MTV follow-up video alongside Mellencamp and a cast of friends and locals. "It's great, I love it," she declared. Soon after, however, she sold her winnings and moved back to Washington. Rural Indiana didn't live up to the allure Mellencamp and his fame had assigned to it, it seems.

For as much as heartland rock espoused back-to-basics, within the context of fame, its figureheads and homebases became so magnified that they morphed into larger-than-life characters, just like pop stars. Mellencamp, the human from Indiana, was a motorcycle-riding hilljack in faded denim and tattered jackets. Mellencamp, the character, was a sexy proletarian ideal rooted in sentimentality and radical optimism for everyday Americans' place in the country's future. The character was effective. WMMS's 1982 rock music poll named Mellencamp the best male vocalist of the year. It also declared *Nebraska*, Springsteen's introspective jewel that is decidedly not a rock record, the worst album of 1982 because Springsteen had broken character.

The downside to that character is that heartland rock's mythical people and places are nearly impossible to live up to in the real world. They reflected the dogged optimism and contrarian spirit of those born in the heartland and other embattled locales where commitment to community, and hardworn roads to prosperity, are forged in service of a state, county, or hometown that has been consistently overlooked and underestimated. In the heartland, folks embrace what outsiders dismiss. The writer Thomas Wolfe first posited the idea that a person can never really return home because nostalgia causes humanity to view the past in an overly idealistic light. To put it another way, for those born and raised in the heartland, one can never truly leave home. To be born in the heartland, Rust Belt, or other marginalized or embattled area, is to be imbued with a polite but fighting spirit that embraces self-mocking titles like the Second City. It is to be steered by an against-all-odds pride that is rendered on T-shirts declaring "Midwest is Best" and "Ohio Against the World." Heartland rock echoed and amplified the feelings and experiences of the American listener. In the process, it constructed a mythical world.

So did MTV. In its infancy, the station had just one Black video jockey, J. J. Jackson, who stayed with the channel for five years before returning to rock radio in Los Angeles. The channel also didn't play videos by Black artists until 1983 with "Pass the Dutchie" by British-Jamaican act Musical Youth and, more famously, Michael Jackson's "Billie Jean." "There seem to be a lot of Black artists making very good music videos that I'm surprised aren't on MTV," David Bowie said to MTV VJ Mark Goodman during an interview the same year.

MTV's response to Bowie was that it was a rock-focused channel with a responsibility to play what the average American viewer wanted. "We have to try and do what we think not only New York and Los Angeles will appreciate but also Poughkeepsie or Midwest," Goodman stated, demonstrating how little New York knew about the Midwest. According to the 1980 US Census, Midwestern states were about 21–26 percent Black on average.

Though they were both predominantly white in this period, heartland rock and MTV differed in their regard and understanding of what constituted an "average" listener. The former sought to spotlight racism, speak out against it, and herald its own Black influences to multiracial and multigenerational fans. Heartland rock's tactics may not hold water in today's climate of low tolerance for appropriation, and mocking reactions to Bruce Springsteen releasing an entire album of soul music covers. But in the 1980s, such open unions and attributions were still radical. The rock vs. disco wars of the late 1970s had carried over into the new decade, and music remained deeply bifurcated between races. Racism was essentially baked into the music industry. The American Music Awards, which carried much more influence in the Reagan years than it does today, included categories such as "Best Black Album" and "Best Black Male Artist."

MTV, on the other hand, hadn't featured Black people and music until being denounced for it. A demonstration in ignorance aside, there was no barring the forces of Michael Jackson and especially Prince. Just ask Mellencamp, who was such a fan of the latter that he played "Little Red Corvette" during multiple tour stops. That's not to say he and his band performed a cover of the song. Instead, Mellencamp literally lifted a boombox to a microphone and played Prince's recording of "Little Red Corvette" for midsized arenas before *Purple Rain* was released. He loved it that much. He also reportedly asked Prince to sing on fan favorite "Pink Houses," but the Purple One declined. Tom Petty was also inspired by Prince, and has explained that the Minnesotan's synth-driven psychedelic funk directly inspired his 1985 hit with the Heartbreakers, "Don't Come Around Here No More."

Bruce Springsteen has long discussed the importance of Black soul and pop music in his life and career. He began performing his cover of Arthur Conely's "Sweet Soul Music" during *The River* tour and has since made his "Detroit Medley" a staple of his concerts. Bob Seger was similarly raised and inspired by Black artists he listened to on the radio, namely Wilson Pickett and James Brown, and their heart-on-sleeve, raw performances that he soon channeled into his own. Seger was also thrilled to be on the same tickets as Howlin' Wolf and Muddy Waters as his career began to take off. "I made my own decisions very young, and I decided that racism was totally idiotic," he said in 1980. Bonnie Raitt's entire career changed when she began playing slide guitar inspired by Delta bluesmen such as Robert Johnson, Son House, and Fred McDowel, and she became a crucial ally of female blues icons such as Sippie Wallace.

Though the heartland "character" created and promoted by the likes of Springsteen was all but impossible to achieve in the real world, that it exists at all is remarkable. As the 1980s grew in service of Wall Street, heartland rock's stars proved that the everyday worker and the underdog could hold their own alongside what had been deemed important or exceptional by the decade's prevailing sentiment. Heartland rock posed an important and enduring counterpoint to the era's narratives of wealth and materialism. In the 1980s, as now, farmers, factory workers, and their family and friends, deserved respect, dignity, and celebration. Through heartland rock's songs, they actually received it.

CHAPTER 3

1982

MACHINES OF THE YEAR

We see a couple of good things going on in the '80s. One is
that people are starting to think about others more than ever
before. And the other is that technology is helping to bring us
closer together.

—STEVE WOZNIAK, APPLE COFOUNDER

"While everyone else talks about the revolution that's coming, you
can experience the revolution that's here." This tagline for the
Commodore 64 personal computer, introduced at the annual trade show CES during the first weekend in January 1982, embodied wider attitudes toward technological advances as the Reagan era pressed on. There were those for whom such consumer technology was a distant reality, a development that was far too expensive, advanced, or impractical to entertain. Others understood it for a real and present truth, one that would quickly evolve in its capabilities and influence, and shape our future lives.

When the Commodore 64 hit retail stores it stirred a revolution. It was the only high-powered machine offered for less than $600. At the time, home computers by Apple, Atari, and IBM cost between $900 and $1,500, prices that were beyond the reach of most Americans. Commodore's model spurred mass demand. One executive claimed that the company was producing nearly half a million machines each month for a couple of years at its height.

New technology aimed at the home consumer rippled throughout American industry. Machines such as synthesizers, drum machines, home recording devices, and digital sequencers became popular, but they split artists much as the rock vs. disco divide had. For many in the rock world, such machines were inauthentic, the tools of amateurs, shallow pop producers, performance-art flakes, and toothless new wave bands. For few others, they were an opportunity to make music on one's own terms, or an occasion to experiment and demonstrate one's willingness to keep up with the times. Amid the intense technological buzz, heartland rock took up residence in both camps.

Bruce Springsteen, John Mellencamp, Bonnie Raitt, and a few others had used synthesizers as light brush strokes on a song's canvas, but Tom Petty was the first canonical heartland rock artist to center them in his instrumentation. For a new single, "You Got Lucky," released in the fall of 1982, he used Roland and Oberheim synthesizers to build its framework and drive the song forward. It peaked at No. 20 on the Billboard Hot 100, and Petty became the first heartland rock figurehead to serve as an ambassador for advances in technology at large. With the song, and his headlining spot at the US Festival in 1982, a confluence of music and technology dreamed up by Apple's Steve Wozniak, he demonstrated how such machines may be used to sate both rock and pop audiences.

Discussing music fans and industry figures preoccupied with notions of "authentic American" music amid rapid technological advances, Petty posited that the US and its artistry has always centered ingenuity. "I think they've gotta be careful that American rock doesn't mean Chuck Berry, or as long as they're no synthesizer, it's American . . . being old enough to remember the '60s, I just remember that the people I looked up to were liable to do anything at any given time musically, which made it interesting."

★ ★ ★

John Mellencamp's combative liberalism has long been an unexpected plot twist for casual fans, politicians, and country music stars who've misinterpreted his populist lyrics as base expressions of American chest-beating. Today, he's been met with some version of "How about you stick to music?" for so long that commenting is restricted on many of his social media accounts.

Amid the Reagan presidency and throughout the subsequent decades, Mellencamp's antiracist, pro-farmer, anti-capitalist diatribes were tantamount to a bag full of hornets: intimidating in principle, and punishing when released. Mellencamp has regularly reminded Americans, through a torrent of *fucks*, that musicians also participate in the political process.

Before he became a vocal ally of leftist causes, however, the singer reached a do-or-die crossroads. By the early '80s, he'd come to understand that success was determined by radio play, and that radio play was achieved by a sound much bigger and slicker than the uneven albums he'd been releasing. He knew that he needed to have a hit that could reach as many people as possible.

This didn't stop him from lining his commercial breakthrough, *American Fool*, with deeper meaning; with a kind of mutiny. The same can be said of his performances in this era. As an elder, Mellencamp often jokes about how many tours he was fired from in his salad days, usually because the headlining acts (KISS, REO Speedwagon, British hard rock act Rainbow) and their audiences didn't take to his kiss-off attitude and misfit energy. What may sound apocryphal—like an old man crafting a fiery archetype—has been verified by at least one notable fan.

Gregg Turkington, who performs standup comedy as the misanthropic character Neil Hamburger, recalled an October 1982 gig at Sun Devil Stadium in Tempe, Arizona, where rising radio rocker John Cougar opened for Loverboy and the Who:

"He came out and started doing 'Jack & Diane,' his big hit. Somebody threw a bottle at him and hit him in the head. It just exploded, shattered right on his head, and blood was pouring everywhere. It was insane. Somebody comes and drags him off the stage, the band leaves, and there was an announcement over the PA: 'Coming up next is Loverboy, John Cougar will not be returning.' Five minutes later, he comes back onstage with a hardhat on and his head bandaged up like a fucking mummy. He grabs the microphone and says, 'You fucking pussy cocksucker asshole! I'll kick your motherfucking ass!' Just this insane profanity-laden tirade that went on and on and on. Then they played 'Hurts So Good.' My jaw was on the floor. That was as good as [hardcore punk band] Black Flag."

Mellencamp grew up modestly but comfortably in the idyllic town of Seymour, Indiana, the son of a mother who was an artist and nascent beauty queen, and a father who worked a white-collar job with a local electrical contracting firm. Like much of his heartland rock cohort, Mellencamp wrote from his life—the people and places of his formative years burrowing into his lyrics as an adult. Though Mellencamp had a comfortable upbringing, he saw the hardship endured by his extended family and rural neighbors, the farmers and other laborers. If Bruce Springsteen's greatest gift was mythologizing the existential open graves swallowing up blue-collar workers, Mellencamp's was his piercing ability to at once celebrate and dismantle agrarian fantasy.

It's why "Jack & Diane," from *American Fool*, remains a fan favorite. Mellencamp's tale of two lovers on the cusp of adulthood, staring down the barrel of societal expectations—with mortality looming in the background—is rife with the details of an Indiana that raised the singer. In the song, an old-growth tree provides cover from the watchful eye of puritanical church folk; chili dogs and ice cream are an excuse to break free from parents. Listeners who'd never stolen away to a soft-serve stand under the guise of an innocent meetup responded to the song's mellifluous reading of coming-of-age courtship and simpler-days nostalgia. Tastee-Freez, which Mellencamp name-checked, was any diner or drive-in. Jack and Diane were any number of wanton teens.

If there is one place that embodies Middle American disposition, it is Tastee-Freez—"The Tastee-Freez" to many Hoosiers—where frozen confections and encased meat flowed like wind through a field of yellow dent corn. Tastee-Freez was where Middle American children were rewarded, budding adults savored their first morsels of independence, and old-timers gathered to reminisce. It was bad-for-you food at good-for-you prices and more nourishing than its nutritional comportment implied. However, no Tastee-Freez location has ever existed in Mellencamp's hometown. Kovener's Korner, a tiny shop that opened in 1949 about two blocks from Mellencamp's boyhood home at 714 West Fifth Street in Seymour, was most likely the singer's childhood frozen-treats respite, but it was a Tastee-Freez in spirit only. In the "Jack & Diane" video, Mellencamp and his second wife, Victoria Granucci, paw at one another outside of a rustic stand serving big Tastee-Freez energy. But that stand was in fact the Penguin, located at 405 S. Walnut Street in nearby Bloomington, which lives on as beloved local ice cream shop the Chocolate Moose.

Even if Tastee-Freez wasn't part of Mellencamp's regular soft-serve rotation, his invocation of the brand in "Jack & Diane" all but secured its position in the annals of history. It also implied a brilliant strategy on behalf of the singer: to spotlight all people in all small towns, folks who aren't often celebrated in popular music.

In the fall of 1982, "Jack & Diane" spent four weeks at No. 1 on the Billboard Hot 100 singles chart, his only song to do so. *American Fool* also went to No. 1 on the Billboard 200 for nine weeks and became the biggest record of the year. Upon its release, it knocked Fleetwood Mac's *Mirage*, a symbol of overproduced pop excess and the antithesis of heartland rock's back-to-basics essence, from the pole position.

Like the first single from *American Fool*, "Hurts So Good," cowritten with Mellencamp's childhood friend George Green, "Jack & Diane" is a horndog anthem of pre–AIDS crisis dispensation. But the similarities stopped there. "Hurts So Good" and its biker-gang music video only hinted at the heart and rural perspective that became synonymous with the singer. Among the dirtbag fraternity, Mellencamp appears with a red bandana fashioned around his neck—a nod to America's original "rednecks," those miners in West Virginia in the early 1920s who wore them as a symbol of solidarity and resistance amid an ongoing struggle for fair wages and safer working conditions.

Hitching his wagon to the geography of working people was a bold enough choice in a decade marked by widespread social and economic warfare against blue-collar workers and the middle class. But Mellencamp took it a step further when writing "Jack & Diane."

In Mellencamp's original demos, Jack was a young Black man, and Diane was white.

Amid archival research for the songwriter's 2010 career retrospective box set, *On the Rural Route 7609*, it was revealed that the two American kids raised in the heartland are an interracial couple. In 2009, Mellencamp explained that the set's archivist rediscovered this fact when digging through old demos.

Steve Berkowitz, a Grammy Award-winning producer, and the man who signed singer-songwriter Jeff Buckley to Columbia Records in the early 1990s, stayed with Mellencamp at his home in Bloomington, Indiana, for weeks during the research phase of *7609*, and was the guy, as Mellencamp described it, "leaving no stone unturned."

The origins of "Jack & Diane" may be traced to a demo from the late '70s, titled "Jenny at 16." It contains a few lines from the chart topper, and also mirrors its nostalgic spirit. The song's narrator runs with Jenny through a field of Johnson grass, a weed that is particularly invasive in farmland, and can grow up to ten feet high. The pair "suck" on a cigarette outside of Tastee-Freez, and Jenny places her hands between the young man's knees. Bobby Brooks trousers are also summoned.

The demo of "Jenny at 16" included with *On the Rural Route 7609* makes no mention of the young man's race, or Jenny's. But that changed when Mellencamp recast the song ahead of the *American Fool* sessions.

Berkowitz was the first person to whom Mellencamp revealed the song's origin story all those years later. "He says I discovered it," Berkowitz told me. "But he did sing it, and he handed me the cassette demos . . . and I listened." He explained there are at least four different demos of "Jack & Diane" with just Mellencamp and an acoustic guitar in his troubadour mode, wherein he sings, "Jack was Black . . . Diane was white."

However, none of those versions of the demo made it onto the *7609* CD box set, and the line was cut from the studio version of "Jack & Diane" released on *American Fool*. Mellencamp has attributed the edit to both an overbearing record label and his own reluctance to rock the proverbial boat any more than he already did during the protracted and tumultuous making of the album.

Over the years, Mellencamp has claimed that his great-grandmother (or great-great grandmother, depending on the interview) was Black, though public genealogy records show no direct evidence of that. However, he may have distant African American ancestry on his father's side. What is more accurate is that Mellencamp, like many kids in Indiana, grew up with Black friends and witnessed interracial couples in his high school years and in audiences as a young musician.

In high school, Mellencamp joined Crape Soul, a covers band. The group had eight members at its height, a couple of them Black, including founding member and lead singer Fred Booker. Some time after the group formed, Mellencamp signed on as the band's second singer and performed with them at school dances, sock hops, fraternities, and battle of the bands competitions. According to Booker and fellow founding member Duane Zimmerman, the group played its first show at a "splash dance" at a local public pool on July 19, 1968. At one point, they had business cards printed that touted Fred Booker as vocalist, Rod Chavez on bass, and John Mellencamp as another vocalist. "For the Best in Popular Music," the card proclaimed.

As the band's second singer, Mellencamp belted out covers of James Brown, Sam & Dave, and Motown singles, and also pop hits like "I'm Your Puppet," and songs by Mitch Ryder and John Sebastian, in sparkling stagewear and pointy Flagg Brothers oxfords. At times he even donned a cape. But by the summer of 1969, Mellencamp's participation in the group was spotty or had ended. An article in *The Tribune*, Jackson County's newspaper, published on August 5, named members Booker, Zimmerman, Dave Hinton, Dennis Blair, Mike Henderson, Gary Keck, and Rick Schill as the winners of that year's Combo Clash at the Jackson County Fair, where Crepe Soul was awarded $50.

In the 1960s, when Mellencamp was coming of age, Jackson County, which includes his hometown Seymour, hovered around thirty-one thousand residents, with about 1 percent of that population composed of Black families. Demographically, it was a far cry from the more populous and integrated environs of nearby cities like Indianapolis and Evansville. But the singer has often said that his time in the group was an education in both music and prejudice, with audiences cheering on the band during performances, and then hurling punches and racial epithets after their shows. "The interesting thing about being in that band was I learned about race, real quick," Mellencamp said. "There were a couple of times when we played some place, and they loved us on stage. But when we came off stage, it was like the white kids were able to stay inside the building, but Fred and everybody else had to go outside. So I just went outside with them."

As the years wore on, Mellencamp became increasingly vocal about his antiracist stances. In 1983, he released "Pink Houses," a song about redlining specifically and inequality more broadly, whose "Ain't that America" refrain was quickly mistaken for a 10-cent expression of patriotism. A year later, in 1984, he began incorporating Bob Dylan's antiracist anthem "The Lonesome Death of Hattie Carroll" into his live sets. Throughout the succeeding decades, Mellencamp released music videos portraying interracial love and friendship, and often spoke out against America's enduring legacy of racism. In 2008, he released "Jena," a song protesting the trial of the so-called Jena Six in Louisiana. (In the early '90s, he carved the phrase "fuck racism" into the body of his Gibson Dove acoustic guitar.)

When President Barack Obama was elected to his first term in office in 2008, Mellencamp performed at the administration's inaugural "We Are One" concert at the Lincoln Memorial. He also sang the traditional folk song "Keep Your Eyes on the Prize" at Obama's White House celebration of music from the civil rights movement. "It was at that point in my life that I learned about how hate can really affect people," he explained to the audience ahead of the song, referring to his time in the Crepe Soul, when he witnessed racism and discrimination aimed at his Black bandmates.

"I think John Cougar is the best spokesman of our time. The guy's not fucking around," the musician Steve Wynn, leader of the influential Los Angeles–based paisley underground band the Dream Syndicate, told a reporter for *Creem* magazine in 1983. "John Cougar's a better spokesman for our time than any art critic's band. I mean, what has Gang of Four done for the heartlands of America that John Cougar hasn't done?"

Reflecting on the gamble of his 1982 album and its left-wing populist spirit, Mellencamp asked, "Can you imagine if *American Fool* had stunk? I mean with a title like that, I could have been crucified," he said. "But the original name was even worse . . . the name of that record was gonna be 'I May Look Silly, But I've Still Got a Job.'"

★ ★ ★

By 1982, Bonnie Raitt had been a folk chanteuse, a slide guitar luminary, and even a pop-country darling on the hit soundtrack to the film *Urban Cowboy*. She'd spoken out against the Vietnam War and cautioned against nuclear power as cofounder of the group Musicians United for Safe Energy. When Reagan was elected, she was stunned. "I always thought we were in the majority. I thought it was us against them, and it turns out 'us' is the people who voted for Reagan," she explained. "I mean, I never thought the Democrats would lose."

In the late '70s, she was even the subject of an intense bidding war between Warner Bros. and Columbia Records, and renegotiated her contract with the former to terms on par with her male contemporaries. But she'd never been satisfied with any of her records.

That changed with *Green Light*, which could have ferried Raitt to her rightful position of heartland rock monarch whose blend of folk, blues, rhythm and blues, and rock 'n' roll, and evident social consciousness, fit in a burgeoning movement concerned with amplifying the common man specifically, and crafting a new kind of unpretentious rock 'n' roll more broadly. She was also the genre's best singer and most skilled interpreter.

To understand the underwhelming arc of Raitt's career to this point, one must account for the men who had failed her. Most recently, producer Peter Asher, who'd helped sculpt Linda Ronstadt's anodyne sound, paired Raitt's commanding vocals with ultra-slick instrumentation on 1979's *The Glow*. Though its songs like "You're Gonna Get What's Coming" hinted at where Raitt would go next, it failed commercially, and was a particularly tender wound that took three years to heal. She was undermined by suits from the start during the making of *Streetlights*, with Warner Bros. advancing her just 10,000 dollars, and producer Jerry Ragovoy stripping any modicum of joy from the performances via his adult contemporary puppeteering (though her delicious cover of John Prine's "Angel from Montgomery" endures). The making of 1973's *Takin' My Time* was nearly sunk by Little Feat's Lowell George, Raitt's former lover, who couldn't seem to abide a strong woman's perspective on her own music.

Raitt, who referred to herself as a businesswoman in this period, and who managed her own affairs with a small team behind her, wouldn't tolerate the idea that a man had any significant influence over her success or failures, for she was her own North Star. But there is something to be said about a music industry that, for many years, simply refused to hear her. There is something about being the lone woman screaming into the deep black void of white male self-efficacy. It's unjust and quite often a fool's errand. But perhaps more importantly for a musician in the prime of her life, it isn't any fun.

Enter: NRBQ. The sprawling, ever-evolving group of bar band rabble-rousers had, in 1980, released one its most beloved singles, "Me and the Boys," written by founding member Terry Adams. It was a modern rendering of '50s greaser nostalgia, recounting a squad of dudebros whose greatest joy was found cruising around in cars, something Springsteen or Mellencamp could have easily covered, but a tune Raitt took on instead. With her new album, *Green Light*, the aim was joy instead of misery. It was to show the world that she was in the driver's seat.

For this herculean task, Raitt called on Rob Fraboni, who'd produced Raitt's steamy ballad "Once In a Lifetime" for the soundtrack to the widely panned 1980 film *Coast to Coast*. He'd also worked with Bob Dylan and the Band, notably on the soundtrack to Martin Scorsese's film *The Last Waltz*. His studio, Shangri-La, in Malibu, California, was designed and built for the former Big Pink dwellers after they concluded a 1974 tour. It was purchased by producer Rick Rubin in 2011 and has since hosted voices ranging from Adele to Eminem.

It was at this storied location that Raitt gathered her own group of all-stars. Ian "Mac" McLagan of Small Faces, who'd also played with Bob Dylan and the Rolling Stones, helmed keys. His Bump Band, consisting of Johnny Lee Schell on guitar, bassist Ray Ohara, and former Beach Boys drummer Rick Fataar, rounded out the group. Jackson Browne and little-known vocalist Vince Gill, who'd joined country-rock act Pure Prairie League in 1978, each sang on a track, as did Richard Manuel of the Band. "I finally got the right band with the right producer in the right studio," Raitt said of the sessions. "It's the most productive experience I've ever had in a studio. I had a ball." She memorialized the sentiment on the LP's inner sleeve, where a black-and-white photograph shows Raitt and her new band wrapped around one another in a big group hug.

The feeling also rings clear on "Me and the Boys," a sonic rendering of Raitt's excitement about *finding* her rock band, but also *being* in a rock band. The album's tacit mission statement may also be read as Raitt steering a group of young men down the path of her artistic vision, with her agency on full display.

Also threaded throughout *Green Light* are heartland rock's themes of nostalgia and inclusion. Raitt notably applied her smokey blues treatment to Bob Dylan's "Let's Keep It Between Us," detailing the intimate worries of an unnamed interracial couple. Raitt's own "I Can't Help Myself," written in the studio with her band, recalls coming-of-age romance à la "Jack & Diane," with a similarly stripped-back and straightforward rock arrangement; in the song, Raitt sings of former childhood flames; how she'd held hands by the river, and driven around town in search of nothing but fleeting moments of love and freedom. It's a tune that she'd perform at the first Farm Aid benefit concert, cofounded by Mellencamp, in 1985.

Album opener "Keep This Heart in Mind," a rock anthem threaded with the saxophone work of David Woodford, who'd played on Mellencamp's *Nothin' Matters and What if It Did*, was star-making material. Its music video, composed of Shangri-La studio footage interspersed with film of a leather jacket-clad trucker in search of love and meaning, rang of average-joe authenticity and of-its-time production, like the best of the heartland rock movement. Its seamless combination of optimism and sadness could have easily slotted among the twenty tracks of Springsteen's *The River*.

But it instead went to No. 39 and *Green Light* peaked at No. 38 on the Billboard albums chart, far short of Mellencamp's *American Fool*, Springsteen's *Nebraska*, and Bob Seger's *The Distance*, and even albums by heartland rock's forefathers and supporters like Willie Nelson and Crosby, Stills & Nash. It wasn't—as David Letterman had hoped during Raitt's appearance on *Late Night*—the album that would "push her into the star spotlight many feel is long overdue."

For as much as Raitt proclaimed *Green Light* her rock 'n' roll breakthrough, and for as hard and as well as she'd performed her rock songs in the studio and on Letterman, ABC's *Fridays* and MTV, many of the nation's critics decried it as new wave, likely because they'd listened to little more than the album's shaky title track. "Why can't Bonnie Raitt be real and rock out at the same time?" *Rolling Stone* asked in its review, an outrageous criticism similarly aimed at female-led bands of the era like Blondie.

"There were inklings of the direction I was going in all along:

when I started standing up at my shows about five years ago instead of sitting in a chair; when I began to play the Gibson instead of the acoustic, and then a Strat instead of the Gibson; when I moved my up-tempo songs from the encore to the beginning of the set," Raitt explained to one interviewer after the album's release. But once again, it seemed the music world wasn't ready to hear her.

Raitt played around sixty concerts in support of *Green Light*, including big benefit shows like Peace Sunday in Pasadena, California, where she performed alongside Dylan, Tom Petty, and others, and antinuclear concerts Stop Diablo Canyon and the Oregon Nuclear Weapons Freeze. But her rise in the industry of rock music remained stalled, despite palpable support from its biggest artists.

★ ★ ★

As man and machine grew more and more intertwined, *Time* magazine named the personal computer its Man of the Year. Or rather, its Machine of the Year. Silicon Valley also, for the first time, logged in to the world of popular music. On Labor Day Weekend 1982, Apple cofounder Steve Wozniak launched the US Festival, touted as a tech-focused version of Woodstock. The gathering of musicians and technology was conceived as a pollyannaish celebration of togetherness and an antidote to the individualism of the 1970s. It also had the effect of predicting the mingling of music and computers that would spread in the new millennium, and offered a roadmap for future out-there desert fests like Coachella and Burning Man.

Held in Glen Helen Regional Park, a stretch of 1,300 acres between the San Bernardino and San Gabriel Mountains, about sixty miles east of Los Angeles, it was, in the early '80s, a wild experiment. Wozniak, who'd just stepped away from Apple following a plane crash, dreamt up the idea while engaged in a quintessential California activity. Driving on the freeway near his home in Santa Cruz, he meditated on how music moved him and an entire group of forward-thinking minds in ways that were unmatched by other artforms. He thought about how, as Tom Petty once told a British newspaper, "Music is probably the one real magic I have encountered in my life. There's not some trick involved with it. It's pure and it's real. It moves, it heals, it communicates and does all these incredible things."

"I have a habit of going headfirst into risk situations," Wozniak said a few weeks ahead of the festival, while looking out into the 250,000 seat amphitheater he'd built for the occasion, whose stage spanned 240 feet. Under his guidance, and his $12.5 million, the US Festival also boasted a massive three-hundred-thousand-watt sound system with speakers that stretched halfway over onlookers, large-scale Diamond Vision video walls, 110,000 RV and campsites, 1,800 water stations, about forty thousand parking spaces and a cooling area with enough sprinklers to soak five thousand people at a time. The California State Roads Commission also approved, for the first time, the construction and use of a temporary off ramp that funneled traffic directly to the festival. Concert goers could walk freely between the bowl, a beer garden, and five tents that housed a technology fair filled with displays of microprocessors and, at separate points, Herbie Hancock talking about synthesizers, and synthesizer pioneer Robert Moog. An article in the *Silicon Gulch Gazette* explained that festival organizers reserved one tent for "homebrew," or hobbyist projects, and that homebrew creators could compete for prizes in "software and hardware development for microprocessors." They also received a discount on tickets, from $37.50 for three days to $25.

On Day 2, just weeks after a June 12 demonstration in New York City against the arms race and nuclear weapons—the largest gathering of protesters in American history—a satellite link later dubbed the US-Soviet Space Bridge connected the US Festival with folks in the Soviet Union. It was a particularly bold gesture given that, just two summers prior, the US led a sixty-five-nation boycott against the Olympic Games in Moscow. However, by the time the connection was made, and projected on respective large-scale screens in each part of the world, it was too dark outside for the Americans to wave to the Soviets behind the Iron Curtain. One report stated that "the hookup alternated between clips of youths in what looked like a Moscow disco, middle-aged Russian folk dancers and an aerial shot of the U.S. festival concert site."

In evidence of heartland rock's healthy reputation in this time period, hippie-era concert promoter Bill Graham booked Tom Petty and the Heartbreakers as the festival's main event. The band headlined Saturday night of the three-day affair, bookended by the Police on Friday and Fleetwood Mac on Sunday. Following the breakthrough success of *Damn the Torpedoes* in 1979, and 1981's *Hard Promises*, Petty and company were a solid bet. But the frontman was also a fitting headliner for his early embrace of technology, displayed on the group's new album, *Long After Dark*, due for release in November.

Petty was booked after Wozniak lost out to his first choice of a Saturday headliner, Bruce Springsteen, who was about to release his solo opus *Nebraska*. Woz was rumored to have offered The Boss 1 million dollars to perform, which Springsteen declined. Instead, he hid away in New Jersey, working, and making surprise appearances at the Stone Pony, Big Man's West, and other small clubs along the Jersey Shore.

Saturday proved to be the most grueling day of the US Festival, with temperatures reaching 110 degrees and dust clouds that thickened the air. That evening, under a full moon, Petty peered out into the crowd and cracked the driest of jokes to the one hundred thousand or so bodies trapped between mountains. "You guys don't have to be anywhere or anything, right?" he asked in a wry drawl before launching into "One Story Town," his new song about life in the boondocks, and a working-class woman who desired more than what fate had afforded.

The group's pending album, *Long After Dark*, marked the amicable departure of Heartbreakers bassist Ron Blair, who'd been with Petty since 1975, and who had grown tired of the album-tour grind and all of the pressure that came with a rising band. Howie Epstein, part of rock 'n' roll pioneer Del Shannon's band, for whom Petty produced the 1981 comeback album *Drop Down and Get Me* with the Heartbreakers, joined them on bass. Their US Festival performance was a debut of sorts to audiences, with the new bassist playing like a seasoned member.

Epstein had come to LA in the late '70s to play bass with rock singer-songwriter John Hiatt, who released two albums on MCA, which ultimately went nowhere. It would be many more years until his heartland rock breakthrough. Epstein was also a gifted high harmony singer. His backing vocals were peppered throughout *Long After Dark* and soon became a Heartbreakers signature.

Long After Dark also marked Petty's embrace of an instrument widely associated with pop music and new wave. The synthesizer was the hero in era hits like Soft Cell's cover of "Tainted Love" and "I Can't Go for That (No Can Do)" by Hall & Oates. British-American pop-rock act Foreigner's "Waiting for a Girl Like You" featured a synthesizer hook played by little-known Thomas Dolby, which cut through the song's fat like a serrated knife. The synthesizer would appear all over Michael Jackson's forthcoming magnum opus *Thriller*.

John Mellencamp used a Linn drum machine to create the synthetic hand claps that drove "Jack & Diane," and a synthesizer pulsed faintly in the background of a few album tracks from Bonnie Raitt's *Green Light* and *The Glow*. Minneapolis luminary Prince was about to release his master stroke *1999*, whose title track, lyrically conceived as an antinuclear armament protest, thematically fit within the concerns of heartland rock. However, the suite of drum machines and synthesizers used throughout the album amounted to a pure, danceable funk no white boy rock act could rival, let alone recreate. Though the Purple One's vision was singular, what *1999* achieved was a codifying of the Minneapolis Sound that foretold the post-disco, electrofunk motifs woven throughout later pop music. Bonnie Raitt's yearning soulfulness was the closest the heartland movement came to Prince; given the pair's shared soulfulness and worry about nuclear arms, it's no surprise they would team up a few years later.

When it came to the heartland rock coterie of the early '80s, a synthesizer had yet to color a major single in an evident way. Piano, keyboards, and organ? Yes. But Bob Seger, Bruce Springsteen, John

Mellencamp, Bonnie Raitt, and others had not yet released a single that centered a synth in the arrangement.

That began to change with "You Got Lucky," the debut single from Tom Petty's *Long After Dark.* For the song he and Mike Campbell leaned on Oberheim and Roland synthesizers. "Even though some of my purist friends think they should be avoided at all costs, I think they're the instruments of the times," Petty said. Roxy Music's *Avalon* was one of his favorite albums of the year. That atmospheric and densely layered work employed a range of synthesizers, including the Roland Jupiter-8 and the Oberheim OBX, and it shifted Petty's mind toward a new realm of possibility. Of heartland rock's prevailing figures, Petty was the least strident, and it's only fitting that he was the first to rail against the genre's purity tests.

For the first time in a Petty song, guitars ceded the spotlight. He compared the slinky arrangement of "You Got Lucky" to 1976's "Breakdown" but with a stabbing hook made with an Oberheim OBX brass patch. This was much to the chagrin of keyboardist Benmont Tench, who, according to Petty, played it begrudgingly. In a 1980 interview with *Rolling Stone*, Tench explained that his preferred instruments were a Hammond C-3 organ, a Wurlitzer electric piano, a Steinway grand piano and an ARP String Ensemble. He said he used the ARP because "I can't stand synthesizers; they're too cold. Also, the string ensemble is basically just an organ with string sound, and if you fuck with it right, you can make it sound like an old pump organ."

Mike Campbell, who wrote "You Got Lucky" in his home studio to a drum loop, added tremolo guitar work that landed somewhere between surf music and Ennio Morricone, providing an earthen counterpoint to the synthesizer blasts. This mix of old and new was visually rendered in the song's music video, which raised the creative bar for the burgeoning format. Before Michael Jackson's "Thriller" video made MTV a household name, Petty crafted a mini music movie of his own.

Inspired by the postapocalyptic desert setting of the movies "Mad Max" and "Mad Max 2," which was released in 1981, Petty and the Heartbreakers paired a barren stretch of sand with modern technology. Dressed in a blend of classic Western wear and biker leather-daddy chic, Petty and Campbell pull off to the side of a desert highway and descend from their white hover car, borrowed from the TV version of the film *Logan's Run*. After being joined by the three other Heartbreakers, who arrive on a motorcycle with a sidecar, the group stumbles upon a mysterious tent. Filled with TVs, an arcade game, sequencers, and other machines with multicolored lights, drummer Stan Lynch flips a breaker, and the group proceeds to watch some of their past performances on the screens, as if to silently comment on how far they've come. Petty's cinematic interpretation of a music video became a hit on MTV. Reportedly, Michael Jackson called the band-leader to sing its praises. The song also reached No. 20 on the Billboard Hot 100.

Long After Dark also marked the fracture of a crucial relationship. When Tom Petty discovered that producer Jimmy Iovine was working on Bob Seger's *The Distance* at the same time he was producing *Long After Dark*, he felt betrayed. According to Petty, Iovine had seemed distracted throughout the session, taking phone call after phone call in the studio—so much so that Petty cut the wall phone's cord more than once. But this was a bridge too far. "As I saw it, I'm a fulltime job," he told biographer Warren Zanes.

After performing "One Story Town," "A Woman in Love (It's Not Me)," "Kings Road," "Breakdown," "Refugee," a cover of the Isley Brothers' "Shout," and "So You Want to Be a Rock 'n' Roll Star," Tom Petty and the Heartbreakers concluded their US Festival set with the beloved Everyman anthem "Even the Losers." On its surface a song about bygone sexual yearning and simpler-days nostalgia, in this setting, with the band flanked by futuristic graphics, multiple spotlights, strobes, a state-of-the-art sound system, and tents filled with cutting-edge computers, one line from the song rang differently—its teen angst transformed to something predictive and wise. On September 2, 1982, it was very much a drag to live in the past.

★ ★ ★

If 1982 was a point of no return for the digital age—incubating the hope, fear, possibility, and dread that comes with technological advances that would, for better or worse, define and steer life as we know it—Bruce Springsteen's work in this period cast back the whole truth of this new kind of life. It demonstrated the antisocial isolation prompted by consumer-grade machines long before chatrooms and social media, and conveyed the dehumanizing effect of digital gloss on even the most human of subjects. It also rallied against the kind of tech that could destroy entire nations.

Springsteen offered a prophetic look into a future America where everyone is connected, and everyone is lonely, and all we can do is move toward an uncertain future. "There are two parts to the American character," Springsteen said in 2016. "One is very isolated and one is in search of community. So how do you make your peace with both of those things?"

By the time he completed the tour in the fall of 1981, Springsteen lost the lease on the Holmdel farmhouse where he wrote *Darkness on the Edge of Town* and *The River*. On a whim, he rented a modest ranch home with orange shag carpeting in nearby Colts Neck, New Jersey. He was, for the first time in his life, financially solvent. He was also on the brink of an existential crisis and a major depressive episode.

When you grow up with very little, it's hard to imagine a life where money is no object. For most, that day never arrives. A clock-punching, discount existence amounts to something humble, but also something honest. The statistical anomaly who attains the so-called American dream, who rises out of the ashes of poverty to a life of riches, is hit with the wallop of guilt: for having more than his parents, for having separated himself from the people and places that raised him, for amassing wealth from the hard-earned dollars of the common man. For Springsteen, the status was even more complicated. Nearly every single person he called a friend was on his payroll. There was basically no one whose livelihood didn't depend on his continued success, on the commodification of his art.

After much internal debate, he bought his first new car, a Camaro

Z28, which, as he wrote in his autobiography *Born to Run*, "felt as conspicuous as if I were driving a solid gold Rolls Royce." As if by a magnetic pull, he often steered the gilded peacock through the streets of his origin, Freehold, New Jersey, where he surveyed "the little town that had its crushing boot on my neck in whatever mental time, place or moment I chose." The poverty of his youth maintained an outsized presence on his psyche as he became one of the most beloved musicians in America.

One night, while flipping through tv channels in that humble little ranch house, Springsteen happened upon filmmaker Terrence Mallick's 1973 directorial debut *Badlands* and became fascinated with the murderous spree of Charles Starkweather and Caril Ann Fugate across Nebraska and Wyoming. He read the Southern Gothic short stories of Flannery O'Connor and soundtracked its imagery with the music of Robert Johnson, John Lee Hooker, and Elvis Presley's Sun Sessions.

With *The River*, he annotated the chasm between the American dream and the American reality, tapping into the worlds of his grandparents, parents, and siblings as his own place in that realm came into question. With the album that became *Nebraska*, Springsteen dove into the depths of America's shadow sides, recounting the conflict, paranoia, and criminality of life in the margins, a hyper-literary spin on the childhood ghosts he rode with, and the disenfranchised of America more broadly. As with much of heartland rock, he channeled the past in order to say something about the present. But here there was no moral. There was only the quiet of the rearview mirror.

Over the course of about three months, he wrote with a fever. He wrote only for the sake of exorcism. Then, in January of 1982, with the help of his guitar tech Mike Batlan, he procured a TEAC 144 Tascam Series four-track recorder, the first model to use a standard cassette tape—the kind you could buy at a drugstore. With it, he began to track demos.

Alone, hiding from the spotlight of his newfound celebrity, he sang of murderers ("Nebraska"), mobsters, corruption, despair and mortality ("Atlantic City"), the closing of the Ford Motor plant in Mahwah, New Jersey, and its spiritual fallout ("Johnny 99") and the complicated love of brothers ("Highway Patrolman"). He meditated on the clinging web of his youth ("Mansion on the Hill," "Used Cars," and "My Father's House") and offered one of music's greatest misdirections with "Reason to Believe," which is rife with dismal images. He channeled the itinerant spirit of Woody Guthrie, and the blues, country, and rhythm and blues amalgam of Presley's Sun Sessions, and colored his narratives with a suite of acoustic six- and-twelve string guitars, harmonica, mandolin, and even glockenspiel.

In the midst of his writing spree, another song surfaced that would eventually take on a very different shape. After meeting Ron Kovic in the late '70s, Springsteen funneled his empathy and advocacy for veterans into a new song. "Born in the U.S.A." recounted the plight of men who'd returned from war to little more than a pat on the back, who suffered from PTSD and economic hardship and were left in the nation's shadows. Like many of Springsteen's *Nebraska*-era exorcisms, its specific tale of down-and-out also reflected the spirit of a working America alienated by political bluster. Its protest rang out from that same place of shock and desperation.

When Springsteen finally decided to share his new songs with the E Street Band, in April of 1982, it was quickly apparent that much of the spare, ghostly material of *Nebraska* wasn't fit for a full-band production. It is fairly common knowledge that the group recorded an "electric" version of *Nebraska* that Springsteen shelved until the release of an archival reissue, *Nebraska '82*, released in the fall of 2025. However, while tracking the song "Born in the U.S.A." at the Power Station in Hell's Kitchen, the group hit upon a sound that was undeniable. Drummer Max Weinberg had been revisiting the work of the Rolling Stones, particularly 1968's "Street Fighting Man." "I was getting back into Charlie Watts's drumming and the beauty of it and the simplicity yet complexity of it," he said. So he decided to play a similarly spare but powerful intro composed of a series of snare hits. Session engineer Toby Scott ran Weinberg's snare microphone through a reverb plate and into a noise gate, creating the explosive "gated reverb" snare sound that became the song's signature. When paired with keyboardist Roy Bittan's opening riff, played on a Yamaha CS-80—considered one of the best and most expensive polyphonic analog synthesizers— the music of "Born in the U.S.A." became as powerful as its message; a prescient fusion of technology and humanity.

About two months later, on June 12, 1982, about one million people gathered in Central Park to protest nuclear weapons as the United Nations held a special session on disarmament. Part of the wider Nuclear Freeze Campaign that had been building since the late '70s, the demonstration proved to be the largest peace rally in United States history, eliciting a diverse array of support from religious groups, professional associations, politicians, environmentalists, academics, and creatives, and across races and nationalities.

Reagan had come into office as a vocal critic of the Strategic Arms Limitation Treaty II and an American detente with the Soviets. Instead, he sought to modernize the US weapons program by building a new missile defense system. Over the eight years of his presidency, American spending on nuclear weapons saw a 39 percent increase over the previous eight-year period, and many Americans feared mutually assured destruction. In May of 1982, Congress passed a Freeze Resolution by a wide margin, but concern about nuclear war with the Soviet Union remained.

During the summer of 1982, Springsteen, amid working on *Nebraska* and the album that became *Born in the U.S.A.*, embarked on a series of small club gigs along the Jersey Shore. From May to October, he made thirty-three surprise appearances, often in the twilight hours, at the Stone Pony and Fast Lane clubs in Asbury Park, Brighton Bar in Long Branch, and his bandmate Clarence Clemons's club Big Man's West in Red Bank. He even popped up at the Monmouth County Fair. Most often, these weren't solo gigs. He usually joined the night's local band. Cats on a Smooth Surface, the Stone Pony's rock 'n' roll house band, was his favorite.

During the Rally for Nuclear Disarmament, he extended that same spirit. On Central Park's Great Lawn, Springsteen reunited with Jackson Browne to perform "The Promised Land" from *Dark-*

ness on the Edge of Town and Browne's "Running on Empty." Joan Baez, Linda Ronstadt, James Taylor, Bonnie Raitt, Carly Simon, Graham Nash, Peter, Paul and Mary, and Springsteen's friend Gary U. S. Bonds, among others, also performed. This was between a lineup of guest speakers, including the actor and director Orson Welles, who denounced nuclear arms and the Reagan administration.

The scene was a visual rendering of 1960s activism reimagined for the burgeoning digital age. It also demonstrated that the new guard of rock icons had the same level of consciousness. Springsteen's image most often had more to do with the 1950s, but his actions projected something deeper than classic cars and Elvis. Working local clubs and a peace rally near the height of his powers was demonstrative of his internal struggle with fame, and his fear of a loss of normalcy. But with that fear came a boots-on-the-ground awareness, a desire to be with the people and to address the issues of the day. It was, as the musician Nina Simone once said, his way of reflecting the times.

The same was true of his art. Though the song "Born in the U.S.A." and the album *Nebraska* demonstrated very different ways of working, and incorporated contrasting moods and instrumentation, both convey a desire for contemporary relevance; a desire to use the latest tools. "You know, my music utilizes things from the past, because that's what the past is for. It's to learn from," Springsteen told the critic Dave Marsh in 1981. "It's not to limit you. . . . I don't want to make a record like they made in the '50s or the '60s or the '70s. I want to make a record like today, that's right now."

When Springsteen released *Nebraska*, the rock press rushed to place its violent and ghostly qualities within the nation's current state of affairs. It was difficult to indulge a lonely, unraveling man when there was so much political and social strife. *Nebraska* arrived at retail stores amid high rates of unemployment and homelessness, and nuclear paranoia. Reagan had also recently survived an assassination attempt. It seemed that brutality was the new norm. Greil Marcus drew parallels between *Nebraska* and Reagan in his review for *New West* magazine, placing incendiary quotes from the president alongside lyrics from "Used Cars" and "Mansion on the Hill." He explained that *Nebraska* was the "most complete and probably the most convincing statement of resistance and refusal that Ronald Reagan's U.S.A. has yet elicited, from any artist or any politician."

After Springsteen jettisoned the idea of a bipolar double album—one LP of somber singer-songwriter music, and the other filled with full-band rock—he released his collection of ghostly demos as the album *Nebraska* in September of 1982. For as spartan and insular as the songs were, they were a daredevil follow-up to *The River*, a filled-to-the-brim double LP featuring one of the world's best bar bands, and his most successful album to date. Through the lens of time, *Nebraska* was also a pioneer that helped launch the four-track revolution; a thousand lonely bedroom poets singing into their machines for no one.

In a letter sent to his manager Jon Landau, Springsteen explained, "You sent me the Paul Schrader script which I did not have the chance to read yet, but I did whip up this little ditty purloining its title." Ultimately, Springsteen didn't participate in the film that became *Light of Day* starring Michael J. Fox, Gena Rowlands, and Joan Jett in her film debut. But the song whose title he stole from that script, "Born in the U.S.A.," became a larger-than-life symbol of a fraught man in an anxious world. It would also become perhaps the most misunderstood song in American history.

After its release, *Nebraska* saw mixed reviews but sold well enough to reach No. 3 on Billboard's pop albums chart. In its yearly critics' poll, Pazz & Jop, the *Village Voice* named the album the third-best of the year with sixty-seven votes, bested only by Elvis Costello's experimental opus *Imperial Bedroom* (at first place) and Richard and Linda Thompson's folk-rock masterstroke *Shoot Out the Lights* (coming in second).

The video for "Atlantic City," Springsteen's first to air on MTV, echoed the album's ghostly timbre. Composed of black-and-white footage that contrasted the resort town's casino glamour with the living reality of its working-class neighborhoods, the singer was depicted in spirit only. His boots and denim were missing from each frame, but his fragile psyche loomed large.

His absence extended to the album's cover, a black-and-white photograph of a lonesome highway, taken from the window of an old pickup truck in the dead of winter. Photographer David Michael Kennedy shot it in 1975, amid an existential crisis quite similar to Springsteen's. "I had just finished a rough couple of months in New York City," Kennedy said. "I decided to take a road trip and have a bit of rest and relaxation. At that time, I was doing a lot of fashion and advertising work as well as beginning to shoot covers, but I really needed to get back to my roots and just do some images for me. So off on the road I went."

Taken together, the video and the album cover said a great deal about the music's physical and spiritual terrain, even if the man behind it was absent. Anything else would be missing the point. Springsteen's version of a solo debut wasn't a clash-of-egos band firing, or a greedy cash grab. It wasn't even planned. It was a secluded deluge of crisis-adjacent creativity that needed to live on in that form. If the imagery of *Nebraska* didn't make that abundantly clear to fans, a hype sticker affixed to many copies of the album provided clarification. It included just three words: The Solo Album.

★ ★ ★

By the end of 1982, Michigan held the bleak distinction of having America's highest unemployment rate. The downturn wasn't a recent phenomenon. Double-digit unemployment had been a trend in the state for about two years amid a recession whose impacts were compared to the Great Depression. In Detroit, unemployment rates among Black workers were so high that *Time* magazine described community leaders there as living in "fear that they are sitting on a smoldering powder keg of urban unrest."

GM, Ford, and Chrysler—dubbed the Detroit Three—had devolved from fruitful houses of Midwestern labor to brittle shells of bygone prosperity, laying off or furloughing large segments of their workforces. At the height of the crisis, the number of Michiganders displaced by the auto industry was around two hundred thousand by some estimates. At the same time, Bob Seger made a pledge to himself and to his new producer. He'd selected Jimmy Iovine on a recommendation from Don Henley, Eagles drummer and singer, who'd just worked with the Italian-American mover on a Stevie Nicks duet, "Leather and Lace." Iovine had also engineered Springsteen's *Born to Run*, and produced Tommy Petty and The Heartbreakers' *Damn the Torpedoes*, *Hard Promises*, and *Long After Dark*.

Seger's promise? No mediums.

Taken in the context of his most recent studio album, *Against the Wind*—which was loaded with mid-tempo hits like "You'll Accomp'ny Me," and rested at No. 1 on the Billboard 200 for six weeks after its release—it was a self-conscious assuaging of old-school Seger fans who'd accused him of selling out, going soft, playing into the music industry's hand. But read within a survey of what was actually happening around Seger, how so many in his homeland were professionally, financially, and spiritually hamstrung, the singer's promise to return to his hard-rocking roots was tantamount to a rallying cry. A time of such crisis demanded a muscular soundtrack, a sonic reminder of his homeland's strength. Or, in its more tender moments, a soft, soothing ballad. Nothing in between. No mediums.

Seger's twelfth studio album, *The Distance*, became an important punctuation mark in the narrative of heartland rock, a return to form for the most avuncular member of the heartland rock cohort. It was also a prime example of the era's so-called recession rock, a wave of songs crafted by musicians across genres reflecting the specific period of 1981–1983 and all of the hardship it brought upon American workers. It was a microgenre within the heartland rock era.

As heartland rock produced naturalistic sonic portraits of everyday Americans in a celebratory and often romantic sense, recession rock, created in the early years of the new decade, took a more detailed approach, recounting the real and present truth of Rust Belt open graves and the struggles of manual laborers. Unlike socially conscious music of the 1960s, the songs didn't propose solutions, call for rose-tinted unity, or engage in antigovernment finger wagging; they simply proffered evocative vignettes of those without work or much hope.

Singer-songwriter Billy Joel released "Allentown" in November 1982, with lyrics that laid bare the fallacy of meritocracy by way of shuttered factories in eastern Pennsylvania. Seventies party rockers J. Geils Band, recently rebranded a new wave act, issued "Rage in the Cage" on its 1981 album *Freeze Frame*, about the dead-end trappings of small-town, blue-collar life. "My Town Was Gone" by the Pretenders, whose leader Chrissy Hynde hailed from Akron, Ohio, described the paving-over of bucolic locales, like a modern take on Joni Mitchell's "Big Yellow Taxi," while Gary U. S. Bonds's "Out of Work," written by Bruce Springsteen, and produced by the singer and his right-hand man Steven Van Zandt, was perhaps the most dead-on portrayal of the era's regrettable unemployment trends.

Springsteen's *Nebraska*, released three months prior to *The Distance*, included evocative descriptions of a shutdown auto factory in New Jersey, and the desperation of man more generally. It took a more meditative approach to the neorealism practices of heartland rock and recession rock to explore the psychic fallout of the unemployed and disenfranchised.

Locally, in Detroit, power-pop act Toby Redd released "Can't Get a Job" with bassist Dennis Martz explaining, "I see it all around me; nobody's working. Guys who are laid off asked us to dedicate a song to them. And that's why we wrote it. We wanted to write something of importance." Akron, Ohio, new wave band The Waitresses were similarly inspired by the blue-collar malaise they observed in frequent trips to the Motor City. Guitarist Chris Butler wrote "Bread and Butter" to chronicle the disparity between the city's workers and bosses.

With *The Distance*, Bob Seger channeled his own heartland nostalgia to evoke better days on the auto assembly lines. The album's second track, "Makin' Thunderbirds," a hard-driving rock anthem with a scorching guitar riff, saxophone, piano, and backing vocals by Bonnie Raitt, summoned a time, in the mid '50s, when Michigan automotive factories were as abundant as they were deafening. When a job on the line meant pride of ownership, in the halcyon days before Ford, GM, and Chrysler workers waited for the next round of furloughs or layoffs to be announced, living in fear of their name appearing on a list.

Seger, the son of a musician and medic at the Ford Motor Company, who grew up in near-poverty after his father abandoned the family when he was twelve, experienced firsthand the advantages of the American auto boom. As a broke, neophyte songwriter and singer, he took on jobs at Ford and GM to make ends meet. At General Motors, he loaded the conveyor. His job installing windshields at Ford was much shorter lived because he repeatedly cut his hands installing rubber around the large pieces of glass, and the company wouldn't move him to a different position.

His stints on the line were but a scene or two in the movie of his life, a financial bolster until his art could pay the rent. Though his adolescence wasn't easy, Seger didn't begrudge Detroit, and never really left the state of Michigan, citing a strong base of friends and a desire to remain tethered to Middle America. "If you get too close to the music industry, you get blinded of what's happening in the rest of the country," he explained to a *Creem* magazine reporter. "You can get caught up in southern California, and it's sort of like a big Disneyland."

It is possible to love and respect the people and places that raised you, and to also want more than your humble origins. Two things can be true at the same time. Though the Upper Midwest may have had a smaller creative industry, and may have lacked the business connections and acumen of the nation's coasts, it flourished in the quiet, everyday virtues that steer souls through the heaviest of existential fog. Seger's life in Michigan was rife with tribulation and quiet mercies, the physical and spiritual forces that contour a person into adult form and leave behind faint reminders of their story. Michigan was Seger's home but also the basis of his character.

Though "Makin' Thunderbirds" was the most obvious nod to the better-days nostalgia Seger was famous for, a way of amplifying the past in order to calm fear, uncertainty, and dread about the present, it wasn't the only recession rock notable on *The Distance*. "Boom-town Blues" held a mirror to the phenomena of Michigan auto work-ers heading to Texas and California in search of jobs, not unlike Dust Bowl migrants in the 1930s or farm workers of past and present. The yearning of "House Behind a House" echoes Seger's lyrical assertion that hope is necessary and also a painful feeling on which to hold.

"Roll Me Away" offered temporal escape. The lyrics, relayed over anthemic piano played by the E Street Band's Roy Bittan, and delivered via Seger's explosive rasp, describe a motorcycle trip across Michigan and into the Great Divide. Such geography doubled as a metaphor for individual freedom, and a point of no return, signaling an exorcism of personal demons. Its music video, depicting a motorcycle journey across Midwest highways, bridges and water, and into the moun-tains, relayed a palpable sense of home and the liberating effects of blue-collar odyssey. Motorcycles were a relatable motif in the visual branding of heartland rock. They recalled '50s era greasers and James Dean, and also were an emblem of autonomy, community, and good fortune—the opposite of the Hells Angels outlaw caricature.

Two-wheelers had featured in Mellencamp's videos for "Hurts So Good" and "Jack & Diane," and Tom Petty and the Heartbreak-ers' "Into the Great Wide Open." Photographs of Springsteen taken throughout the mid '70s demonstrate how his budding rocker iden-tity was bolstered by Triumph motorcycles. He bought a late '60s Tri-umph Trophy from the last standing dealership in New Jersey, owned by three brothers who quickly became his friends, and rode it through the Garden State's wilds. In at least one famous photo, Springsteen wears a heather-gray Triumph T-shirt.

The making of *The Distance* was fraught with challenges, mostly driven by Seger's self-doubt and indecision, and Iovine's demands for perfection. It took fourteen months to complete. *The Distance* also saw a major change in personnel, including the absence of the Silver Bullet Band's longtime guitarist Drew Abbott and drummer Dave Teegarden. For the first time, Seger invited polished session players to join his updated Silver Bullet Band at Studio 55 and Crystal Sound

Recording in Los Angeles. These were folks he'd always wanted to work with, including drummer Russ Kunkel, guitarist Waddy Wachtel, and E Street Band pianist Bittan. Seger also spent time in Alabama with the Muscle Shoals Rhythm Section, as he had for previous records.

Given all the songs he'd recorded—nineteen total—the singer thought of making a double album. According to Seger, the most ardent supporter of this ambitious idea was Springsteen, who'd found runaway success with his two-LP work *The River* and its subsequent tour. Springsteen had recently purchased a cottage in the Hollywood Hills and was spending his first winter out West, working in a garage recording studio. Amid his time in Los Angeles, he palled around with Seger, taking long drives and going to movie theaters to see films such as Robert Altman's *Come Back to the 5 & Dime, Jimmy Dean, Jimmy Dean*. Springsteen also, for the first time in his life, found himself in therapy.

Bruce Springsteen and Bob Seger perform "Thunder Road" in Ann Arbor, Michigan, in 1980.

PHOTO COURTESY MEDIAPUNCH INC.

Though Seger's discography predates Springsteen's, the two had essentially risen alongside one another; the Jersey native's commercial breakthrough came in 1975 with *Born to Run* and Seger's about a year later with *Night Moves*. They were two working-class rock musicians crossing the Rubicon from a life of very little to one of abundance, by drawing from the sounds and simplicity of earlier rock 'n' roll. They sang of and for their respective regional corners, laying the bricks that formed the path for the heartland rock that followed. The pair officially met backstage at the Pine Knob amphitheater, about forty miles outside Detroit, in 1978. Two years later, Springsteen invited Seger to sit in on "Thunder Road" during a performance at the Crisler Center in Ann Arbor.

Seger was known as the most easygoing of the heartland rockers, with a greater willingness to play ball with music industry suits than Springsteen, Mellencamp, and Petty. But that's not why he and his manager Punch Andrews abandoned the double album idea. Taking stock of what was happening around him, particularly in Michigan, the state of physical and emotional economies, Seger decided, "We simply didn't want our fans to pay that much for a record." Releasing a double album that was out of reach financially for fans would be bad for business. It would also be an anathema to Seger's heartland ethos. He also insisted that *The Distance* be released on eight-track, in addition to LP and cassette versions. It was a fast-fading format, but an affordable one that a segment of his fans preferred.

After Seger pared the album down to nine tracks, including a stirring cover of singer-songwriter Rodney Crowell's "Shame on the Moon," a country-adjacent ballad that became the album's highest charting single, Springsteen was one of the first people to give *The Distance* a thumbs-up. Before it was released, the two musicians navigated LA streets in Springsteen's car, a '69 Ford XL with a rag top, previewing their new music for one another on the stereo. "He said he liked it!" Seger told *Rolling Stone*, apparently with enough excitement in his voice to warrant an exclamation point.

After *The Distance* was released in December of 1982, and he'd completed the cycle of press and promotion in Los Angeles, Seger headed to the airport and boarded a plane bound for Michigan. He happily returned to his ordinary life where there was no delta between right and wrong, between true and false; where there was the sacred hum of a realer, working America. Where there were no mediums.

CHAPTER 4

HOMETOWN HEROES

Is this a picture of Cleveland? Is this what they do there?

—DICK CLARK, *AMERICAN BANDSTAND*

On August 5, 1983, moviegoers in more than six hundred theaters watched twenty-one-year-old Tom Cruise dance in his tighty whities. *Risky Business* was a teenage coming-of-age tale and a watershed moment for the explosion of such films. Grossing more than $4 million in its opening weekend, it was a critical and commercial success that set a debaucherous teenage preppie against a soundtrack of acclaimed music. The electronic collective Tangerine Dream composed its ambient score and songs by Bruce Springsteen ("Hungry Heart"), Prince ("D.M.S.R."), and Phil Collins ("In the Air Tonight") appeared throughout.

The film's most memorable scene, however, was soundtracked by Bob Seger. "Old Time Rock & Roll," released on the singer's *Stranger in Town* album in 1979, was reinvigorated in a major way after Cruise, as the film's main character Joel Goodsen, lip-synced to it, barelegged, while shimmying through his parents' living room. Placed in this context, the song was a reminder of America's grand traditions and rock 'n' roll's liberating energy.

In October, Seger released a music video for the song that combined scenes from Cruise's romp with footage of the singer and his Silver Bullet Band performing live. The pairing visualized an unquestionable truth as heartland rock became a cultural force; nostalgia for a not-so-distant past had become a contemporary phenomenon unbound from time itself. It coursed through at least three generations at the same time, and each molded the sentiment to suit its particular vantage point. It was the sound of youth and the sound of wisdom. It was the sound of the past and the sound of the present. It was also, as much of rock 'n' roll, the sound of Black artistry as interpreted by white voices. George Jackson, the Black Muscle Shoals–based hitmaker, cowrote the song. Its "funky old soul" came courtesy of the Swampers—the iconic Muscle Shoals–based house band—who recorded the demo. Though the dynamic was customary throughout American history, white men laying claim to the labor of Black men, it also reflects two consistent themes presented throughout heartland rock's height. There was a conscious effort by its figureheads to spotlight the hypocrisies of the American dream. There was also a desire to amplify the historical Black artistry that inspired them as they took up these positions.

"Old Time Rock & Roll" hung in the American singles charts through 1987 on account of the popularity of *Risky Business* and the nostalgic undercurrent of heartland rock throughout the decade. As Reagan began mounting a bid for a second term in office, old time rock 'n' roll had become a present-day big business.

★ ★ ★

Months before the release of his second successful album, John Mellencamp stormed off the set of CBS's *Nightwatch*, the network's late-late-night news program, which ran for ten years and had a hybrid format that mixed a live newscast with in-studio interviews and debate segments. On the heels of his No. 1 album *American Fool*, and well-received tour opening for Heart, the thirty-one-year-old sat down with the journalist Felicia Jeter, who proceeded to ask pointed questions about the musician's "salacious" biker-bar video for the single "Hurts So Good," and his moral responsibility as "the establishment."

Mellencamp's rejoinder? "I don't go to PTA meetings. I don't go to the Nazarene Church. I don't vote. I don't do any of that stuff." Then, he unclipped his microphone and left the set muttering profanities. "I'm not gonna hang on nobody's cross," he told *Rolling Stone* that December, by way of an explanation.

This, combined with the fact that Mellencamp and his band walked out of a concert in London, Ontario, on August 30, 1982, initiated the musician's reputation as either an arrogant SOB or a tough guy who doesn't take shit from anyone, depending on one's point of view. As Mellencamp later explained to a reporter for *Creem* magazine, such binaries are reductive. Misunderstood is what he actually was, and it had been getting worse as his star rose. According to the singer, people may have been listening, but they refused to truly hear him.

He blamed the Ontario incident on the concert's promoters who, according to Mellencamp, coerced him into playing the package gig between Del Shannon and the Beach Boys while he was on tour with Heart. "I find out that before I got on the bill, they'd only sold 2,000 seats. I get added, and 10,000 seats are sold-out," he explained. "But the real dastardly deed came when they told my brother Ted—he's my road manager—that we had to cut our set from 55 minutes to 35, because they were running late. I thought the people who paid 10 bucks to see this mess are going to be bummed out when the act they paid for only plays 35 minutes." And on reports that he threw the promoters' rented gear into the crowd, injuring two women? "It was inaccurate reporting, because we didn't heave it out in the audience. We handed it to security guards who handed it out to the audience. If somebody got hurt, don't you think they'd have sued me right away? *Rich rock star, let's get some of his money,*" he said. "I never even got a letter . . . we went back and did two free shows in London about three months ago to make up for it, and it cost me a lot of money. But it taught me a good lesson."

And on walking off the set of CBS *Nightwatch*? "It was the woman not accepting my answers," he explained. "She asked me the same question five different times, I answered it five different ways, and it was like hey, what the fuck else do I have to say to you?"

These two events may have been very public examples of Mellencamp acting out and, according to him, being misread. But the most enduring arrived with the release of his 1983 album *Uh-Huh*, which produced the singles "Crumblin' Down," "Authority Song," and "Pink Houses." It was the first and only album he released under the name John Cougar Mellencamp, a step toward shedding the stage name that had been foisted upon him by a former manager.

Uh-Huh is also the first example of Mellencamp recording a hit album on his own terms. Instead of the tortured out-of-state processes of *American Fool*, Mellencamp and his band worked in an unassuming hole-in-the-wall dubbed "The Shack" in Jackson County, Indiana. Producer Don Gehman, who'd guided Mellencamp through the tumult of his previous LP, joined them. Little Bastard, the caustic moniker Mellencamp adopted as a nod to the Porsche 550 Spyder that killed Indiana icon James Dean, and a sly vengeance on those who misunderstood or underestimated him—much like the state of Indiana adopting the nickname Hoosier—is also credited as a producer for the first time.

The group recorded twenty-five songs in sixteen days, ten of which made it onto *Uh-Huh*. Their mission was spontaneity. Mellencamp wanted the end result to sound homespun, like *Exile on Main Street* by the Rolling Stones. The LP's credits even thank the Stones for "never taking the living room off the records when we were kids." This quality is most evident in guitarist Mike Wanchic's audible epithet in the intro to "Lovin' Mother Fo Ya" and Mellencamp's directive "Take it Kenny" during the bridge of "Jacki O." Mellencamp wrote the peculiar ode to Jacqueline Kennedy Onassis with singer-songwriter John Prine, who broke out of the folk music scene in Chicago in the early

'70s, became an inspiration to heartland rock and its artists, and was a longtime friend to Mellencamp. Prine's "Storm Windows," from the 1980 album of the same name, slots into the heartland rock genre for its piano-oriented childhood nostalgia.

For many less gifted and less rehearsed ensembles, such speed and spontaneity results in a garbled, out-of-sync mess. But the Zone were finely tuned to Mellencamp and to one another. The success of *American Fool* prompted more touring than the group had ever done in the past. Mellencamp had also put the band on an aggressive practice schedule as he determined to break out to national audiences. According to drummer Kenny Aronoff, Mellencamp insisted the band practice from 11 a.m. to 11 p.m. five days a week when the band wasn't on tour. He gave them a break from 5 p.m. to 7 p.m. for dinner.

In interviews, Mellencamp attributed much of the sound of *Uh-Huh* to Aronoff's skill behind the drum kit. The drummer explained that a Mellencamp recording session always began with John strumming an acoustic guitar and singing a demo, or hitting play on a demo cas-

John Mellencamp puts the crowd on notice during the *Uh-Huh* tour.
PHOTO COURTESY MEDIAPUNCH INC.

sette he'd recorded. After that, the process moved to the drums. "The challenge for me was always to come up with a simple, cool beat that would make the song special and inspire John and the band to come up with cool hook lines, parts, and arrangements for the song, and to ultimately get his song on the radio to be a number-one hit single," Aronoff explained in the documentary *Hired Gun*. "He wanted my drum parts to be hook lines, and they were for a lot of his songs."

This is most obvious in Aronoff's "gunshot" snare sound that rings with singular *whomp!* During the *American Fool* sessions, Mellencamp insisted on magnifying Aronoff's drums in the mix, which infuriated recording engineers and blew out studio speakers. The singer has stated that the idea was to defy the gentle drum mixes established by legacy acts like the Eagles. "I loved it," Aronoff said in 1999. "I thought it was great, because at that time, songs like 'Eye of the Tiger' and 'Ebony and Ivory' were on the radio, and when 'Hurts So Good' came on it completely blew those songs off the radio. I mean, sonically, the drums were so present, and that really made a big statement." Though the presence of Aronoff's distinctive drum sound originated on *American Fool*, it was solidified on *Uh-Huh*. Here, his snare shoots out of the mix like commercial-grade pyrotechnics.

Thematically, *Uh-Huh* found Mellencamp at a personal and professional crossroads. He'd suddenly become one of the most famous musicians in America and was reckoning with what it meant to be a public figure. Such conflict manifested in "Crumblin' Down," which recounts the frictions that arrive with fame, public perception, and the business of music. In the tune, the singer discusses how people in his life treat him differently now that he's successful, though his status hasn't erased his position as a "whipping boy" in broader society. "Authority Song" reinterprets "I Fought the Law," the classic combat hymn popularized by 1960s rock act the Bobby Fuller Four. Instead of the "Law" Mellencamp and company fights "Authority." The outcomes of such brawls, however, remain the same.

Mellencamp was inspired to write "Pink Houses" after traveling home to Bloomington, Indiana, from the Indianapolis airport. The musician was driving on an elevated stretch of highway and spotted an old man sitting in his backyard with a dog on his lap. The man looked directly at Mellencamp with a "real contented look on his face," the singer told a reporter for the *Dayton Daily News*. "It was obvious he thought he'd really made it in life. But there he was with a damned six-lane highway running right through his backyard."

According to a report by WRTV in Indianapolis, interstate construction in and around the state capital throughout the 1960s and '70s displaced about seventeen thousand residents, primarily in places where Black and low-income people lived. It also caused the demolition of about eight thousand community buildings, including a recreation center owned by former Negro Leagues baseball player Will Owens. Moreover, it divided and disenfranchised Black neighborhoods, from the city's Southside to downtown and all the way to the historical neighborhood Ransome Place on the city's Northside, with concrete pillars, exhaust, and noise pollution. It was a classic example of the practice known as redlining.

In 2021, Pete Buttigieg, former mayor of South Bend, Indiana, and US secretary of transportation under President Joe Biden, told the African American media outlet TheGrio that "there is racism physically built into some of our highways." His statement set off a wave of jeers from conservative politicians and publications—a lot of the same folks who've willfully misconstrued Mellencamp's "Pink Houses" as a jingoistic pro-America anthem. The fact is, the two Hoosiers are closely aligned on the point that American exceptionalism is available only to certain people due to the country's legacy of implicit and explicit discrimination. Mellencamp was asking Americans to open their eyes. "The majority of the public is going to fall right in line with the way Reagan wants them to think," the singer said. "I don't mean to get political, but I do get wound up about these kinds of things because so many people see it as it's really not. They believe the propaganda. And that's sort of what 'Pink Houses' is about." The song's music video clearly conveyed this. Shot in various locations throughout rural Indiana, it depicted how the other half lives, among fields and highways and trailer parks, cut off from the privilege of the ruling class.

When *Uh-Huh* was released in August of 1983, the Reagan administration was preparing the president's reelection campaign. In an effort to appeal to the youth vote, Reagan played Bruce Springsteen's "Born in the U.S.A." and praised "the message of hope in songs of a man so many young Americans admire, New Jersey's own Bruce Springsteen," at a stop in the Garden State. As it happened, Reagan also wanted "Pink Houses."

The February 15, 1984, issue of London's *Evening Standard* newspaper reported that a Reagan staffer asked Mellencamp's London-based record label Riva for a copy of the song's music video—shot in rural Indiana—with the thought of using "Pink Houses" as his campaign's theme song. "White House officials called us and asked for a copy of the lyrics and the video," said Bill Stonebridge, managing director of Riva. Speaking to a reporter from Memphis's *Commercial Appeal* newspaper on March 9, 1984, Mellencamp explained that he heard Reagan wanted "Pink Houses" through watching MTV. "I don't know anything about it," he said. "If it was true, I wouldn't agree to it."

"Reagan doesn't know nothin' about workin' people in the Midwest or anywhere else," Mellencamp would later tell a reporter for *Penthouse* magazine. "So when I got a direct approach from his people for permission to use 'Pink Houses,' I made it clear from day one that he just had to forget it. I couldn't bear gettin' involved that way with any politicians, least of all Reagan, and corrupt what is essentially a basic, humble dream of contentment he can't even understand."

It's possible that Mellencamp was being contrarian in his reworked telling of Reagan and "Pink Houses." Or maybe, he simply couldn't remember the original version. Dig through early '80s interviews and you'll also find Mellencamp proclaiming that his music is "bullshit" and politics are a waste of time, a far cry from the older man in the new millennium who describes Ronald Reagan as his greatest enemy.

Though Mellencamp and his team managed its use by Reagan, numerous other figures whose beliefs run contrary to the heart of

"Pink Houses" have attempted to use it at their events. Republican candidate John McCain played "Pink Houses" and Mellencamp's "Our Country" during his 2008 run for president. He stopped when Mellencamp's team contacted his campaign staff to point out that the singer is an outspoken leftist. Two years later, the conservative National Organization for Marriage (NOM) played the song at its events protesting gay marriage. To that, Mellencamp's publicist sent a cease-and-desist letter that in part stated, "Mr. Mellencamp's views on same-sex marriage and equal rights for people of all sexual orientations are at odds with NOM's stated agenda." It also suggested that NOM "find music from a source more in harmony with your views than Mr. Mellencamp in the future."

Beyond politics, country musicians have also seemingly misconstrued "Pink Houses." Vocal Trump-supporting stars such as Jason Aldean and Luke Bryan have performed "Pink Houses" in concert, as has Detroit's Kid Rock, who sometimes dabbles in the country genre. Mellencamp "has always been country," musician Chris Janson told *Billboard* in 2018. "He wears cowboy boots, jeans and T-shirts. He looks like a guy that you went to high school with, went to college with, went to Tootsie's with and went to the arena with. He looks like an everyday guys' guy, and he sings songs about how we all live in modern-day country music and have been living for years. It's a natural fit." This was two years after Janson performed at the Republican National Convention in Cleveland, Ohio, where he sang a cover of Tim McGraw's "Truck Yeah" but altered its lyrical hook to "Trump Yeah."

In the decades since Mellencamp's rise to fame, an inextricable bond has formed between the singer and modern country music, more so than with any other heartland rock musician. Whether it is his Indiana home, his Everyman style, his advocacy on behalf of farmers, or his songs' general themes, the singer has become so beloved by Nashville and beyond that more than one original song has been written about him or his music. Australian country-pop musician Keith Urban released the single "John Cougar, John Deere, John 3:16" in 2015. Urban once told me that seeing Mellencamp perform in Australia when he was in a fledgling bar band helped define his entire career trajectory. "I looked onstage and thought, 'Oh, I get it. You take your influences, put them all together and make your own sound and do your own thing. That's what you gotta do, Keith,'" he said. "And it was profound. It was literally like the clouds parted."

On Mellencamp and his music's appeal to country musicians, young country artist Tegan Marie may have put it best with this bird's-eye observation. "It's about everything in between New York and LA, that big chunk of land," she told *Billboard* when she was fourteen years old. This is also heartland rock's appeal to listeners across regional, cultural, and economic lines. Heartland rock made the themes of America's midsection relatable, sympathetic, and desirable. Though heartland rock is often viewed as a proxy for Middle American ideals, its artists are often exceptions to the prevailing views and attitudes of such areas. The "blue dot in a red state" phenomenon is perhaps most common in the American Midwest and South, where entire states may blare crimson save for a few specks—like Bloomington, Indiana, which Mellencamp calls home, or Gainesville, Florida, in which Tom Petty was raised.

Though "Pink Houses" and "Born in the U.S.A." may be the two earliest examples of heartland rock's left-wing populist anthems being upended for political purposes, they do not stand alone. George W. Bush played Tom Petty's "I Won't Back Down" at campaign rallies until he received a cease and desist. So did Donald Trump. "Both the late Tom Petty and his family firmly stand against racism and discrimination of any kind. Tom Petty would never want a song of his used for a campaign of hate. He liked to bring people together," his estate posted on the social media platform X, then known as Twitter, in 2020. In 2008, Jackson Browne sued the Republican National Committee, Ohio Republican Committee, and Senator John McCain for using "Running on Empty" in a campaign ad without his permission. In response, McCain's camp cited "fair use," filed a motion to dismiss the suit, and filed an anti-SLAAP (strategic lawsuits against public participation) suit against Browne, accusing the singer of trying to suppress free speech. The matter was settled about a year later when a California district court ruled in Browne's favor. He was awarded an undisclosed sum of money and, more importantly, an apology.

As their music survives the passage of time, Mellencamp and his heartland rock associates will continue to be misinterpreted, misrepresented, and coopted for political gain. Unscrupulous politicians will play "Born in the U.S.A.," "Small Town," "Pink Houses," "Rockin' in the Free World," and "I Won't Back Down" at their events, suspending such songs' left-wing populist roots in a liminal plane between the artist's intent and the listener's bias. It's almost as if Mellencamp knew this as he wrote "Pink Houses," with its anthemic chorus that so shrewdly encapsulates the nation's contradictions.

★ ★ ★

On December 10, 1983, television host Dick Clark sat in the audience of his long-running music television show *American Bandstand*, looking perplexed as he studied the cover of the Michael Stanley Band's new album, *You Can't Fight Fashion*. The black-and-white image depicted an industrial landscape in the foreground, and Cleveland's Terminal Tower—once the second-tallest building in the world—in the distance. "Is this a picture of Cleveland? Is this what they do there?" Clark asked out loud to no one in particular.

The Michael Stanley Band then launched into "My Town," the group's new song glorifying the unifying force of a native land. Cleveland natives naturally adopted it as a form of hometown pride, and for native son Stanley it was. But the song doesn't mention Cleveland or anything about it specifically save for a vague reference to the east side and west side. Instead, its in-spite-of-itself framework can be projected onto any town in any region where residents proudly embrace a home base that has struggled but has survived. Its chorus is akin to the writer Nelson Algren's sentiment about being devoted to Chicago: It's like loving a woman with a broken nose.

The Michael Stanley Band formed in Cleveland in 1974 as a four-piece and then experienced several personnel changes. By the time it was dropped from Arista, signed to EMI America, and released its 1980 breakthrough *Heartland*, the group boasted seven members: principal songwriter Stanley on lead vocals, guitars, and percussion; coprincipal songwriter Kevin Raleigh also on vocals and percussion, as well as organ and piano; Michael Gismondi on bass; Gary Markasky on lead guitar; Bob Pelander on piano, organ, synth, percussion, and vocals; Tom Doback on drums and percussion; and Danny Powers on guitar and vocals. But they did not operate in worship of the sprawling, future-thinking ensembles of Frank Zappa or Funkadelic. MSB, like many of the era, were Springsteen's and Seger's progeny—a band that crafted earnest and upright songs of and for the heartland.

By the time of the Reagan presidency, Cleveland had endured a series of hardships that may have ended a less sturdy place. It entered the 1970s as the city whose river—the Cuyahoga—had caught fire due to pollution. Cleveland closed out the decade with a war between the Italian and Irish mafias, defaulted on its loans due to industrial decline, and lost nearly 25 percent of its population. In the process, it earned the pejorative title "Mistake by the Lake."

But the city had also established its NBA team which, after a six-year losing streak, achieved the "Miracle at Richfield," defeating the Washington Bullets to win the Eastern Conference Semifinals in 1976. Like New York and Los Angeles—cities that also experienced major declines in the '70s—it had also earned a national reputation as a stronghold for rock 'n' roll by incubating a swath of celebrated punk, new wave, and experimental local bands. Its vibrant club scene, which stretched across venues such as La Cav, the Piccadilly Inn, Pirate's Cove, Viking Saloon, Traxx, and the Cleveland Agora, attracted national touring acts that played legendary shows, like the Velvet Underground in the late '60s and Bruce Springsteen in the '70s.

None of this had done much for MSB, except provide creative fuel. After releasing a series of albums that sonically shapeshifted between a series of era specific touchstones, like the soft rock of Fleetwood Mac, the fusion of Herbie Hancock, the arena rock of Foreigner, and a live album meant to ride on the coattails of Peter Frampton's *Framp-*

ton Comes Alive, the band hit the proverbial reset button in the late '70s. They'd been dropped by two record labels and one producer, and had parted ways with their management. Though MSB wasn't part of the Cleveland punk scene, it decided to go the punk route: producing and recording on its own, and shopping its next record around that way, too. Its members had also decided that they'd self-release the album that became *Heartland* if labels weren't interested. This is how committed the group was to its last hurrah, and the degree to which it believed it was its last stand.

Stanley recalled that in an environment of very low stakes, and with no major label puppeteering, it was a magical time in the group. There were no ego clashes. No infighting. The kismet that occurred amid the sessions seemed to reflect that. The first of these events was the E Street Band's Clarence Clemons, who blew sax on three tracks that made it on *Heartland*, during a tour break with Springsteen. According to Stanley, Clemons was seeing a woman who lived in Cleveland and didn't charge the band for his work. All it cost MSB was a roundtrip plane ticket from New Jersey. The second small miracle was the last-minute inclusion of the ballad "Lover," one of the band's most beloved songs, which went to No. 68 on the Billboard Hot 100.

With *Heartland*, MSB had finally found its voice and, more importantly, its style. Upon its completion, four major labels bid on the album, and EMI America won out. The company was responsible for getting MSB in early rotation on MTV, which also helped solidify its reputation as a heartland rock act out of Cleveland. The Michael Stanley Band had finally reached its goal of transcending its hometown's borders while remaining true to its ideals. They weren't yet a household name, but MSB felt more optimistic than ever.

For its next album, *North Coast*, which was composed of several songs left over from the *Heartland* writing era, the group brought on producer and recording engineer Eddie Kramer, the South African who'd worked with the Beatles, the Rolling Stones, and Led Zeppelin. And for its third album for EMI America, *MSB*, the band coproduced with Don Gehman of Criteria Studios in Miami, who was about to have a mammoth hit with John Mellencamp's *American Fool*. For *You Can't Fight Fashion*, the group again aligned itself with Springsteen in hiring Bob Clearmountain, who mixed *Born in the U.S.A.*

You Can't Fight Fashion had all the markings of a great heartland rock album, with its mix of hometown pride, lovelorn ballads, and hell-on-wheels party anthems, all steeped in a nostalgic patina that summons bygone, simpler times. It didn't receive much press, and EMI was unwilling to put much money behind the band's fourth attempt with the label. But the reviewers who lent it an ear clearly understood its place in the culture. "Like the Houserockers, the Stanley Band needs to flex its working-class muscles," a critic for the *Pittsburgh Press* wrote.

By the time of the album's release in 1983, MSB had built solid momentum but had yet to crack the Top 10 of *Billboard*'s important album and singles charts. The band had reached another crossroads, a make-or-break moment as its label saw it. As Tom Petty and The Heartbreakers' *Long After Dark* shot to No. 9, and John Cougar Mellencamp's *Uh-Huh* hit the same position in early 1984, MSB's *You Can't Fight Fashion* topped out at the 69th position. Despite appearances on *American Bandstand* and *Solid Gold*, "My Town" reaching No. 39 on the Hot 100 (the band's second highest position to date), and concerts with opener Donnie Iris & the Cruisers (a band that had similarly failed to truly break out of Pittsburgh), EMI America dropped the Michael Stanley Band. The group endured more personnel changes, self-released two more albums, and decided to break up in 1986, but not before completing a series of twelve farewell concerts at the Front Row Theater in Cleveland. Michael Stanley pivoted to radio disc jockey, spending most of his career at WMMS competitor WNCX, a classic rock outfit. He released about twenty albums as a solo artist in the '90s and 2000s, and played himself on the television sitcom *The Drew Carey Show*, which was set in Cleveland. In the fifty-plus years he dedicated his creative efforts to his hometown, he became one of its most cherished local celebrities.

Though MSB failed to transcend its Upper Midwest region, it joined the pantheon of heartland rockers whose mythopoetic lyrics have elevated humble enclaves to larger-than-life fairytales. "My Town" stands alongside John Mellencamp's "Small Town," Bruce Springsteen's "My Hometown," Bob Seger's "Mainstreet," Bruce Hornsby's "The Valley Road," and other songs that have immortalized places that most people will never visit.

The Michael Stanley Band also took it a step further. Aware of the common appeal of "My Town," and how its broad underdog sentiment may apply to most any American municipality, Stanley and keyboardist Bob Pelander traveled to a New York studio to record—according to Stanley—two hundred different versions of the song that inserted a specific city's name. These versions were distributed only to local radio stations to play on air. If someone in St. Louis purchased *You Can't Fight Fashion* or the "My Town" single in 1983, that person would've heard the original version—a song that will forever be claimed by Cleveland. Today, "My Town" is the state's fight song, played by the Ohio State University Marching Band since the '80s. Moreover, it's a torch song. It's a tune the people of Cleveland sing on March 25, which was declared Michael Stanley Day in 2021. Though MSB isn't as widely recognized as other bands of its era, it has achieved something that is perhaps more important. MSB is synonymous with a strong working town. Detroit has Bob Seger; Asbury Park has Bruce Springsteen; Bloomington has John Mellencamp; and Cleveland will always have Michael Stanley.

★ ★ ★

As heartland rock's bullhorn sounded across the country, a group of musicians from the California underground began to echo its sonic cues and lyrical motifs. The Blasters' *Non Fiction, More Fun in the New World* by the band X, both released in 1983, and Rank and File's *Sundown*, released in November 1982, flung open the gates for punks and other DIYers to combine American tradition and fervent blue-collar solidarity—as if to trace the country's punk roots directly to its progenitors like Woody Guthrie, Sister Rosetta Tharpe, Lead Belly, and Johnny Cash.

The scene that became known as "cowpunk" wasn't heartland rock but it was a crucial ally and sonically adjacent, embracing the themes of Springsteen—working class-struggle, disillusionment, nostalgia— and blending its versions of rock music with elements of folk and country music. The main differences between the two genres were budgets and production values. Whereas heartland rock's goal was to reach as many people as possible through very listenable pop-rock distributed through mainstream channels, cowpunk's was to unite the freaks and the squares by bringing the underground to society's surface. And then there were acts like Jeffrey Lee Pierce's the Gun Club, whose swamp-rock noir was rooted in tradition but far too spooky and strange to ever appeal to mainstream audiences.

This is not to say that the heartland rockers didn't carry their punk influences forward via electrifying live performances and auditory clues. Springsteen's love of New York minimalist art-punk band Suicide and its song "Frankie Teardrop" surfaces throughout *Nebraska*, on songs such as "Johnny 99" and "State Trooper." Mellencamp spent a brief period as a teenager in a glam-punk band called Trash, inspired by the New York Dolls—and if there is anyone who has embraced punk's in-your-face civics, it is John Mellencamp. Bob Seger and his band the System earned comparisons to fellow Michiganders the Stooges and the MC5 for its hell-on-wheels live performances and ferocious 1970 garage-rock single "Lucifer." Before he was dunked in heartland rock's baptismal font, Tom Petty was mentioned in the same sentences as Blondie and the Ramones as part of the so-called new wave. These heartland rock artists unite with the cowpunks for their shared epiphany: for most, punk rock means toiling away in the margins. "If we'd remained independent we would have broken up by now," John Doe of X said in 1983 after the band signed to Elektra Records. "After a while you don't want to travel miles to play to 600 kids and find out none of them can buy your record." For the artists inside and on the margins of heartland rock, there was a desire to find a happy medium.

Brothers Chip and Tony Kinman were part of one of LA's earliest punk bands, the Dils, based in Carlsbad, California, and then

San Francisco. Though the group is perhaps best remembered for its appearance in Cheech and Chong's 1978 comedy *Up in Smoke*, its proletariat-core mission was clear via songs like "I Hate the Rich" and "Class War." After a stint in New York City, the brothers landed in Austin, Texas, where they formed Rank and File with fellow former San Francisco punk Alejandro Escoveda. Though The Dils preceded the "hardcore" punk scene that became synonymous with Southern California, and were decidedly more melodic, Dils fans questioned Rank and File's change in sound. Would it affect its social and political outlook? "There's all the politics you need right on that record," Chip Kinman explained of *Sundown* shortly after its release. "It's just that now we're not singing to an audience who all think like we do. We're not singing to an audience who're going, 'Yeah, I hate the rich.'" "We're singing to all kinds of people; we're reaching more people with basically the same thing."

With *Non Fiction*, the Blasters, whose first two albums were largely received as good-time rockabilly rippers, began to garner some of the best reviews of its career due to leader Dave Alvin's skill for composing lyrical vignettes detailing the lives of common people. With its third album, released in 1983, the Downey, California-originated group demonstrated its range with songs like "Bus Station," which recounts a struggling couple seeking new life in a different town, and "Jubilee Train," detailing four scenarios of the down-and-out in America: a farmer who is foreclosed upon; a white-collar brat who loses everything in a stock market crash; a woman who loses her job after a factory shutters; and a small-business owner who goes bust. Though each character's origin story differs, with *Non Fiction*, Alvin seems to deliver a punchy narrative throughline: The American Dream is an illusion for many and no one is safe from its pitfalls.

"I just always felt that as a songwriter you should use as many of the colors on the American musical palette as you can," Alvin said. Drawing upon various traditional styles, such as country, folk, blues, rock 'n' roll, and R&B, Alvin also experienced the polarization that grew in American society under Reagan. Early on in the band's career, he wrote, and the Blasters recorded and released, the song "American Music" on its 1980 debut of the same name. The rockabilly energizer celebrates the singularity of the country's sonic traditions while also highlighting the marginalized communities from which those traditions sprang. As the nation became increasingly divided under Reagan, however, "American Music" was met with mixed reactions as more and more people discovered it. Some critics received it how Alvin had intended, as a celebration of the "greatest thing we've given the world," as he put it. Others interpreted it as pro-Reagan jingoism, similar to how "Born in the U.S.A." was misunderstood, but on a smaller scale.

Alvin recalled how the country seemed to split apart as the years wore on in the '80s. "There was this jingoistic thing happening on the right, Reagan's 'It's Morning in America' and all that," he told me. "On the other hand, you had this anti patriotism on the left that was also distasteful." Reflecting on the way country, folk, blues, and rock music blended in the Los Angeles scene in the 1980s, and more commercially within the work of heartland rock's big names, Alvin said most of his friends and peers were trying to portray the everyday people who were caught in the middle. "There is this effort to balance the narrative," he said of his songwriting. "I think most of the people in my songs, or Springsteen's songs, or Mellencamp's songs are all caught between the country's extremes."

"I'd refer to us as rock 'n' roll the way God and Chuck Berry intended it," X singer and lyricist Exene Cervenka explained to a Florida newspaper in 1983, amid the band's tour in support of its new album *More Fun in the New World*. The group had been together for about five years and had received widespread critical support for its first two albums, *Los Angeles* and *Wild Gift*, before signing with a major label. The move came with accusations of selling out, but also higher production values and, with *Fun*, a shift from the personal to the observational. X moved away from confessional songs to those dealing with social and political issues.

Cervenka described the early LA punk scene as formed from a kind of blue-collar desperation. It was composed of people who had "shitty jobs" and were "trying to play music at night and make enough to get the car repaired." Doe added that X gigged around LA before the Sex Pistols released *Never Mind the Bollocks Here's the Sex Pistols* in October 1977. This placed its frame of reference outside the accepted "birth of punk" on the international stage and with American rock acts they viewed as antithetical to the likes of Peter Frampton and Elton John. "For us it was the Ramones, Tom Petty, Blondie," he said. In 1983, X wanted to clarify that they were not art school aesthetes, musical anarchists, or conservative sellouts. They were, as Alvin said, somewhere in the middle. They wanted to update tradition, and hopefully gain a more material form of success, beyond a critic's hot superlatives.

For *More Fun in the New World*, Doe, Cervenka, guitarist Billy Zoom, and drummer DJ Bonebreak sought to emphasize their rock 'n' roll bona fides by reaching even further into music's history for inspiration—to artists such as Berry, Merrill Moore, Otis Redding, and Robert Johnson—and to shed any Anglophilic notions about X while also appealing to "normal" Americans, as Doe put it in several interviews. Its music video for single "The New World," a thinly veiled reproach of Reagan (aka "what's his name"), incorporated a series of heartland rock touchpoints: factories, workers, the countryside, and the open road and its vehicles. "Poor Girl" found the group in the Petty and Springsteen category, detailing the tragic life of a young woman who desired more than what life had dealt.

X's cover of "Breathless," a song composed by Otis Blackwell and popularized by Jerry Lee Lewis in 1958, was included in the end credits of the 1983 remake of Jean Luc Godard's opus, starring Richard Gere. As a band whose commercial performance had yet to match its critical accolades, the placement connoted the potential for a crossover; as did the band's debut on *Late Night with David Letterman*, where they performed the song. A North American tour of more than thirty dates received widespread praise from local newspapers. *More Fun in the New World* was voted No. 4 in the *Village Voice*'s year-end Pazz & Jop critics' poll. But the album stalled at No. 86 on the Billboard 200.

Though these acts didn't achieve the runaway success and subsequent ubiquity of the core acts of heartland rock, what they did achieve was a marked shift within the Los Angeles scene, from a fledgling hodge podge of aggro punks to substantive and interconnected groups rooted in tradition. Such traditionalist spirit expanded in the succeeding years via acts such as Jason and the Scorchers, Los Lobos, the Long Ryders, Steve Wynn and Dan Stuart's Danny & Dusty, and Lone Justice, who'd work with Jimmy Iovine and Tom Petty. Future country music star Dwight Yoakam also became a presence in the cowpunk scene, where he performed at DIY clubs such as Chinatown's legendary Madame Wong's.

In 1984, the hardcore punk record label SST, based in the Los Angeles area, released *Meat Puppets II* by Arizona rock act the Meat Puppets. It remains one of the most celebrated and enduring weirdo fusion albums, unrivaled in its demented blend of country, folk, psychedelia, and punk. A year later, as if to double down on their traditional turn, Cervenka, Doe, and Bonebrake of X, Alvin of the Blasters, and Johnny Ray Bartel of popular blues-rock band the Red Devils released their first album as the Knitters, paying homage to country and rock 'n' roll pioneers via original songs and covers.

As these artists set a high bar for cutting-edge fusion in Los Angeles, Bob Dylan attempted to pole vault. On March 22, 1984, the singer made his own appearance on Letterman's experiment in late night television, becoming the first big-name legacy artist to do so. It was a rare act by the folk music icon, the result of the comedian's rising celebrity and Dylan's diminished relevance. After his conversion to Christianity in the late '70s, the songwriter released three gospel-influenced albums exalting his faith, *Slow Train Coming* (1979), *Saved* (1980), and *Shot of Love* (1981), which also alienated a large portion of his fanbase. Instead of calcifying into a Christian relic, however, Dylan soon felled those experimental woods and began tinkering with island sounds. He finished a new album, *Infidels*, with collaborators Mark Knopfler (Dire Straits) and Mick Taylor (Rolling Stones) by June of 1983. Like cowpunk, *Infidels* wasn't explicitly conceived or marketed as a heartland rock album, but seems to embrace elements of the movement's left-wing populism, something that attempted to reach those who felt caught between the extreme right and far left.

Widespread speculation about the true identity of the "Jokerman" from *Infidels* has pointed to Jesus Christ, the biblical King David, the Antichrist, Caribbean jumbie spirits, and Bob Dylan himself, among others. More broadly, it describes demagoguery and the conflicting faces of man. It's no wonder so many have interpreted it as a political protest against Ronald Reagan. More explicit is Dylan's critique of capitalism and corporate greed in "Union Sundown," whose lyrics object to imported goods, overseas manufacturing, and unions that favor profit over people. Its concerns were not far from those in Bob Seger's "Makin' Thunderbirds." The band X expressed some of the same worries as they embraced traditional country and rock 'n' roll with *More Fun in the New World*. In interviews, they opined that original rock 'n' roll music was an extension of an American mythos around its singular capability to make things—the instruments, the songwriters, the performers, the cars they drove, the scattershot regional recording studios filled with American gear. What would rock 'n' roll mean if those operations closed and were made overseas?

Dylan also, as it happened, began driving an hour from his Malibu retreat to punk clubs in Hollywood to take in the youth culture. Through a series of unlikely sliding doors, he artistically clicked with two members of the Chicano punk band the Plugz: drummer Charlie Quintana and bassist Tony Marsico, and their friend, a guitarist named J. J. Holiday. The foursome jammed together at Dylan's home studio in Point Dume after Quintana received random calls over the course of a year from Dylan's management when the musician desired their presence. Instead of Dylan's catalog, the group played improvised, stretched-out versions of classic soul and blues songs accompanied by difficult-to-decipher instructions from the Bard of Minnesota. According to Holiday, Dylan once asked them to play a song "to a stripper beat but with a marching band added onto it."

Though they'd released records on influential local label Slash—as had the Blasters, Los Lobos, and X—the Plugz were mostly unknown outside of LA's tiny scene—making its members' collaboration with Dylan all but impossible to believe. After many spontaneous rehearsals, Dylan laid down the ultimate wild card. Instead of Taylor and Knopfler, he brought his new twenty-somethings to Letterman. There, the quartet executed fierce, angular takes on Dylan's new songs "Jokerman" and "License to Kill," and a sizzling cover of Sonny Boy Williamson's "Don't Start Me Talking." In fitted black suits accessorized with either a skinny tie (Dylan), bolo tie (Quintana and Marisco), or headband (Holiday), they also looked hip while doing it.

With "Jokerman," Dylan also stepped into the now by making his first music video, even as artists such as Joe Jackson derided the format as shallow and tasteless. It was directed by George Lois, the art director and designer who long claimed to have created the "I want my MTV" campaign. In an interview with the magazine *Musician*, Lois expressed that his enthusiasm for the Dylan collab was as much about the artist as it was about the chance to help pivot the music video into a serious art form. "Because of music videos, every commercial director in America froths at the mouth," Lois said. "They're all starry-eyed. It's almost revolting. They feel they can take a song and wing it. Discipline is gone. Videos are seen as hot stuff where you can use symbolism that doesn't mean anything. Perhaps I'm exaggerating, but that's been the feeling."

In the process of working with Lois, Dylan made several concessions. He didn't want to lip sync in the video, but he did, mostly in profile. He didn't want to look at the camera, but Lois included a split second of his piercing bedroom eyes. He was uncomfortable with his lyrics being shown on screen, but they were, over a series of iconic artworks and historical images. Lois also included a series of well-known images of the singer, as if to stress his icon status and singularity at a time when it had been obscured. "This is Bobby saying, 'Here's what I think about life, about my own life, about the past and about the future. And here's what I think about music videos. I don't have to look like the rest of the world because I've got something to say with words, visuals, and my intensity when I sing to you,'" the director offered as a summary of the pair's intent.

Though Dylan and the Plugz's performance on Letterman was objectively good, exciting even, its volte-face quality was a lightning rod for debate, much like when Dylan "went electric" at the Newport Folk Festival nearly twenty years earlier. The haters needn't have worried. Dylan abandoned this version of himself shortly after his appearance on *Late Night.* He hired Tom Petty and the Heartbreakers as his backing band two years later.

By reaching back into history and rebelling against punk's "loud, fast, angry" archetype, cowpunk musicians made tradition edgy while also creating a new form of it. In the process, they embraced and echoed heartland rock's Everyman influence and iconoclasm throughout the Reagan years. There wasn't a scene for their vision and so they made their own, similar to what Tom Petty once said of his own band's roots: "We had to be in the new wave, because we weren't in the old. I just don't like clubs. We didn't join no clubs. We're our own club."

CHAPTER 5

NEW PATRIOTISM

I'm a cool rocking daddy in the U.S.A. now.

—BRUCE SPRINGSTEEN

The 1984 Summer Olympics torch relay, which stretched from New York to Los Angeles, was the first such event to include ordinary citizens alongside world-class athletes. Over eighty-three days, 3,636 torchbearers ran more than nine thousand miles. At the Los Angeles Memorial Coliseum, decathlete Rafer Johnson, who rose from humble origins to become a gold medalist in the 1960s, became the first Black athlete to light the Olympic cauldron. When asked if he felt powerful as he ascended the stairs and held out the torch that day, Johnson demurred. "Just the opposite," he said. "I felt very, very humble."

The Los Angeles Summer Olympics exuded a sense of triumph after previous Summer Games were beleaguered by a terrorist attack (Munich 1972), considerable financial woes (Montreal 1976), and a sixty-six-nation boycott (Moscow 1980). The blending of ostensibly average and extraordinary Americans at the beginning of the international sporting event broadcast to the world America's foundational promise: In the land of the free, anyone willing to work hard could become exceptional.

Though its opening ceremony—with marching bands, a gospel choir, and New Orleans jazz musicians, plus performers dressed as Revolutionary War–era patriots, pioneer folk, and cowboys—drew equal parts enthusiasm and mockery, the Games spurred a demonstration of national pride that was novel amid a social and political era rife with uncertainty. Amid Reagan's second bid for the presidency, a flag-waving fanaticism surfaced under a banner deemed new patriotism. Red, white, and blue was all the go, and the year's biggest heartland rock album, *Born in the U.S.A.*, echoed that. Or did it?

★ ★ ★

Bruce Springsteen's *Born in the U.S.A.* is one of the best-selling albums of all time. Its title track, about the plight of Vietnam veterans, is one of the most misunderstood songs of all time. The album's pop appeal brought heartland rock's back-to-basics ideology to the masses while also incorporating synthesizers and gated reverb drum sounds. The music video for "Dancing in the Dark," featuring young Courtney Cox, is further evidence that straight white men can't dance.

These are some of the things most of us know about *Born in the U.S.A.* As an album that's been written about, discussed, debated, and documented on par with the Beatles' *Sgt. Pepper's Lonely Hearts Club Band*, rehashing the framework of Bruce Springsteen's commercial juggernaut feels tantamount to believing that the earth is flat: There is no point because all of the factual details about its makeup are widely available. If a Bruce fan wants this information, a Bruce fan can easily find it. This is not to discount the album's importance, but to say that beyond the facts of its writing and recording lies a different fact that is less known and perhaps more interesting: Bruce Springsteen's *Born in the U.S.A.* was the first compact disc manufactured in America, and the factory that made it was located deep in the heartland.

The Sony Digital Audio Disc Corporation announced plans for its first American manufacturing plant in Terre Haute, Indiana, in 1983. Test production began the next year, in mid-August 1984, just after mayor Pete Chalos presented the key to the city to basketball star Larry Bird; the native Hoosier had just dedicated his 1984 National Championship win with the Boston Celtics to the city of Terre Haute on national television.

Located seventy-seven miles southwest of Indianapolis, Terre Haute is best known as the home of Indiana State University, where Bird played for three years before going to Boston. It was also a hub of music manufacturing. Columbia Records was the first major record label to operate in Terre Haute. The company built one of its three vinyl pressing plants there, which opened on June 15, 1954. According to reports from that time, Columbia Records chose Terre Haute for its proximity to several key railway lines, which allowed the label to get its records to distributors within twenty-four to forty-eight hours of pressing them.

Sony DADC officially began making CDs about thirty years later, in the first week of September 1984. The facility boasted six CD presses and about one hundred employees in its infancy, and grew quickly. Its aim was to produce three hundred thousand discs a month by the end of the year. Amid a time of economic uncertainty, when many factories were stalled or closing across the heartland, its opening was a boon. In the early '80s, CDs were a cutting-edge format that had until then been manufactured solely in Japan and Germany. Sony's decision to open in Terre Haute also had the effect of positioning the state of Indiana as a center of cutting-edge technology.

Before the advent of 4.7-inch plastic discs, the city demonstrated its singular ability to crank out other formats. In March 1966, Columbia Records began manufacturing tapes in Terre Haute in a second building, which it leased. Soon after, the company announced that it would spend $2 million to buildout its tape operation in a permanent space near its vinyl pressing plant. There, it produced prerecorded four and eight-track tape cartridges, prerecorded two-track cassettes, and prerecorded four-track reel-to-reel tapes.

By 1973, Columbia Records had spent $4.5 million while expanding its warehouse operation to a single structure near its vinyl pressing plant, folding in the contents and workers of several warehouses it had been renting in Terre Haute. In the process, the company became the largest employer in the city, and a visible presence in the community through charitable causes and community organizations. Its Babe Ruth League recreational baseball team was often covered in the local newspaper; so were its collaborations with the local symphony orchestra and Indiana State University.

As the 1980s set in, and vinyl records began to fall out of fashion, Columbia Records ceased its pressing operations in Terre Haute. But its building didn't lie fallow for long. Sony's new CD plant was a joint venture with CBS, Columbia Records' parent company, which the Japanese manufacturer bought out in 1985; Sony DADC soon took up residence in Columbia's former pressing plant. The move marked a morale boost for those who'd lost their jobs but were now employed in the making of CDs. The format was also viewed as a lifeline for the music business more broadly in the wake of vinyl's decline.

"It could be one of the things to save this industry," said Walter Yetnikoff, then president and CEO of CBS Records. "There's a lot of money behind this configuration—these aren't two-bit companies involved in the launch of the format—and I'm getting the initial feeling that the format's introduction may be better than expected." Separately, the head of Polygram Records predicted in a speech that the CD would totally replace vinyl records by the year 1990.

Sony DADC's opening in Terre Haute was also the starting pistol for the CD wars that took place in America between competing record clubs. Along with Columbia Records in Terre Haute had come the Columbia Record Club, an experiment by the label in direct-to-consumer vinyl record sales. By the 1980s, the company had morphed into the Columbia House Record Club, and in the fall of 1984, Columbia House announced that it was folding CD sales into its existing vinyl record and tape club. At the same time, RCA Records announced its own venture, the RCA Victor Record Club, which touted one free CD to new members upon its announcement in 1984. Two years later, in 1986, RCA sold its club to the Bertelsmann Music Group, which created the BMG Music Service. This club became the Columbia House Record Club's main competitor.

By the mid '80s, the Columbia House Record Club had become the largest private employer in Terre Haute, and famously offered a stack of CDs for next to nothing to new members. Usually, its deal was eight CDs for a penny; after purchasing one CD at full price, new members would also receive three additional free CDs. That meant twelve CDs for the price of one. All the lucky respondent had to do was tape a penny to Columbia House's promotional mailer and return it to an address in Terre Haute, where the company's manufacturing, distribution, and customer service operations were located.

If this deal sounds too good to be true, that's because it was. Columbia House's "penny deal" mailers were loaded with asterisks and other fine print that surely almost no one read. That penny essentially forced the respondent into a contract that required the purchase of a certain number of CDs each year at full price ($17.98–$19.98) plus unspecified "shipping and handling" costs. This could add up to as much as $10 more than CDs sold at retail stores.

Each month, Columbia House mailed members a catalog of CDs available through the club, which also contained a card with its CD of the Month pick. Members were to write in if they did—or did not—want the club's featured CD, and then mail the card back to Columbia House. If the member was late or forgot about the club, or became disorganized or lazy about returning the mailers, Columbia House sent its CD of the Month whether the person wanted it or not. It also charged for it, a practice known as negative option billing. If customers didn't pay the club's bills, Columbia House tacked on a labyrinthine tangle of penalties and fees. The club also made money by paying reduced royalties—and sometimes no royalties at all—to record labels and publishers in exchange for its substantial presence in the market.

Columbia House sometimes sent multiple catalogs of different genres of music, with different CD of the Month picks, to the same address. According to the documentary *The Target Shoots First*, made by a former Columbia House marketing department employee in New York who struggled with the club's sales tactics and comportment, Columbia House intentionally chose lowest-common-denominator titles for its "CD of the Month" so that members wouldn't try to return them.

Columbia House touted that if its members kept up with the club, its CDs cost about $8 each, much lower than prices at traditional retail. That may have been true. But many people thought that the club's CDs were also often inferior in quality to discs sold in stores. Many were packaged with a paltry version of an album's original insert. They were also often housed in cheap cases that easily cracked. Also, there were untold numbers of Americans suspended in a vortex of music and bills they didn't want and couldn't afford. Columbia House's financial honey trap prompted a windfall for the company.

Karmic comeuppance arrived in the form of savvy American teenagers who'd narrowed in on the fact that the record club didn't require a credit card to sign up—just a name and address to which Columbia House would send a bill. Such unscrupulous individuals cashed in on the penny deal many times, under multiple names and addresses, to no accountability, allegedly. Other folks discovered the effectiveness of writing "return to sender" on the packaging of unwanted Columbia House CDs.

At its height in the late '90s, the Columbia House Record Club accounted for 15 percent of record industry volume in the United States. But as the CD fell out of fashion, so did the club. It officially ceased its record club operations in 2005, when it was rebranded as a mail order DVD club.

Though Columbia House was once a giant, Sony's CD plant in Terre Haute wasn't just a vehicle for its wares. DADC manufactured CDs for all of the record labels owned by Sony and CBS, including Columbia, RCA, Epic, and Arista, as well as discs for outside labels. The plant's physical presence was an obvious benediction for Terre Haute, and it also marked the beginning of an ideological shift in the state of Indiana.

"The Japanese may have lost the Second World War, but they were going to win the economic battle we were involved in," explained John Mutz, who was lieutenant governor of Indiana from 1981 to '89, and who helped close the deal with Sony. "I say that because Japanese auto manufacturers were taking our market share and were affecting levels of employment in Michigan, Illinois, Indiana, Kentucky, Ohio, and Tennessee. The result of that is that people were scared and may have lacked faith in the future . . . what they saw was a situation in which that American Dream they'd been a part of had been deeply affected and challenged."

Mutz told me that after taking office alongside former Indiana governor Bob Orr, the administration worked to create local economic development organizations in communities throughout the state that "would be concerned about prosperity for people, jobs for the people in the community, and in general, would be a spokesperson for the community when opportunities present themselves." Such a program aided Sony's plant in Terre Haute. According to a report in *Billboard* magazine, a state and local industry group provided $400,000 for a training package for new Sony DADC employees. Tax abatements designed by Orr's administration also made the Terre Haute location more attractive, including a promise to pass legislation that eliminated Indiana's global unitary tax law.

Mutz said that this factory was an important first win that cleared the path for future Japanese manufacturing operations in the Hoosier State. "There were literally over 120 Japanese plants that all came to the state afterwards," he said. "Now not everyone loved this idea because they thought the Japanese were taking over. But in reality, they weren't. They were investing. And we were quite pleased with the results."

The growth of the technology sector in Indiana was so rapid in the '80s that it prompted speculation about the future of manual labor at large. In 1983, announcements about tech expansions in the state occurred almost weekly and caused one local newspaper reporter to write, "The 'blue collar worker' of the new high technology age won't have grease beneath his nails. And he probably won't wear blue shirts."

In addition to CD manufacturing, plants specializing in electronic test equipment, auto industry robots, and communication electronics, among others, opened up shop.

At the same time, concern about American products and the people and places that made them loomed. Under the auspices of protecting US manufacturing, in 1982 the Reagan administration introduced the Buy America Act, which required federally funded transportation projects, such as the construction of highways, rapid transit systems, and railways, to use materials made in the United States. Sam Walton, the chairman of Wal-Mart stores, also began an aggressive "Buy American" campaign in the early '80s in which he ordered and sold products such as electric fans, metal stacking garden chairs, and flannel shirts in large numbers from American-owned factories. The program was "flying in the face of economics," according to *The New York Times*. However, the Arkansas-founded chain was just behind No. 1-ranked K-Mart in sales in 1985.

Heartland rock increasingly spoke to such concerns through the decade. With *Born in the U.S.A.*, Springsteen released "My Hometown," another in a series of his meditations on the psychic reverberations of factory closures. Bob Dylan's "Union Sundown" addressed the issue of unions and offshoring in 1983, a year after Bob Seger's "Makin' Thunderbirds," which detailed Detroit's former auto factory glory. These artists continued the lineage and legacy of Woody Guthrie's "Union Burial Ground," a sentiment that began to resurface in the '70s via John Lennon's "Working Class Hero," Bruce Springsteen's "Factory," and country star Johnny Paycheck's "Take This Job and Shove It," among others. Johnny Cash released "One Piece at a Time" in 1976, about a Kentuckian who goes to work in a Detroit auto factory. Merle Haggard issued "A Working Man Can't Get Nowhere Today" a year later.

As existential questions about American labor began to take shape, Sony DADC and its employees bore a tangible hope for those in Terre Haute as well as other laborers seated on the bench awaiting such technological advances in their own industrial enclaves.

"I remember people who were in other careers at other workplaces coming to Sony and quite enjoying the fact that it was a clean environment and a healthy place to work. People had a lot of positive things to say about working there," said John Macdonald, an audio engineer who was the thirty-first employee hired at Sony DADC.

Sony DADC's twelfth employee, Mike Mitchell, began his work at the plant as a processing engineer hired to help set up the CD-making operation in Terre Haute. "The people that I run into now from the early days that are either retired or have moved on because of the decline in the industry, they all say the same thing," he explained. "They say that Sony DADC was unique. And it was the best part of their working career and in some cases, their personal lives. We hired some amazing people with high school diplomas that did some amazing stuff and had tremendous work ethic, things that are so hard to find today." It's also where Mitchell experienced the version of the American Dream in which dedication is rewarded and meritocracy exists. By the time he retired from the company, Mitchell was its executive vice president and chief technology officer, someone who'd worked his way up through the ranks over decades. If it's a professional arc whose stability and loyalty rings of the past, it is also indicative of what Sony and the CD brought to the heartland.

A ribbon cutting held on a Friday in late September marked the official opening of Sony DADC in Terre Haute, Indiana. In attendance were Governor Orr, Lieutenant Governor Mutz, Terre Haute mayor Chalos, CBS president Yetnikoff, other industry executives from New York and Tokyo, and members of the press. "Terre Haute is my kind of town," said Norio Ohga, Sony's then president and chief operating officer. "I couldn't find the word Hoosier in my Japanese-American dictionary, so I have made up my own definition: I have decided it is the English word that means 'Somebody who makes things happen.'"

Corresponding print advertisements ran in *Billboard* magazine, which depicted a life-size black-and-white illustration of the *Born in the U.S.A.* CD with scaffolding around it and little men in hard hats. "Now Made in America," its headline stated. "CBS Inc. and Sony Corp. are proud to announce America's first compact disc manufacturing plant is open for business," text at the bottom of the advertisement declared.

Sony DADC also manufactured a special edition of *Born in the U.S.A.* for employees and attendees of the ribbon cutting event. A sticker affixed to the front of its case read, "The first CBS Records Compact Disc Made in the USA." These one hundred or so discs are known as the elusive "red text" CD versions because the text on the front of the disc—including the title, track listing, label branding, and manufacturing codes—is red. The version that went to retail stores has black ink. The plant also produced a second CD for employees. *The Edison CD Sampler: Edison Historical Recordings Digitized on Compact Disc*, contained historical children's songs, John Phillip Sousa's "The Yankee Shuffle," other folk tunes, and political speeches, including President Theodore Roosevelt's "Social and Industrial Justice." The two CDs were packaged together in a blue-and-white cardboard box with the striking DADC logo and the date of the ribbon cutting: September 21, 1984.

In the wake of the new operation in Terre Haute came an industrywide promotional blitz on behalf of the CD format. MTV factored heavily into these calculations. Sony, CBS, Polygram, and WEA (Warner, Elektra, Atlantic) joined forces and spent about $1 million to promote their emerging software, as well as the companies making CD players, in commercials that aired on the network. This campaign also included the use of MTV VJs, who hyped the CD format and a promotional giveaway in which one winner took home a Sony "digital component system" and one hundred compact discs manufactured by the labels. The record companies also gave CD demonstrations on college campuses and at industry trade shows. Depending on who you ask, the CD was a revolutionary innovation in music that made high-quality audio portable, or it was a scam that brainwashed consumers into buying albums they already had on a cheap-to-make format marked up at retail by 600 percent. But for everyday people in Terre Haute, it was a lifeline, one unlocked by the best-selling heartland rock album of all time.

At its height in the 1990s and 2000s, Sony DADC was the largest private employer in Terre Haute, Indiana, with about 1,300 employees. According to the company, it has manufactured about twenty-three billion discs including CDs, DVDs, Blu-Rays, and Sony Playstation games. However, as physical media has become outmoded in the streaming era of the new millennium, Sony DADC has diminished. Today, a used CD copy of Bruce Springsteen's *Born in the U.S.A.* sells for about $5 on the website Discogs, and the company that made it is a shell of its former self. The manufacturing facility now employs fewer than two hundred people in Terre Haute, and no longer makes CDs.

★ ★ ★

Born in the U.S.A. also marked a major shift in Bruce Springsteen's E Street Band. His longtime friend, guitarist, and musical advisor Steven Van Zandt decided to leave the group about halfway through its making. Thankfully, he convinced Springsteen to keep "No Surrender" on the album ahead of his departure.

The pair had been together long before Springsteen's fame, having gigged at the same clubs in Asbury Park since they were teenagers. Van Zandt as a principal songwriter was directly responsible for the rise of Southside Johnny, and both men had played as part of the Asbury Jukes. Van Zandt had been Springsteen's right hand through most of his life when he decided that his contributions weren't being taken seriously enough and that he should try going out on his own. He released his second—and best—solo album, *Voice of America*, in May 1984, a month before *Born in the U.S.A.*

Van Zandt's departure from the E Street Band also marked an awakening in his political consciousness. What began with a horrifying experience in South Africa ended with Van Zant leading an influential political campaign that is at least partially responsible for the fall of apartheid. USA for Africa's "We Are the World," released in 1985, may endure as the most successful charity single in American history, but Van Zandt's "Sun City" has contributions from a more diverse range of musicians that included Miles Davis, Run-D.M.C.,

Steven Van Zandt at
Los Angeles mayor Tom
Bradley's office in 1988,
where the politician
praised the musician
for the song "Sun City."
PHOTO COURTESY
MEDIAPUNCH INC.

Jackson Browne, Bonnie Raitt, Ruben Blades, Peter Gabriel, and Joey
Ramone, among many others.

Around the same time, Van Zandt began speaking out about a
term that was being batted around in American culture: the new patriotism. On October 25, 1983, President Reagan ordered the invasion of
the Caribbean island nation Grenada as part of the revised Cold War
against communism, which began with the Soviet invasion of Afghanistan in 1979 and became more acute after Reagan's infamous speech
in which he called the Soviet Union the "Evil Empire." There was also
the idea that American medical students studying on the island were
in danger, and that the country didn't want a repeat of the Iran hostage crisis. Multiple branches of the US military joined troops from
Jamaica and the Caribbean Regional Security System to overthrow the
People's Revolutionary Government of Grenada in just a few days.

The United Nations called the action a "flagrant violation of international law" in its adoption of Resolution 38/7 by the General Assembly. In the US, protesters marched on Washington, DC, and college campuses around the country. The Congressional Black Caucus denounced the invasion. Seven Democratic congressmen moved to impeach Reagan on "the high crime or misdemeanor of ordering the invasion of Grenada in violation of the Constitution of the United States."

Their efforts were unsuccessful. Reagan touted the invasion as an antidote to the Vietnam Syndrome that had a widespread demoralizing effect on the country's view of US forces. (The feeling Springsteen addressed in "Born in the U.S.A.") The president commended the "gallantry and heroism" of the "young men" who'd fought in Grenada in what amounted to a nationalist makeover for the military, now framed as powerful anticommunist warriors who would dominate anywhere the US perceives a threat to freedom.

The sale of American flags boomed. Military enlistments climbed. Sickly ROTC programs on college campuses fattened up. Olympian Carl Lewis won the gold medal in the 100-meter dash at the 1984 Summer Olympics in Los Angeles, then grabbed an American flag out of the crowd and ran down the track waving it. The country music singer Lee Greenwood released his syrupy patriotic anthem "God Bless the U.S.A." that summer. It went to No. 16 on the Billboard Hot 100 and quickly became a favorite among Republicans. The party used the tune in a film about Ronald Reagan that played at the 1984 Republican National Convention. Greenwood also performed the song at the GOP's 1988 convention.

With *Born in the U.S.A.* and its provocative cover art, Bruce Springsteen's ass became an unwitting ambassador for new patriotism and its denim, stars, and stripes. The album's imagery was all but inescapable, splashed across magazines and promotional signage from Lewiston to San Diego. Springsteen also played the song in front of an American flag on tour. Old Glory was the hottest accessory of 1984.

The new patriotism and its unifying message were enticing after the individualism of the 1970s and amid economic uncertainty that hung in the air like smog in the distance. So, a sizable portion of America pledged allegiance to a Hollywood gunslinger, and got drunk on a cocktail of red, white, and blue. Patriotism was the easiest way to press against equivocation. Cowboys and soldiers are also universally accessible forms of heroism.

Van Zandt wasn't going to absolve his fellow Americans that easily. With *Voice of America* came an open expression of resistance. Each of the album's ten songs speaks to a specific social issue, such as state-sponsored abductions in El Salvador, the Berlin wall, American dissent, and ultranationalism. His lens was secular humanism, the idea that every person is entitled to dignity and is capable of moral righteousness regardless of religious beliefs or political affiliation. In the song "I Am a Patriot," he rattles off an entire list of things that actually aren't required to be a proud American—capitalism, imperialism, and the Republican and Democratic parties, among them. The song became a favorite of Jackson Browne, who covered it on his 1989 album *World in Motion*.

During an appearance on the German music television show *Rockpalast* in 1984, Van Zandt gave the following speech, in an unmistakable Jersey patois, before his performance of "I Am a Patriot":

"Some wild things going on these days. We got something going on in America. They call it new patriotism. But it don't look like no new patriotism to me, it looks like blind nationalism. And that ain't right, that ain't what patriotism's all about. It ain't about accepting everything you hear on television and everything your government tells you. That ain't being a good patriot. Being a good patriot means you question every motherfucker, everywhere, every time. Make sure your country stays your country. And it don't mean you stop being a member of the world community, either. And it sure ain't about parties, you know: loyalty to the party instead of loyalty to the truth. But if we don't like things, it's up to us to change things, you know. Politics ain't nothing to be scared of. It's just freedom, and human rights, and democracy. That's all it's about. That's righteous politics."

In an address to the nation on October 27, 1983, just after the US

attack on Grenada, Reagan framed "freedom" as something to be pro-
tected with violence and hyper militarization. Van Zandt argued the
opposite in his songs, that freedom is best harbored by intellectual
honesty and human decency. Though America had yet to truly bifur-
cate into the red-blue dichotomy of the new millennium, the question
of freedom and how to preserve it was becoming a kind of fulcrum
on which everything else rested. Bonnie Raitt, John Mellencamp,
Bob Seger, Bruce Springsteen, Steven Van Zandt, Tom Petty, Jackson
Browne, the stars behind "We Are the World," and many other musicians called for resistance, collective action, civility, or all three.

Scholar Nancy Mitchell argued that Reagan's overarching foreign policy strategy could be summarized in one word: *vigilance*. She
wrote that it is an "accessible metaphor" because it "describes the
mood of America today—the 'new patriotism.' This is a patriotism
charged with vigilance: We have experienced weakness and we have
perceived danger; we are now on guard." It's a term that worked for
both conservatives and liberals, she argued. For the right it, "evokes
vigil, alluding to America's messianic mission to keep the world free
for democracy, to protect it from the Evil Empire." For the left it
"evokes vigilantes, alluding to the administration's lawless and summary invasion of Grenada."

Though Van Zandt's *Voice of America* was often compared to
conscience-driven protest rock of the 1960s—"Little Steven shared
concerns about America's conduct here and abroad in a way that hasn't
been heard since the fall of Saigon," wrote one newspaper reviewer—
heartland rock musicians traded the 1960s' peace and love aphorisms
for a belief in the strength and good sense of everyday people. "I don't
think you should take anything in rock and roll as gospel but you
should find out for yourself," Van Zandt told an audience in New Jersey before he performed the song "Los Desaparecidos." And he meant
it. He was a rock star who encouraged his audiences to read and pon-
der those facts in good faith.

Van Zandt imbued rock 'n' roll with political meaning without for-
getting that the songs also needed to be good. He gave Reagan's Amer-

ica a highly listenable rock record with punk rock shoring. The only common criticism of *Voice of America* is Van Zandt's singing voice, which is thinner and more reedy than Springsteen's mighty rasp.

"I deeply respect Steven Van Zandt's brave translation of rock and roll libertarianism into internationalist antiwar propaganda, and I don't think he's done badly by the songwriting—somebody cover 'Fear,' or 'Justice,' or 'Among the Believers.' But please, please, please don't make me listen to him sing them anymore. His voice is devoid of dynamic or dramatic zip. When he's not bellowing, he's plodding. And he's got a band to match," critic Robert Christgau wrote in his 1984 review.

On his pivot from Springsteen, the E Street Band, and soul music revivalism with *Voice of America*, Van Zandt may have put it best. He was well positioned because his profile as a solo artist wasn't high enough to disappoint a huge fanbase. And, the voice of his conscience mooted the messages of standard rock fare. "In the 1980s," he told a *New York Times* reporter, "the world didn't need love songs from a sideman."

★ ★ ★

If *Born in the U.S.A.* is the defining heartland rock album of the '80s, Don Henley's "The Boys of Summer" may be its defining song. With it, the Eagles' cofounder tapped into the firmament of youth celebrated by heartland rock, as well as its tuneful sense of uncertainty. As synthesizers and drum machines became acceptable tools in the wake of *Born in the U.S.A.*, and heartland rock embraced a more diverse sonic palette free of rock 'n' roll purity tests, "The Boys of Summer" aligned with the movement's spirit for its lyrical motifs and electronic color palette. "Guitar solos, to me, are getting as boring as drum solos," Henley told one interviewer.

Though strongly associated with Henley's post-Eagles comeback, the origins of "The Boys of Summer" didn't begin with Henley. The song that swept the nation, reaching No. 5 on the Billboard Hot 100 and No. 1 on the Billboard Top Rock Tracks chart, and winning Video of the Year at the MTV Video Music Awards, began with Tom Petty and the Heartbreakers.

In 1984, the band was on a short break after months of touring in support of *Long After Dark*. During this period, guitarist Mike Campbell was admitted to a hospital for exhaustion and Petty had surgery on his hand, which he'd broken in a flush of anger. They also worked on the album that became *Southern Accents*, a protracted and tortured process due to Petty's charge to push himself artistically. Though the group was on a break, it wasn't a chill scene.

After regaining his strength, Campbell returned to his creative practices and recorded piles of demos at home using a four-track recorder. As was his way, he played all of the instruments, but left out the vocals. Petty had already written the song "Rebels," which became the new album's lens: a look at the American South, the place of his origin, through the clarity of life experience and the passage of time. As they often did, Petty and Jimmy Iovine, who'd been called in to help course correct the album, paid Campbell a visit at home. It was then that the guitarist played for the pair a particular demo, one steered by the very first drum machine built by his friend Roger Linn: an Oberheim OBX.

At the time, the demo's chorus was written in a minor key; Petty and Iovine felt that it was too jazz influenced for the album. "I remember sitting at the piano and showing him that if it went major there when the chorus comes in, it would be much more effective," Petty told the author Paul Zollo. Given Campbell's gift for "working in bulk," as he once said to Petty, this little demo could've easily been lost in a pile of other scattershot ideas, left unrealized for eternity. But Iovine had a different idea. "Jimmy called me a week later and said that Don Henley was looking for some music for his solo record," Campbell said.

He and Iovine drove to Henley's house and played that same demo, which Campbell had tightened up and dubbed to a different cassette tape. According to Campbell, the Eagles member was undemonstrative as he listened, and the Heartbreaker left the meeting believing Henley hated the tune. As it happened, Henley was actually inspired and deep in thought. He wrote the lyrics of "The Boys of Summer" in mere hours.

Campbell was tasked with copying his demo because Henley wanted it exactly as it was, no easy feat as it had arrived in a stream of consciousness. After about a week of playing and overdubbing with Henley on vocals; Campbell on synthesizers, guitars, drum machine, and percussion; session pro Danny Kortchmar (best known as a member of the so-call Mellow Mafia of session musicians who played on countless soft-rock hits, and who'd become Henley's writing partner) on synthesizers and guitars; and Larry Klein, who was then married to Joni Mitchell, on bass, Henley decided he wanted to change the song's tone. Making it higher would add more drama, he believed. It would help the emotions land. As Petty had suggested, he took the chorus to a major key.

After another week of work the song was finished, but not before nail-biting near-misses with the drum machine, and in mastering, during which two different tapes were almost destroyed. For all of the modernity and resonance of its instrumentation—how the bridge's plucked guitar riff twinkles like sun on water; how the song's dah-dah-dah synth motif sweeps its way into one's memory—it's the song's lyrics that make "The Boys of Summer" timely and also timeless. In a few swift verses, and a monster chorus, Henley summons better-days nostalgia, ridicules sellout hippies, and offers a palpable sense of personal insight. These are, after all, the words of a deeply nostalgic man who used to wear an embroidered peasant shirt, but who now drove a black Porsche.

In addition to Campbell, Henley invited a host of other iconic musicians to contribute to his new album, *Building the Perfect Beast.* Heartbreaker Benmont Tench played keyboards, piano, and synthesizers on four songs, and the band's drummer Stan Lynch cowrote the album's tenth song, "Drivin' with Your Eyes Closed." Randy Newman played synthesizers; Lindsey Buckingham of Fleetwood Mac played guitar and sang backing vocals; soul music legend Sam Moore sang backing vocals; so did Belinda Carlisle of the Go-Go's and Martha

Davis of the Motels; longtime Eagles friend and cowriter J. D. Souther appears in the album credits, as do legendary studio and touring musicians Charlie Sexton, Tim Drummond, Jim Keltner, and Waddy Wachtel; there were also two members of Toto and one member of King Crimson in the studio.

For *Building the Perfect Beast*, Henley reunited with David Geffen, the cofounder and former head of Asylum Records, who helped orchestrate the Eagles' rise to fame. After the label head stepped down in 1975 to work in film, the fresh blood at Asylum went on a signing spree. Henley has said he felt lost in the pack of new artists, and partially blamed the label for the comparatively modest response to his first solo album. However, Henley had also been arrested in 1980. As the Eagles broke up and Henley brought on Kortchmar to help write new songs toward a solo debut, Henley threw a party at his Sherman Oaks home with the ensemble's crew, roadies, and others. Around 9 a.m. on November 21, 1980, Henley called the Los Angeles Fire Department as a sixteen-year-old sex worker was having a seizure due to the aftereffects of combining cocaine and quaaludes. Henley was taken into custody hours later by police, on suspicion of furnishing cocaine to a minor. Police also reportedly found twenty-two grams of cocaine, and "quantities" of marijuana and quaaludes in his home. A fifteen-year-old girl was also arrested for being under the influence.

In 1991, Henley told *GQ* magazine that the firemen had "just flat-out lied" to him. "They said, 'Well, by law, we're supposed to take this little girl to the hospital, but if you'll take care of her, we'll leave her here. We're not here to get anyone busted,'" Henley said. "She was fine by the time they got there. I had no idea how old she was. I had no idea that she was doing that many drugs; I didn't have sex with her, you understand." He also framed himself as the victim because he was being "clobbered in the press." Henley pleaded no contest to the charges, and carried on with his life and career, joining a long line of rock stars who've been accused in the court of public opinion of sexually assaulting minors.

And "The Boys of Summer" became a massive success. Its French new wave–inspired black-and-white music video, directed by Jean-Baptiste Mondino, demonstrated that Henley was a capable and even excellent artist in his own right. At the 1985 MTV Video Music Awards, Henley took home top honors and also three other "moonmen," for Best Cinematography in a Video, Best Direction in a Video, and Best Art Direction in a Video. "I had very little to do with the video," Henley explained at one point during the ceremony, as if to spotlight Mondino and fall in with all of the other stars who were also ambivalent about how they were represented on MTV. Tom Petty and the Heartbreakers cannot be lumped in with that cohort. Petty had long overseen the creation of the band's videos before MTV even existed. This was also true of the band's creepy rendering of *Alice in Wonderland* for its hit song "Don't Come Around Here No More." That year it won for Best Special Effects in a Video, but lost to Henley twice, along with two other snubs. Bruce Springsteen won Best Male Video and Best Stage Performance in a Video. John Mellencamp wasn't nominated but performed his new song "Lonely Ol' Night," whose black-and-white music video, shot in Indiana, is a charming backwater companion to Henley's Southern California beach opus. Henley and Canadian heartland rocker Bryan Adams both presented. Steven Van Zandt accepted one of Springsteen's awards on his behalf. Amid the incomprehensible saturation of David Lee Roth, heartland rock was a victor during the music television channel's second awards ceremony.

"The Boys of Summer" also earned a Grammy Award for Best Male Rock Vocal Performance, beating Bryan Adams, John Mellencamp, John Fogerty, and Mick Jagger. More importantly, it functioned as a wildly successful bait and switch. Listeners who'd enjoyed Henley's openhearted reminiscence of simpler days, and then purchased the full album, were soon walloped by left-wing political commentary. This would become a Henley trademark: wistful love songs interwoven with musical reprimands. He may have owned the car and the estate, but he wasn't going to accept Reagan and the corruption, as he saw it, of America's soul.

According to Campbell, Petty later regretted his decision to pass on the song, which he admitted when the pair was working on "Don't Come Around Here No More" for the album that became *Southern Accents*. "We go out to the car and listen to the mix on cassette like we used to do back in the day," he recalled. "The two of us were sitting in the car and we turn on the radio and there's 'Boys of Summer.' I go, 'Oh!' and I change the channel. There it is again before I can even turn the cassette on. And he looks at me and goes, 'Boy, you know, you were really lucky with that. I wish I would have had the presence of mind to not let that get away.' That was a real brother moment we had."

Alongside the runaway success of "The Boys of Summer," Henley released three other singles. "Sunset Grill," the album's ninth song and fourth single, was drawn directly from a hamburger stand Henley formerly enjoyed in relative anonymity. At the Sunset Grill, located near Grauman's Chinese Theater in Hollywood, he'd ordered possibly hundreds of cheeseburgers over the years. In the song, he animates the restaurant, its patrons, and its neighbors: two lovers who are hanging on by a thread, the immigrant owner who cooks and calls all of his regulars by name, and the sex workers and unhoused individuals who walk the street outside. Each character evoked an individual strain of cinematic desperation and human grit. Henley remarks on how the city has grown mean, and has become all but unrecognizable. He described how such an environment has stripped everyday people of their dignity by virtue of its callousness and greed. Though his observations were local, like most good stories, they were also universal.

Despite releasing his solo debut just two years earlier, Henley's visibility as a solo artist remained fairly obscure. This is partially because he didn't participate in an aggressive press cycle around that album's release, and the Eagles were strongly identified as a band, not by its individual members. As far as many fans were concerned, Henley was just the guy in the back on the drums with the nice voice. With "The Boys of Summer" and *Building the Perfect Beast*, that began to change.

There is perhaps no greater evidence of this than an encounter he had in 1984 at the Sunset Grill. Henley picked up a music journalist in his Porsche, and drove the pair to the dive for burgers. "Are you somebody? I think you're someone!" the owner-slash-cook's wife declared as the pair entered the restaurant. She hadn't recognized him until the popularity of his second solo album, and the song that specifically name-checked her restaurant. "You are Don Henley!" she decided.

He'd never be anonymous again. As Henley became a popular voice of the people in 1984, he also became one of them. No longer was he the consummate drummer of one of the most ubiquitous bands of all time, a relic of the mellow '70s. Now, he was a lone wolf, with a lot of big-name friends, who was troubled by where the country was headed. "The way people relate to each other on a one-to-one level," he said, "is directly related to the way the world is and the way the times are." So on that day, at the Sunset Grill, he met the excited woman's gaze and gently said, "yes."

★ ★ ★

The best heartland rock songs make the listener sentimental for a youth they never had. John Mellencamp's "Jack & Diane," Bob Seger's "Night Moves," Bruce Springsteen's "Glory Days," Bonnie Raitt's "Can't Help Myself," Tom Petty's "Even the Losers," Lucinda Williams's "The Night's Too Long," Don Henley's "The Boys of Summer," Bruce Hornsby's "Mandolin Rain." Each evokes a specific time and place to the artist, but are rendered in such a tender and evocative way that they become personal, cozy even, to the listener. These songs imprint on the psyche like a handknitted scarf or a mother's lasagna.

As heartland rock and its story songs swept through America and toward its apotheosis in the mid '80s, Canada began to experience its own kind of working-class musical phenomena. Tom Cochrane's Red Rider had its third straight platinum album in Canada with 1983's *Neruda*, which reached No. 11 in Canada, and No. 66 on the Billboard 200 in the US. Its three singles, "Crack the Sky (Breakaway)," "Power (Strength in Numbers)" and "Human Race" are antecedents to the synth-laced direction the genre's American artists would take in the succeeding years. The latter, with its driving beat and sparkling guitar, seems to have directly influenced the most popular heartland rock of the new millennium, the War on Drugs. Robbie Robertson of the Band was preparing to make an important comeback as a solo artist, guided by the hand of a fellow Canadian, producer Daniel Lanois. The Tragically Hip and Cowboy Junkies were also preparing their distinctive interpretations of the genre.

In the midst of this surge across the northern border was the biggest-ever Canadian breakout in the history of heartland rock. Bryan Adams was the son of a Canadian foreign service officer and a homemaker, both originally from England. Adams had traveled with his parents to postings around the world before attending secondary schools in Ottawa and Vancouver. He has described his child self as "completely incorrigible." "I didn't bother to go to classes. I'm the same way today," he told a newspaper reporter in 1985. "If I get the feeling that someone doesn't care, then I'm just not interested." His parents divorced when he was young, and as a teenager Adams took on varying jobs to help his mother make ends meet. He left school in the twelfth grade and became a dishwasher in a restaurant as he began gigging in the local scene in Vancouver, finding moderate success with the glam-rock band Sweeney Todd. He also hung around with addicts, though he wasn't one himself, and got in trouble with local police for unspecified crimes. Later, Adams linked up with Jim Vallance, formerly of the Canadian rock band Prism, who became a longtime songwriting partner.

Adams's first two solo albums received respectable buzz in Canada. He broke out in 1983 with *Cuts Like a Knife*, whose title track and single "Straight from the Heart" shot up the American charts and found moderate success in the UK. With his fourth full-length album, *Reckless*, released on his twenty-fifth birthday in 1984, Adams became a global phenomenon. The album spawned six singles, all of which charted within the top 20 of the Billboard pop singles chart, and one of them, "Summer of '69," became immortalized due to its faultless reading of the heartland rock formula. Red-blooded vocals? Check. A shotgun snare? Check. Guitar rock threaded with a synthesizer's lilt? Check. A lyrical vignette with an earworm hook that triggers memories across geography and time, which also name-checks specific people? Check. Check. Check.

Adams's roughneck origin story bore several similarities to those of his heartland rock peers. He also wore a leather biker jacket like Springsteen, and had boyish good looks like Mellencamp. His ballads elicited big sloppy feelings, like Seger. Though he traveled to New York to work with Bob Clearmountain, who mixed Springsteen's records, and found his greatest success in America, he did not go the route of Neil Young and Joni Mitchell. He has lived in Canada or England for most of his life, an extension of the same spirit that tethered Seger to Michigan, Mellencamp to Indiana, and Springsteen to New Jersey.

The man ticked off a lot of boxes. For the general listeners that heartland rock actively courted, this was appealing. For the rock press, this was a problem. "Summer of '69" climbed to the top 20 of charts in Australia, Canada, Ireland, Sweden, New Zealand, Belgium, Austria, and Norway. It went to No. 5 on the Billboard pop singles chart in

Bryan Adams performs in Germany in November 1984, just after the release of *Reckless*.

PHOTO COURTESY DPA PICTURE ALLIANCE.

America. But Adams's 1985 tour of stadiums was met more often by biting ire than not. In London, a writer for the *New Musical Express* likened Adams's performance to a sissy beer: "for if ever a glass of shandy played a gig, then 'twas tonight," he wrote. "Bryan Adams could be your kind of concert—if you're into mediocre," read the headline of the *Sacramento Bee*'s review, though it conceded that his performance of "Summer of '69" was "not at all unlike that of Bruce Springsteen."

Amid Adams's runaway success, reviewers in his native land even began to question his authenticity. "The U.S.A. may have Bruce Springsteen, but we've got Bryan Adams, the fresh-scrubbed kid from Vancouver," wrote one. "And that's the essential contradiction. While Springsteen may champion the ideals and attitudes of working class America, Adams's Canadianism is barely recognizable." These sentiments presaged a drastic turn six years later when the Canadian Radio-television and Telecommunications Commission decided that Adams's 1991 megahit "Everything I Do (I Do It for You)," from the *Robin Hood: Prince of Thieves* soundtrack, wasn't "Canadian enough" to have been made by a Canadian artist, thus denying it more frequent airplay throughout the country.

In 1994, on the heels of his *Robin Hood* hit, Jon Pareles of *The New York Times* described Adams as drawing all of his ideas from English and Midwestern acts the Rolling Stones, Rod Stewart, the Who, Bob Seger, and John Mellencamp . . . with a touch of Bruce Springsteen (who is neither English nor Midwestern). "And after more than a decade of Top 10 hits, Mr. Adams has made a trademark of his own facelessness; he is heroically ordinary," the critic concluded. In other words, Adams was like a pre-Broadband AI hoovering up and dissecting classic content in order to spit out mechanical forgeries. And the millions of people worldwide who disagreed were cultural vulgarians. Never mind that Mellencamp, Seger, Springsteen and others have also openly declared their love of the Stones and the Who. Mellencamp's *Uh-Huh* was even recorded in a way to mimic the live spirit of *Exile on Main Street*.

If this says more about the rock press of the '80s and '90s than it does about Bryan Adams, that's sort of the point. As Bob Seger had endured sellout insults upon releasing *Against the Wind*, Adams's tender ballads and pop sheen had critics singing "fraud" in a round. Though the biggest heartland rock artists have never hidden the fact that their goal was to sell as many albums as possible, Adams, who also fulfilled that brief, was received differently from those acts. Springsteen was lauded for his horny and entirely vulnerable ballad "I'm on Fire," but Adams was dismissed for his similarly hot desire in "Run to You."

Though Springsteen remained the standard by which all other heartland rock was measured, he also is directly responsible for the genre's tipping point and subsequent demise. *Born in the U.S.A.* set a new template for high production values and synthesizers within the genre, which Adams applied with Clearmountain to *Reckless*. But Springsteen's widespread popularity in the wake of *Born in the U.S.A.*, and his subsequent oversaturation in America and beyond, prompted heartland rock fatigue, with fans and within the artist. On the *Born in the U.S.A.* tour, Springsteen played for about five million people over sixteen months. He'd become a household name, even among music listeners who'd never cared about rock music before. Now, he lived among the ranks of Madonna, Prince, and Whitney Houston as a celebrity.

In September of 1984, *The Washington Post* conservative columnist George F. Will recounted his experience at a Bruce Springsteen concert. After a disclaimer about how unhip he was, in which he admitted that he could not identify the smell of marijuana smoke, Will extolled the virtues of the show within the framework of old-fashioned American values and toxic masculinity. He wrote that Springsteen hadn't a "smidgen of androgyny" and that he resembled "Robert De Niro in the combat scenes of *The Deer Hunter*." He noted that the concert was implicitly dedicated to US steelworkers because Springsteen's tour was hard, honest work that evinced the "astonishing vitality of America's regions and generations." Will was also knocked out by the presence of American flags at the concert, in line with the new patriotism that was sweeping the nation. "I have not got a clue about Springsteen's politics, if any, but flags get waved at his concerts while he sings songs about hard times," he wrote, flagrantly waving his own cluelessness. "He is no whiner, and recitation of closed factories and other problems always seems punctuated by a grand, cheerful affirmation: 'Born in the USA!'"

Some of Adams's Canadian reviewers were similarly drawn to his virility and his concerts' demonstrations of patriotism. "Like Springsteen, Adams brings some honest masculinity back to rock 'n' roll," one wrote. "It was an evening when the Canadian flag received nearly as many cheers as the beloved guest of honor," another noted of a concert in Toronto. Yet another critic included a scene of Adams draping the Canadian flag over a drum kit in his review. Differing from Bruce's show was the unbridled presence of sex. In Ottawa, one critic estimated that ninety young women jumped on stage to hug Adams throughout the evening, one of which he slung over his shoulder like a caveman carrying his kill. At the same show, he stuffed a microphone down his pants à la Mick Jagger, more John Mellencamp than Bruce Springsteen.

If Adams's chart dominance injected a youthful energy into the emergence of homegrown heartland rock in Canada, it did little to quell fears that old folks were attempting to co-opt it in the United States. This was particularly true in the wake of Reagan's missive on Springsteen during a stump speech in Hammonton, New Jersey, in September 1984. "America's future," the president told the audience, "rests in a thousand dreams inside your hearts. It rests in the message of hope in the songs of a man so many young Americans admire— New Jersey's own, Bruce Springsteen."

Reckless went four times platinum in a little over a year, and sold about fifteen million copies worldwide. Though those stats amount to about half of the numbers *Born in the U.S.A.* tallied, it remains one of the strongest showings in the history of heartland rock. In succeeding years, when distaste for the genre's earnestness and ubiquity was moving toward the rear view, "Summer of '69" began to take on a life of its own.

Popular Christian pop-punk band MXPX released its appropriately sloppy cover in 1994. Boy band One Direction performed "Summer of '69" on the British music competition show The X Factor in 2010, ahead of being propelled to global stardom largely due to social media. Then, in 2018, Bryan Adams performed the song with Taylor Swift at a sold-out concert at the Rangers Centre in Toronto, amid the pop star's Reputation Tour. She called it "one of my favorite songs ever written," ahead of their onstage collaboration. In 2015, prevalent roots-rock revivalist Ryan Adams, long saddled with Bryan Adams–related heckling by crowds, finally caved in and covered "Summer of '69" at the Ryman Auditorium in Nashville. He stripped it back to a simple folk tune, just a guy with an acoustic guitar whose sounds barely carried over the crowd's audible show of enthusiasm. This entire process—how the singer claimed that the throngs of jokes over the years had nearly given him a mental breakdown, and how his cover marked a kind of defiant reclamation of his own identity—created a years-long press cycle.

In the years since the song became one of the best-known rock singles of all time, its authors have diverged on its original meaning. Jim Vallance, who met Adams as a punk kid all those years ago, has long held that he was envisioning the summer he experienced when he was seventeen years old, how singular and memorable it was. Adams, on the other hand, has stated that 69 is not in reference to a year, but to a sexual position. "Well, I was going to call the song 'Best Days of My Life,' but mentioning '69' felt a bit more provocative," he said in 2023. Luckily for both of them, "Summer of '69" has inhabited innumerable meanings over generations of listeners, summoning memories and feelings largely rooted in nostalgia—as the best heartland rock songs do.

CHAPTER 6

1985

THE YEAR OF AID

It's the same old story—Reagan helps the rich, and the Lord helps the rest of us.

—JIM HIGHTOWER,

TEXAS AGRICULTURE COMMISSIONER,

DEMOCRATIC NATIONAL CONVENTION

After *Born in the U.S.A.* permanently altered American culture, delivering heartland rock from roots-tethered classicism to pop music's fickle affections, 1985 saw a wave of musicians and albums that embraced heartland rock's lyrical sentimentality and synth-laced populism. Its reach was wide and its grip was solid, even as its sound became fluid and malleable. Heartland rock's impact in this period is well demonstrated by its influence on even more legacy musicians who were inspired by its proletariat doings. 1985 saw the release of commercially victorious albums by Creedence Clearwater Revival's John Fogerty and English guitar-rockers Dire Straits. Tom Petty released a well-meaning if thematically wobbly paean to the South, and John Mellencamp matured with a masterstroke about his home in the Midwest.

Ronald Reagan was sworn in for his second term in office on January 20 after winning every state except Minnesota and the District of Columbia, and amid a phenomenon of flag-waving new patriotism. "As we gather here tonight, the state of our Union is strong, but our economy is troubled," he said in his state of the union address five days later. "For too many of our fellow citizens—farmers, steel and auto workers, lumbermen, Black teenagers, working mothers—this is a painful period. We must do everything in our power to bring their ordeal to an end."

Views of Reagan among labor unions were mixed. Many workers had chosen to believe Reagan's folksy assurances and absorb his socially conservative agenda. Others were skeptical, framing a union vote for Reagan as tantamount to a turkey endorsing Thanksgiving. Corporate management and its attorneys relished the president's hands-off approach in the midst of major negotiations, which left the issue of wages and job security to the individual efforts of collective bargaining, rather than the president intervening to set a national tone as presidents such as Roosevelt and Truman had.

On the campaign trail, farmers who were navigating a major crisis of debt and foreclosures attended Reagan's rallies to voice their concerns while also pledging their support. Former vice president Walter Mondale, who ran against Reagan in 1984, and who dared to choose a female running mate, was widely viewed as an accessory to former president Carter's partial grain embargo against the Soviet Union, which had hurt American farmers. Reagan had also promised to reduce the national deficit and cut taxes in an effort to help alleviate farmers' financial woes. Instead, congress passed the Reagan administration's Tax Reform Act of 1986, which significantly lowered the tax rate for top earners, while passing a tax increase or no change at all to about 40 percent of American families.

As Bruce Springsteen continued his massive world tour in support of *Born in the U.S.A.*, the album's title track continued to be misinterpreted until the song became a nationalistic anthem in spite of itself. It was and is what the postmodern philosopher Jean Baudrillard called hyperreal—a representation without an original referent, endlessly remixed to suit a particular world view.

"It makes no sense whatsoever. What Reagan wants to do has nothing to do with 'Born in the U.S.A.,' 'Pink Houses,' or working class people," Mellencamp said shortly after Reagan took office. "But Reagan doesn't appeal to logic. He appeals to the emotional. Let's not forget the guy was an actor, and he's not stupid. You even see this stuff in beer commercials right now—'Made the American way.'"

America and heartland rock, in 1985, was an elastic band stretched between ideological extremes: jingoism and protest, prosperity and calamity, exceptionalism and globalism. At any point the whole thing could snap. As heartland rock ascended its cultural throne, and its reigning leaders edged toward burnout, bands such as Lone Justice, the Replacements, and R.E.M. folded heartland rock flavors into their alternative-rock batter, bringing an even more palpable punk spirit and attitude to the genre.

★ ★ ★

Los Angeles roots-rock quartet Lone Justice sprang from the same LA cowpunk scene as X, the Blasters, and Dwight Yoakam. David Geffen enveloped the group under his wing after Linda Ronstadt met the band through a mutual acquaintance, watched a gig, and then made a phone call. Geffen Records paired the group, led by twenty-year-old singer Maria McKee and guitarist Ryan Hedgecock, with producer Jimmy Iovine, who applied heartland rock's radio-friendly polish. For its self-titled debut, the band recorded "Ways to Be Wicked," written by Tom Petty and Mike Campbell, which was released as one of its two singles. A classic lament about the darker sides of relationships, the song also had the effect of upending the dehumanizing "evil woman" archetype when sung by McKee, who placed the wickedness on a male lover. The group also recorded "Don't Toss Us Away," which became a hit for country singer Patty Loveless in 1988. As a whole, *Lone Justice* paired '60s-indebted rock sounds with an outlaw country spirit and rockabilly flourishes. Its lyrics covered timeless themes: love, heartache, betrayal, work, and rebellion.

McKee said that the sudden buzz around her band was overwhelming at the time, but that her naivety and punk roots served as an unlikely protector. She described Stevie Nicks and Bob Dylan attending their shows or recording sessions and attempting to coach her. "I mouthed back to him, basically," she said of Dylan. "And because of that, he liked me. Bob likes to test people to see how much he can get away with because most people kiss his ass so much. And I didn't give a shit that it was Bob Dylan. I was like, 'This is my mom's favorite. I don't care.'" Dylan liked her so much that he wrote a song for the band, "Go Away Little Boy," which they recorded but didn't include on the album. They proceed to open for U2 on its *Unforgettable Fire* tour, and for Tom Petty and the Heartbreakers.

With its fourth studio album, *Tim*, Sire records head Seymour Stein placed big bets on Minneapolis quartet the Replacements, along with hip '80s acts such as the Cure, Depeche Mode, and a dance-pop singer in New York named Madonna. The Replacements' fourth work represented a make-or-break moment. Would they be remembered as a niche regional band from Minneapolis, formative but underground? Or would the Replacements reach the mainstream beyond college radio stations? Seemingly set on orchestrating their own implosion via heavy drinking and generally delinquent behavior, could Paul Westerberg and company pull it together long enough to make a widespread and lasting impression?

Like Mellencamp, Westerberg was a big fan of the Rolling Stones' *Exile on Main Street*, and cited its "Tumbling Dice" as a sonic reference point for the new album: something a bit slower, poppier, and with a heavier groove, all while maintaining the band's rock 'n' roll bona fides. Bruce Springsteen was also a formative influence. *Tim* incorporated heartland rock's recurring themes and refracted them through punk's cracked prism: the indignities suffered by blue-collar laborers ("Waitress in the Sky"), intense feelings of alienation ("Bastards of Young"), flyover country iconography as a subversive valhalla ("Here Comes a Regular"), a character study whose fictional tribulation speaks for an entire segment of the American populace ("Little Mascara").

This isn't to say that the band was in any way amenable to playing by the music industry's rules. In November of 1985, about two months after *Tim* received near-universal praise from the cultural cognoscenti, Westerberg told a reporter for *Sounds* magazine that he actually disliked the attention he was receiving and that they'd signed to Sire records because it seemed like the most lenient major label in terms of creative control. "I mean, we know in the end that we're going to do whatever we want no matter who we're signed to and it just seemed like the thing to do," he said. And on whether or not the band was aiming for a mainstream breakthrough á la bigger heartland rock acts, Westerberg offered a prescient response. "No, I don't know what we're doing to be quite honest," he said. "I guess we wanna feel like we're in control of what we're doing but whenever it gets to *that* point, I think we'll call it quits or do something that will destroy the band."

R.E.M., from Athens, Georgia, a hippie-adjacent guitar-rock act that has never been shy about name-checking its 1960s influences, began its shrug toward heartland rock with its third album, *Fables of the Reconstruction*. It was produced by Joe Boyd, who also worked with British folk-rock icons Nick Drake, Sandy Denny, and Richard Thompson, as well as Pink Floyd. Steered by the shyest of frontmen, Michael Stipe, the album was received as a letdown by fans in its day, but has since become a favorite. Its murky sense of tradition is widely viewed as a necessary transition for the band, and deserving of cultural reappraisal for the massive bet it placed. The group incorporated regional flourishes and folk-rock's updated sense of tradition in its lyrics and sound; the album evokes the kind of eerie gothic qualities that pervade the South's literary and musical legends, and begins to introduce auxiliary brass, woodwind, and stringed instrumentation to its guitar-centric sound. Though anyone listening could hear its production value was muddy and did little to draw out these new elements, the turn hinted at the eventual leap R.E.M. took when it hired Don Gehlman, John Mellencamp's producer, for its next album.

This next generation of torch bearers held little resemblance to the teetotaling, against-all-odds, workaholic predilections of Mellencamp and Springsteen, or hometown avuncular qualities of Bob Seger. There wasn't the sense that they would take on the big business of music like Tom Petty. What it did indicate was a near future where heartland rock was less ardent, largely aesthetic-driven, and derived from countercultures that ran contrary to mainstream needs or understanding. It seemed in this period that heartland rock had few direct heirs and, instead, a gaggle of misfit cousins who were less interested in propping up America's good qualities in an effort to sway hearts and minds. These artists reflected an iconoclastic spirit that would go on to reshape popular culture in the 1990s, from nostalgic and earnest, to modern and dejected. They were more jittery than jingoistic. "It's a really weird time that we're living in," Stipe said of America in the Reagan era. "It's kind of scary. I'm not sure that I like it too much."

As their aesthetics and messages were becoming more influential, the likes of R.E.M. and the Replacements remained relegated to the world of so-called college rock, whose audiences were mostly composed of students at universities and high schools. They were hip youth music, but they were not yet dominant. The latter designation was reserved for John Mellencamp, who was voted College Act of the Year in 1985 by the College Media Journal. "You also see a lot of people my age at the shows," he said. "I'm real proud of that, and I think the greatest thing that ever happened to me is the fact that my audience is so widely spread."

* * *

In any professional stadium or arena in the United States, a few rock songs are guaranteed to carry across the stands during sporting events: Queen's "We Will Rock You," "Welcome to the Jungle" by Guns N' Roses, and Gary Glitter's "Rock 'n' Roll (Part 2)," of all things. And there are other anthems that have come to define individual sports. The NBA has the jaunty synthesizer number "Roundball Rock," originally written for television broadcasts of its games on the NBC network, which has taken on a life of its own via internet memes, a *Saturday Night Live* spoof, and rapper Nelly's "Heart of a Champion." "Song 2" by Britpop royalty Blur has become a must at National Hockey League rinks, and no one can summon the NFL without hearing the opening brass stabs of composer Johnny Pearson's 1970 piece "Heavy Action."

Since John Fogerty of Creedence Clearwater Revival reemerged as a triumphant solo artist in 1985, Major League Baseball has adopted his hit "Centerfield." As a song that teeters on the brink of novelty, the enthusiastic ditty could have sunk his rock 'n' roll credibility. Instead, it helped carry him from being a ferocious, class-conscious voice of the antiwar movement, to being an elder in heartland rock's inclusive populism. The album *Centerfield* went to No. 1, making Fogerty one of five artists to have a top album in the 1960s, '70s, and '80s, along with John Lennon, Paul McCartney, the Rolling Stones, and Barbra Streisand. It was a boon after his solo debut for Asylum Records, *John Fogerty*, failed to connect with fans.

The album's heartland rock credentials were enhanced by Fogerty's homage to America's national pastime, but they were also strengthened by an ideological feud behind the album's first track, "Old Man Down the Road." With one of the biggest albums of 1985, Fogerty ended up taking the baton from Tom Petty in the fight against greedy record labels. As such, *Centerfield* also became a referendum on the misdeeds of American capitalism and its working-class predation, beyond its nostalgic, simpler-days patina.

Saul Zaentz, the head of Creedence Clearwater Revival's record label Fantasy Records, believed that "Old Man Down the Road" sounded almost exactly the same as the Creedence song "Run Through the Jungle," also written by Fogerty. In essence, Zaentz was saying that John Fogerty had ripped himself off. Due to a contract Fogerty signed while in CCR, the singer had relinquished most of his rights to CCR's catalog to Fantasy Records, including "Run Through the Jungle," and didn't own the copyright to the song. Zaentz filed a lawsuit claiming infringement.

Fogerty and Zaentz were far from friends at this point, in part due to the well-publicized collapse of a Bahamian tax shelter in which Fantasy had invested the band's revenue, which caused Fogerty and his ex-bandmates' income to virtually disappear. For *Centerfield*, the singer had written two new songs that underlined his displeasure. "Mr. Greed" and "Zanz Kant Danz" took aim at powerful men who seek to own everything and lie, steal, and manipulate in order to do so. Zaentz naturally took this as a personal attack and also filed a defamation suit, seeking $144 million in damages.

In 1988, a jury quickly ruled in Fogerty's favor, stating that "Old Man Down the Road" did not infringe the copyright in "Run Through the Jungle." However, the court ruled that Fogerty was not eligible to recoup payment for his attorney's fees, which amounted to more than $1 million. He fought that ruling all the way up to the Supreme Court and eventually won a decade later. Zaentz prevailed on his defamation claim, and the suit was settled out of court; Fogerty also changed the title of his musical right hook to "Vanz Kant Danz."

Centerfield hit No. 1 on March 23, 1985. "Old Man Down the Road" was praised as a delightful return to form for the swamp-rock icon, and became the only Top 10 hit of Fogerty's solo career. The album's third track, "Rock and Roll Girls," speaks directly to heartland rock's gift of sentimentality, setting escapist lyrics against rock music derived from the 1960s. The song's chord progressions during its verses nearly mirror those of Chad and Jeremy's 1964 single "A Summer Song," and Fogerty's lyrics illustrate an old soul whose greatest pleasure is getting lost in the nostalgia for old time rock 'n' roll. About twenty-five years later, in the summer of 2010, Fogerty became the only musician to ever be honored at the Baseball Hall of Fame's induction ceremony, when "Centerfield" was inducted among iconic ball players in Cooperstown.

Zaentz, who worked primarily as film producer in succeeding years, became known for financing the Miloš Forman–directed

One Flew Over the Cuckoo's Nest starring Jack Nicholson, and for his litigious nature. He died in 2014 from complications related to Alzheimer's disease. In response, Fogerty posted one link to his official Facebook and Twitter accounts, without a caption or other context. It directed his followers to the official music video for "Vanz Kant Danz." In the wake of a decades-long battle for his self-respect and livelihood, the storied musician could muster but one tribute to his former nemesis: a fleet of animated dancing pigs.

★ ★ ★

It took Tom Petty and the Heartbreakers three years to release its sixth studio album. *Southern Accents* was loosely based on Petty's reflections about the American South, and was overburdened by the pressures of its ambition. The group had made a successful transition from new wave–adjacent upstart to a reliable author of catchy rock songs that would endure beyond their era. *Damn the Torpedoes, Hard Promises*, and *Long After Dark* vaulted the group to canonical status, connecting with a wide listenership—Middle American laborers and coastal elites.

For his next work, Petty sought to transcend his 1960s rock and pop references—and lyrics whose characters could dwell in any number of towns between Pennsylvania and Colorado—with something deeper, richer, and more thoughtful. "I think I was trying to become a better writer," he told biographer Warren Zanes. "I felt I had enough going for me that I could do that. I'd touched on it, but my focus had been on writing good rock 'n' roll songs. This was the first time, I think, that I started to push beyond."

But there was the issue of his personal life and his professional neurosis. Petty's marriage to his first wife Jane was troubled. A cohesive suite of new songs wasn't coming very fast or very easily. When they did materialize, Petty labored over them, and then wasn't happy with the way they were written, produced, recorded, or all three. Once, in a fit of frustration, he hurled his fist into a wall and broke his hand. There was also the issue of drug use. Of *Southern Accents*,

Petty said: "When I hear that one, I can taste the cocaine in the back of my mouth."

All of this, combined with tensions within the band, prompted Petty to bring in new collaborators. Dave Stewart, of the British pop duo Eurythmics, cowrote the album's wildest curioso, "Don't Come Around Here No More," which was originally meant for Stevie Nicks. Instead, Petty retained it because he wanted to make something whose electronic psychedelia emulated Prince. It became the album's most successful single, though it in no way fulfilled its brief, while "It Ain't Nothin' to Me" and "Make It Better (Forget About Me)," two more Stewart cowrites, are unquestionably the worst songs on the album.

The album's title track is one of the songwriter's most tender and yearning compositions, a piano ballad with string arrangements by storied arranger and conductor Jack Nitzsche, who was Phil Spector's right-hand man for many years. Those strings are the momentum that carry the two main sentiments Petty's character relays, which are also felt by many of those who reside in the middle of the country: an unyielding antagonism for fancy people who dare to underestimate him, and an equally stubborn love-hate pride for his particular region's ways. A decade later, Johnny Cash would transform the song into a front-porch folktale set to acoustic guitar on his second album with the producer Rick Rubin, *American II: Unchained*. In 2024, Dolly Parton made the song her own for a country music tribute to the musician, *Petty Country*. The bonds between country music and heartland would be strongest in ensuing decades, but were forged in the mid '80s.

There was a song about a badass Southern biker who wears a dog collar in "Spike" and a pair of misfit dreamers in "Dogs on the Run." Dogs were also a long-running shorthand among the band. "We used to have dogs everything, and still do," Petty said in 1989. "Dog songs and dog humour. I don't know why—it's one of those dumb things." These three songs, combined with opening track "Rebels," are the vestiges of Petty's original intent, before he was distracted by his anger and anxiety. The album displayed its ambition through a wider palette of textures, too, including horns. And there were several songs that were cut from the album that, if they had been included, would have made for a far more cohesive listen than the indecisive, self-conscious version that was released. "Trailer" became a B-side; "The Apartment Song" was discarded; "Walkin' From the Fire," about the trials of two brothers, wound up on the box set *An American Treasure*, released in 2018.

"Sheets," a frank telling of the racism that pervades the American South, was never recorded. This omission is a particular shame because it may have also clarified the underlying sentiment of "Rebels," about a louse who blames his unemployment, drinking, and generally unlikeable constitution on the fall of the Confederate South. What Petty had sketched was a contemptible cliché, a hillbilly whose ugliness had alienated him from society. Petty's intent was an implicit call for his fellow Southerners to do better. The song was received by some, however, as celebratory; a sonic glorification of the stars and bars.

Fans didn't come to this conclusion on their own. In an incomprehensible lapse of good judgment, Petty and his art director decided to incorporate the confederate battle flag in the album's promotional material and on its tour. The *Southern Accents* tour book included the flag, and so did Petty's stage wear. He also raised the flag when he played "Rebels" in concert. An album composed of live recordings from the tour was released under the title, *Pack Up the Plantation: LIVE!*

Petty has explained that his intent was to visualize the regressive mindset of his broken characters, yet another layer in his artistic social commentary. A more appropriate judgment may be about his naivety in assuming that this nuance would resonate with the Budweiser-swilling public in the stands of a large arena. Like Springsteen's "Born in the U.S.A." and Mellencamp's "Pink Houses," "Rebels" became another widely misunderstood entry in the canon of heartland rock, but one with much more grave effects. It is one thing to mistake an antiracist song as a pro-America anthem, as was often the case with "Pink Houses." It is very much another to mistake an antiracist song as a pro-segregation hallelujah, as was often the case with "Rebels."

The cover art wrapped the album's thematic confusion into a tidy bow. "The Veteran in a New Field," a painting by Winslow Homer made just after the end of the Civil War, depicts a Union soldier in a field of wheat. It's a storied symbol of postwar fallout—death, grief, fear, transformation, determination, hope—that had little to do with the past or present South. Confederate soldiers wore red, after all, and the South grew cotton, not wheat. In short, *Southern Accents* was like *Gone with the Wind* if Victor Fleming had developed a cocaine habit, soundtracked the film with Glenn Miller and His Orchestra, and stuck Abraham Lincoln on the movie poster. When fans began waving confederate flags at his concerts, Petty quickly regretted his branding choice, and four years later, in 1989, he reinvented himself as a Southern California cool guy for his debut solo album, *Full Moon Fever.* The following year, in 1990, at a concert in North Carolina, a fan hurled a confederate flag onstage during his performance of "Rebels." Petty picked it up, and then verbally lamented using the flag on the "Southern Accents" tour. "A lot of the people that are flying this flag these days—I don't want anything to do with it anymore," he said, tossing it aside.

"I wish I had given it more thought," he added in an interview that ran in *Rolling Stone* in 2015. "It was a downright stupid thing to do."

★ ★ ★

As the divide between heartland rock's purists (Mellencamp, Seger) and heartland rock's innovators (Springsteen, Petty, Henley) widened, English songwriter Mark Knopfler and his band Dire Straits, formerly known for its earthen pub rock, morphed into a stadium leader best known for its embrace of music's most cutting-edge technology. *Brothers in Arms*, released May 1985, was one of the first albums recorded on a Sony 24-track digital tape machine, which meant that it sounded great when played through high-end audio equipment, particularly on CD.

Its audiophile ambition exemplifies how heartland rock transcended the rank and file, and reached men in gilded towers whose worst fear was becoming out of touch. Combined with the lyrical content of his songs—one that slyly mocks the necessity and prominence of music videos ("Money for Nothing") and another that heralds the ingenuity of penniless upstart rock 'n' rollers ("Walk of Life")—and arrive at the state of heartland rock in 1985: too nostalgic to truly be modern, too modern to truly be retro.

"Walk of Life," in particular, slotted in alongside Fogerty's "Centerfield," Springsteen's "Glory Days," Mellencamp's "Cherry Bomb," and others for its use of sports as an emotional device. Springsteen and Mellencamp summoned athletics in order to evoke the past, but Fogerty and Dire Straits used it to demonstrate modern enthusiasm. In the latter's case, the "Walk of Life" video spliced Dire Straits' live performances with imagery from stadium matches as if to equate their preparation, execution, and energy. The video framed Dire Straits' music as an accessible medium for everyday folks and their common pleasures—even if said music was made on and for high-end, financially inaccessible machines.

★ ★ ★

On December 10, 1985, farmer Dale Burr of Lone Tree, Iowa, population 550, killed his wife, the president of a local bank, and a neighbor before taking his own life with the same shotgun. The sixty-three-year-old had formerly been an honorable member of the community, one who owned about eight hundred acres of land with his son, which he'd farmed for most of his life. By the mid '80s, however, Burr had racked up more than a half million dollars in debt. A note he left by his wife Emily's body explained that he could no longer manage his problems.

Burr was an extreme and tragic byproduct of a crisis in American farming that swept the nation. It annihilated small towns, family farms, local businesses, and farming-related manufacturing. John Deere laid off thousands of workers, and rural banks and small stores folded en masse. Rates of murder, alcohol abuse, and domestic violence increased in rural areas. More than nine hundred male farmers who lost their farms to foreclosure committed suicide. By the end of the decade, it was estimated that more than three hundred thousand farmers had defaulted on loans. In 1977, amid the Carter presidency, the American Agriculture Movement began a series of rallies aimed at increasing the prices of certain crops. The farmers behind the group argued that the revenue they received for their crops did not align with the costs associated with growing them. These protests culminated in the so-called Tractorcade demonstration of 1979, in which three thousand American farmers drove their tractors to Washington, DC, in a show of solidarity. A few months later, in January 1980, President Carter enacted a partial grain embargo against the Soviet Union after it invaded Afghanistan. This had little effect. The Soviets soon discovered they could buy grain from South American countries at a lower cost.

These acts were the first indicators of the problems to come under the Reagan administration's seeming ambivalence and subsequent mishandling of mounting problems that pushed American farming into a full-blown crisis. During tours through the Midwest and other vast stretches of American farmland, President Reagan echoed Republican promises to restore profitability to agriculture, and make life in rural America prosperous again. In his 1984 State of the Union address, Reagan declared "America Is Back." But US workers, particularly farmers and their families and advocates, were beginning to see through that murky claim.

Though the problem had many branches, the farming crisis' roots grew from the fact that the market set the prices for food, not farmers. The 1970s also saw the emergence of large-scale corporate farming, which was the first major threat to family farms, and the main driver of overproduction in American farming. Many trace its emergence to Earl Butz, secretary of agriculture during the Nixon and Ford presidencies, who promoted the slogan "Get big or get out." Such surpluses began to lower the prices of goods, and farmers, caught in a cost-price squeeze, had to borrow money against the equity they held in their land to plant for the next season and otherwise make ends meet. Family farmers, in particular, were finding it much more difficult to obtain the credit they needed to plant each season. The rise of corporate farming was so fierce that a report by the USDA in the late '70s predicted that only hay, range livestock, and cash grain crops would be controlled independently by 1985.

The economic climate became particularly disastrous for farmers under Reagan's free-market agenda, whose programs initially did not support paying farmers to halt overproduction. It also allowed the country's largest food retailers, such as Kroger and Safeway, to participate in leveraged buyouts and recapitalization. Such restructuring impelled the formation of so-called supercenters, which demanded lower prices from vendors. So did corporations such as K-Mart and Wal-Mart, which also began to break into food distribution. Interest rates skyrocketed, and Reaganomics caused the value of land to plummet between 1981 and 1986. This was great for the corporations that began to swallow up vast swaths of rural America at bargain-basement prices. It was calamitous for farmers whose only lifeline was the value of their acreage.

"I hope for a moment we can have your voices be the voices of millions of people across the United States who are suffering the exact same thing," John Mellencamp told thousands of farmers and their families gathered in a parking lot in Chillicothe, Missouri, on May 7, 1986. Mellencamp, his violin player Lisa Germano, and multi-instrumentalist Larry Crane came to town to perform at a local protest against the government's treatment of farmers, in particular the local branch of the Farmers Home Administration, which authorized loans. Mellencamp, nearing the apex of his celebrity, naturally attracted the press. This was by design. "I believe we need to change the face of America. These people, farmers, are your people," he told a *USA Today* reporter. "We've got to help each other. I want to help and make the media and people in this country aware of farmers' problems." On a small stage, in front of a homemade banner, the trio performed stripped-back acoustic versions of three of Mellencamp's most populist songs: "Pink Houses," and two new tunes with lyrics that echoed the concerns of the crowd before him.

Since releasing *American Fool* in 1982, the musician had inched closer to something like an epiphany: His songs were most impactful when drawn from his personal province. Most of Mellencamp's biggest hits exemplified this, and they helped transform his sense of responsibility as a musician. As a neophyte, Mellencamp was vulgar, combative, contrarian, or all three. When *American Fool* found runaway success, he insisted that songs such as "Jack & Diane" were devoid of meaning and that fans shouldn't hoist him atop any kind of pedestal. For an artist who long seemed destined to author his own destruction, the singer's mid '80s turn was remarkable. It was then that Mellencamp began to admit that his previous stances were defense mechanisms from years of being dismissed as a joke or a fraud; songs like "Hurts So Good" also did little to spotlight his conscience. Mellencamp was sure that, given his track record, no one would ever take him seriously.

Amid the farming crisis in America, however, he reconsidered the utility of his position. He thought back to the 1960s, when he wore a black armband to school to protest the Vietnam War, and participated in the Vietnam War moratorium actions in 1969. He recalled his favorite music of the decade and how it stood firm against war and discrimination in implicit and explicit ways. Instead of fearing comparisons to artists such as Bob Seger, Tom Petty, and Bruce Springsteen, Mellencamp began to embrace their similarities, how each artist was informed by the culture of the 1960s, and became a singer-songwriter with an eye toward American issues. As someone who long believed that big government was corrupt and had little to do with his home in southern Indiana, he began to realize that some of its actors are worse than others. For the first time, he registered to vote.

This existential lightbulb moment was fully realized on a new album, Mellencamp's version of *Born in the U.S.A.* On July 31, 1985, *Scarecrow*, his most mature, substantive work to date, hit record store shelves. With it, the singer showed that he'd grown up and had also put his money where his mouth was. He also began to carve out an album-oriented identity and sound rooted in the simplicity and imperfections of 1960s rock and the landscapes of his southern Indiana home.

American Fool and *Uh-Huh* were patchy, but contained monster hits. *Scarecrow* was a sonic thesis, rendered in the musical qualities of a black-and-white photograph. "I don't have a smooth voice. I don't want to be a smooth singer," Mellencamp told *NBC Nightly News* reporter Eric Burns shortly before the *Scarecrow* tour began. "I want the band to sound the same way. I want it to be rag tag. I want it to be as garage as we can make it. Because if a kid in Los Angeles can't pick up a guitar and play 'Small Town,' then it's not really any good to anybody."

The album's opening track, "Rain on the Scarecrow," focused on the plight of American farmers via a first-person lyrical account of a tragic foreclosure. Many of its other songs drew from American tradition. The title of single "Lonely Ol' Night" was plucked from a line in one of Mellencamp's favorite films, *Hud*, in which Paul Newman stars as the titular antihero. "R.O.C.K. in the U.S.A." name-checked some of the singer's favorite musical artists from the 1960s, and paid homage to the hard work of musicians across genres and races. And then there were tunes whose themes were self-referential, tracing arcs from past to present. "Between a Laugh and a Tear" is a gripping duet with Rickie Lee Jones whose spirit brings Jack and Diane into adulthood. "Minutes to Memories" summons a bus ride Mellencamp took to Florida as a young boy. Its lyrics recount an older man who sat next to the singer, offering advice that young Mellencamp couldn't appreciate at the time, but as an adult understood and lived by: namely that family and friends are the most important relationships in a life well lived. Those themes also carry over to "Small Town," one of Mellencamp's most enduring songs, which went to No. 6 on the Billboard Hot 100, and heralds rural life in an expansive and genuine way. "That's where my friends are, my family's there, and I guess I don't make friends real easy, so it's easy for me to stay there," Mellencamp said of Indiana on *Late Night with David Letterman* in 1985. "Plus, your head doesn't get out of proportion."

The album was also the start of Mellencamp's use of more varied instrumentation. He played a harmonica on "Small Town," the first time he'd ever done so on a recorded track. There was also trumpet, saxophone, and slide guitar by Ry Cooder. For the album's tour, Mellencamp hired violinist Germano, a fellow Hoosier, who would become an essential component of his next album, *The Lonesome Jubilee*. She played with him until 1993 and again in the new millennium.

In 1984, for $20,000, Mellencamp built his own studio, rehearsal space, and offices in rural Belmont, Indiana, about ten miles east of Bloomington. He jokingly christened it Belmont Mall, because the entire town was no larger than a shopping center. He wrote, rehearsed, and recorded the songs of *Scarecrow* amid the rural ennui, the contours of its local pastures a visible reference point from the studio's windows. This, combined with the fact that Mellencamp tasked his band with rehearsing entire catalogs of artists from the 1960s and '70s ahead of the recording sessions, underscored his desire to transport listeners to the springtime of his life. It also demonstrated his style in the studio, in which little was ever good enough. "He pushes people to their limit and sometimes doesn't back off," the album's producer Don Gehman explained. "So consequently, here was a group of really talented people with a leader that was just maniacal."

Gehman, who'd worked with Mellencamp since his 1979 self-titled album, settled on a more highly produced and bigger sound on *Scarecrow*, which emphasized Kenny Aronoff's muscular drumming. The idea was to emulate the vibe of a hardworking Midwesterner while also transporting the listener to a simpler place in time. On "Rain on the Scarecrow," Gehman proposed that Aronoff hit a metal fire extinguisher with a metal rod to echo the sound of heavy machinery—a tractor or a factory—which is the anvillike quality on beats two and four, alongside the snare drum. Gehman also homed in on the merits of Mellencamp's abilities as a pop star, which is the reason "R.O.C.K. in the U.S.A.," a tune the singer hated, ultimately made it on to "Scarecrow."

Though Mellencamp was raised in the wilds of southern Indiana, his parents were not farmers. But one of his great grandfathers had worked the land, and by 1985 his sister was married to a hog farmer who struggled to eke out a living. Many of his boyhood friends were now grangers. He'd also seen the immediate spiritual effects of farm foreclosures on them. "There was one kid whose parents had a huge chicken farm. He works in a grocery store now. He's not the same guy he was after his family went out of business," Mellencamp explained. Seymour's agrarian imagery—its fields dotted with produce and framed by invasive Johnsongrass; its farmhouses and cabins—was central to Mellencamp's identity. In the *Scarecrow* tour book, Mellencamp included a mention of Seymour's Farmers Club in its opening remarks, a historical clubhouse embellished with Indiana limestone where farmers in Seymour and beyond sold produce as their wives mingled and their children played.

By Reagan's second term in office, the number of farmers in Indiana had dwindled to mid-nineteenth century numbers, and for Mellencamp, the issue was personal. Of all of Mellencamp's albums to date, *Scarecrow* was his most cohesive because it most clearly conveyed its source material—the importance of his friends, family, and community farmers in the rural Midwest. The album also bore the fruit of an enduring songwriting partnership between boyhood friends, whose bond was emblematic of the characters and characteristics in Mellencamp's songs such as "Small Town" and "Rain on the Scarecrow." The singer met George Green in Sunday school class as a child, and the pair eventually graduated from Seymour High School together, in the Class of 1970. Their collaborations date to Mellencamp's 1976 album *Chestnut Street Incident*, but first flourished on *American Fool*. Mellencamp has long said that the idea behind the album's first hit, "Hurts So Good," came to him in the shower. What many don't know is that Green was the first person to whom he relayed the idea. "I was still dripping wet when I got dressed, walked out of my bedroom, and said to my old songwriting friend George Green, 'Hey! I just thought of a great chorus,'" Mellencamp wrote in the liner notes of the compilation *The Best That I Could Do (1978–1988)*.

Green contributed to "Rain on the Scarecrow" and "Minutes to Memories" from *Scarecrow*, two of the album's most lyrically evocative songs that place the listener squarely within the pair's shared homeland. Four days after the album was released in the summer of 1985, Mellencamp and Green attended their fifteenth high school reunion, where attendees mingled around a Seymour swimming pool and shimmied in a dance competition, just like something out of a John Mellencamp song.

Mellencamp has explained that his collaboration with Green on "Rain on the Scarecrow," the album's mission statement, reflects the comfort and community of their longtime friendship. "Our songs always came about the same way: talk around the kitchen table," he told *Rolling Stone*. "I had just played 'Small Town' for him. He said, 'I don't know why these towns are going out of business'—towns like Freetown and Dudleytown, Indiana. We couldn't figure out why they were disappearing. We did our research and wrote this song—Reagan had been using grain against the Soviet Union and all sorts of other things. Talking to people was heartbreaking. Nobody wanted to lose their farm."

Other personal connections are threaded throughout *Scarecrow*. Laura Mellencamp, the singer's grandmother, a gifted musician and storyteller who Mellencamp has often referenced as a formative influence, sings a verse of the traditional folk song "In the Baggage Coach Ahead" on track two, which Mellencamp titled "Grandma's Theme." Propositionally, it's a stirring bridge connecting the plight of rural life in "Rain on the Scarecrow," to Mellencamp's celebration of it in "Small Town." These pieces form a triptych that heralds agrarian life while dismantling its fantasy. On the back cover of *Scarecrow* there is a dedication to Harry "Speck" Mellencamp, John's grandfather, who taught him the merits of hard work and a good fight, and who died in 1983.

"With this record what we're doing is more important than charts," Mellencamp said on MTV the same year. "I think we're reaching a lot of people, speaking to a lot of people, and making a lot of people feel good. I think that's better than chart positions or money." *Scarecrow* fared well among critics and fans. It peaked at No. 2 on the Billboard albums chart, and produced three Top Ten hits. A common observation among critics was that Mellencamp had matured. "At its best, *Scarecrow* brings both Mellencamp's Sixties-rock fixation and his fiercely patriotic distrust of big business and big politics into the muck of the modern world, with scintillating results," *Rolling Stone's* critic wrote. The album was named third in the *Village Voice's* critics' poll of the best albums of the year. It also prompted the biggest tour of Mellencamp's career.

The summer of 1985 remained rife with Bossmania due to the long tail of *Born in the U.S.A.*, but Mellencamp was no longer willing to live in The Boss's shadow. The Hoosier's tour consisted of around one hundred dates in the US, Canada, Japan, Australia, and France, ran between two and three hours, and included a series of 1960s-era covers. Inevitably, his marathons were compared to Springsteen's in the press, but Mellencamp was forging a path of his own. In each North American city Mellencamp played, the singer's team took out an ad in a local newspaper encouraging his fans to write to their senator and congressional representative on behalf of family farmers. He also refused corporate sponsorships, which could have raked in millions of dollars. A person who worked on Mellencamp's team in this period told me that the singer actually had little interest in appearing overseas at all, given the issues facing his own country.

In 1983, the Reagan administration began its payment-in-kind program, which compensated American farmers who stopped producing crops in excess. But the government's lack of foresight cost America greatly, about $35 billion for the same programs that would have cost ten times less a year earlier, before the farming crisis spiraled out of control. This did nothing to stop the growth of corporate farming, which controlled about 50 percent of American farming by the year 1990. In the new millennium, government subsidies for the production of corn and soybeans have created the proliferation of corporate monocropping that has had a widespread ripple effect on the environment, including soil degradation, pollution from pesticides, and a loss of biodiversity. The definition of a family farm and farmer has changed as a result; many small-to-medium family-owned farms have switched to growing soybeans and corn for corporations by necessity or to maximize profits. Though the farm-to-table dining movement has created a surge of interest in farmers markets and CSAs among white-collar consumers who will pay premiums for local and organic meat and produce, many grangers who endeavor to make it in this model have folded or walked away with considerable debt.

The writer Wendell Berry, who was raised on a farm in Port Royal, Kentucky, has advocated for small-scale sustainable farming since the 1970s. In his book *Bringing It to the Table: On Farming and Food*, he argues that a farmer's work is required to extend beyond its obvious task. "Agriculture must mediate between nature and the human community, with ties and obligations in both directions," he wrote. "To farm well requires an elaborate courtesy toward all creatures, animate and inanimate. It is sympathy that most appropriately enlarges the context of human work." With *Scarecrow*, Mellencamp similarly extended his scope to include his homeland's most vulnerable and cherished. In doing so, he gained more credibility than a standard pop-rock work would have afforded. He also presented a strong point of view that set him in relief from the era's other rock stars. In melding the historical spirit of the 1960s with the modern plight of American farmers, and their families and neighbors, Mellencamp tunefully illustrated that so-called progress most often arrives with pain. A quote from the singer, which appears on the back cover of *Scarecrow*, encapsulates this mindset. "There is nothing more sad or glorious," he said, "than generations changing hands."

★ ★ ★

As Mellencamp climbed the charts with an album that honored agrarian life while also emphasizing its modern tribulation, country music icon Willie Nelson, a lifelong supporter of farmers, ranchers, and rural communities, approached him with an idea. Nelson and Neil Young were organizing a benefit concert for farmers. Would Mellencamp join them, and help gather some rock stars?

The concert in question became Farm Aid, a long-running effort headed by rock and country musicians whose proceeds go to programs that assist and advocate for family farmers. Its inaugural run took place on September 22, 1985, in Champaign, Illinois, and drew almost eighty thousand attendees. It also kickstarted a lifelong fight for Mellencamp, Nelson, and Young. It was just one in a run of high-profile charity efforts helmed by musicians and the music industry, leading many publications to declare 1985 the Year of Aid.

Farm Aid was the biggest alliance between rock and country stars to date, and it foretold a future in which the genres were more closely aligned. Most country music stars had been excluded from the huge charity efforts of the year, such as the "We Are the World" single, and the Live Aid concerts for Africa, in which no country musicians performed. "You never see a show with country acts and rock acts, but there's not all that much difference between the two," Petty said backstage at Farm Aid. "The thing that interests me is how easily the audience accepts it."

Nelson was notably the only country singer featured on "We Are the World," a charity single organized by the group USA for Africa and pop stars Lionel Richie and Michael Jackson. The recording took place in the evening after the 1985 American Music Awards, the one window when so many superstars were in Los Angeles and had free time. Amid the session's charged, high-stakes environment, Nelson leaned over to Ray Charles and offered the following: "It might be nice to help some of our own people here at home." Nelson's compadre Waylon Jennings famously walked out of the session and never returned. The "We Are the World" single also notably featured Bruce Springsteen's mid "Born in the U.S.A." tour voice, which was shredded like branches through a wood chipper.

With his new album *Old Ways*, Neil Young also built a bridge between rock and country's cultural gap. It was one that Mellencamp reinforced with his pastoral-rock opus *Scarecrow*, making the two musicians natural allies. In 1984 and '85, Young toured with a country-rock backing band, the International Harvesters, and some of those dates included contributions by country music icons like Waylon Jennings, Jessi Colter, and Johnny Paycheck. The group also played

Nelson's annual Fourth of July picnic concert. Nelson contributed to
Old Ways, adding vocals and guitar to the singer's 1983 recording of
"Are There Any More Real Cowboys?" As part of the album's promotion, Young released a music video in which he and Nelson sang the
song as a duet on a ranch in cowboy hats, and Young's alliance with
America's country music scene, particularly its outlaw country stars,
was solidified in this period. *Old Ways* was released in August 1985, a
few days after *Scarecrow*.

Amid the *Old Ways* touring cycle, a last-minute request carried
Young and company to Cheyenne, Wyoming, where catastrophic
flooding had recently killed twelve people and displaced many others, including farmers, whose lands were waterlogged beyond repair
for the season. Young had already demonstrated a newfound sense of
patriotism, even though he was Canadian, and his willingness to perform a benefit concert for flood victims was an extension of that, he
explained. "For those people that need it, they had a lot of things go
wrong all at once, and they have no way out," he said ahead of the concert. "And even though the money we raise is really going to be a drop
in the bucket, the feeling of doing something like this, and showing
them that we care, and that the rest of the country cares, it's good for
their spirits."

About a month earlier, the mammoth charity concert Live Aid,
organized by the musicians Bob Geldof and Midge Ure, and high-
profile promoters Harvey Goldsmith and Bill Graham, took place at
Wembley Stadium in London, composed largely of UK-based acts,
and John F. Kennedy Stadium in Philadelphia, with mostly North
America–based groups performing. Concerts inspired by the Live Aid
model were also performed simultaneously in the Soviet Union, Canada, Japan, Australia, and other countries. At the time, it was one of
the largest satellite television broadcasts ever. Nearly two billion people tuned in from countries across the globe, and the event raised more
than $100 million. Tom Petty and the Heartbreakers, Bryan Adams,
Bob Dylan, and Neil Young with the International Harvesters took to
the stage in Philadelphia alongside a cast of peers that included rap-

Tom Petty performs
at Live Aid in 1985.
PHOTO COURTESY
ZUMA PRESS, INC.

pers Run-D.M.C., Madonna, the Beach Boys, Black Sabbath, and others. Each concert ended with an Africa-focused charity single: Band Aid's "Do They Know It's Christmas?" in London, and USA for Africa's "We Are the World" in Philadelphia.

Though the concert's foundation was formed by commercial juggernauts, one of its opening acts, Philadelphia locals the Hooters, stood out from its more storied and commercially successful peers in the lineup. Graham was the architect behind the decision, reportedly a thorn in Geldof's side, which gave the hometown heroes a chance to preview its recent hit singles to the entire world. The group had just released its major label debut, *Nervous Night* in April, and was riding high on the strength of "And We Danced," a Springsteen-like tale of young love and lost innocence that opens with mandolin and melodica and crescendos in a bridge rife with "Born to Run" force, which hit No. 21 on *Billboard*'s Hot 100 pop singles chart. The group also performed "All You Zombies," a Dylanesque experiment anchored by light reggae and biblical imagery.

Bryan Adams, who cowrote the Canadian charity single "Tears Are Not Enough," whose proceeds were also donated to help fight famine in Ethiopia, included the song during his set at Live Aid, along with "Kids Wanna Rock," "Cuts Like a Knife," and "Summer of '69." "Tears Are Not Enough" was conceived by Adams's manager Bruce Allen amid the wave of Africa-focused charity work in the mid '80s, and was performed by Northern Lights, a Canadian supergroup that included Adams, Joni Mitchell, Neil Young, Gordon Lightfoot, Anne Murray, Geddy Lee of Rush, and others. Though it was created independently of the USA for Africa project, "Tears Are Not Enough" was included on the full-length *We Are the World* album released on April 1, 1985.

Tom Petty was in low spirits when he arrived in Philadelphia. He and the Heartbreakers were in the midst of their tour in support of *Southern Accents*, and had just arrived in their home state of Florida, when Petty received a call from his manager Tony Dimitriades. He explained that the group would have to cancel its Florida plans and head to the East Coast for a charity concert they knew little about. Though the band delivered one of the concert's most heralded performances, its start was touch-and-go. In the middle of "American Girl," its first song, Petty appeared exasperated and seemed to momentarily flip off someone in the audience.

Bruce Springsteen's notable absence from Live Aid was due to his exhaustion from the *Born in the U.S.A.* tour. He also wanted to spend time with his new bride, Julianne Philips, during the break in his touring schedule. Instead, he donated the stage and rigging from his own Wembley Stadium show, which occurred a week earlier, to the London-based Live Aid, and later stated that he regretted not driving down to Philadelphia for the American gig. Billy Joel also didn't perform because, he said, he couldn't gather his touring band together in time, and didn't want to do the gig solo. He has also since expressed his regret. Mellencamp said in interviews from the time that he didn't think concerts whose only goal was to raise money were a good idea, which is why he had not participated in any of the marquee charity events of 1985 thus far.

Bob Seger didn't make the "We Are the World" or Live Aid lineups, but was a featured participant in Hands Across America, which took place in May of 1986. The event was organized by a USA for Africa cofounder on account of widespread criticism about the organization's international focus when poverty and economic uncertainty also plagued the United States. Estimates from the National Bureau of Economic research showed a 30 percent jump in American homelessness between 1983 and 1985 due to an increase in poverty in the 1980s, and a decrease in the number of lost-cost rental units and other affordable housing. The Reagan administration's widespread deregulation also prompted unchecked discrimination against people of color by banks, real estate agents, and landlords. A 2004 report by *Shelterforce* magazine stated that by the end of Reagan's second term as president, local governments received 60 percent less federal assistance than they had under President Carter. Reagan's administration also "eliminated general revenue sharing to cities, slashed funding for public service jobs and job training, almost dismantled federally funded legal services for the poor, cut the antipoverty Community Development Block Grant program and reduced funds for public transit. The only 'urban' program that survived the cuts was federal aid for highways—which primarily benefited suburbs, not cities," according to the report's author, Peter Dreier.

For those who are aware of Reagan's 1976 speech in Asheville, North Carolina, when he aimed to beat former president Gerald Ford for the Republican nomination for president, these policies and discriminations may come as no surprise. It was then that Reagan excoriated public assistance, stating that recipients were buying expensive steaks with food stamps and living in public housing akin to luxury condos. As an extreme and anomalous example of poor people abusing federal aid, he summoned a "welfare queen" from Chicago who reportedly used eighty different names, thirty different addresses, and fifteen telephone numbers to collect welfare, food stamps, social security benefits, and veteran's benefits for four deceased spouses who didn't exist. She drove high-end vehicles, owned multiple properties, and wore expensive clothing, all on the government's dime. On that day in 1976, Reagan placed her take at $150,000, but in other speeches he stated that she made up to 1 million dollars, without evidence.

His story was based on 1974 reporting in the *Chicago Tribune* about a woman named Linda Taylor, who was convicted of fraud and perjury by a Chicago jury, and who is alleged to have engaged in some of the nefarious activities Reagan described. She was also a sophisticated career criminal who was a pathological liar and likely committed assault, kidnapping, theft, insurance fraud, and possibly murder, acts that stretch far beyond simple abuses of aid programs. But for Reagan, she was a tool to demonize the poor, transmit a detrimental stereotype of Black women, and cut federal programs that helped those who struggled.

USA for Africa's domestic program hoped to help alleviate the problem of homelessness and hunger in America by replicating its previous success, and aimed to raise 50 to 100 million dollars for a great number of local charities across the country focused on those issues. The event called for Americans nationwide to create a human chain from Manhattan to Los Angeles in a show of solidarity. Participants were asked to donate $10 in order to join others in holding hands. USA for Africa also produced a new single, titled "Hands Across America," composed by jingle writers with lead vocals by session singers Joe Cerisano and Sandy Farina, and music by the band Toto. The organization's plan was to unveil the song and a star-studded video at Super Bowl XX, but none other than Michael Jackson protested because he didn't want it to upstage "We Are the World." The organizers relented, and Hands Across America raised just $15 million, a fraction of the $60 million "We Are the World" secured.

At Live Aid in Philadelphia, Bob Dylan discharged a populist sentiment similar to the one that flew from the mouths of USA for Africa's critics. Dylan's closing set was largely a disaster with out-of-tune guitars, a broken string, and generally deflated posture. Ahead of performing a shaky rendition of "When the Ship Comes In," backed by two clearly intoxicated members of the Rolling Stones, Keith Richards and Ronnie Wood, he stepped up to the mic. "I hope that some of the money that's raised for the people in Africa, maybe they can just take a little bit of it, maybe one or two million, maybe, and use it, say, to pay the mortgages on some of the farms that the farmers here owe to the banks," he declared.

"Willie and I both noticed that. We were talking about it last week," Young said in the wake of Dylan's remark. "Then Willie got to talking with the governor of Illinois, and he said that he and I had talked and we thought we could get together all the country acts, because there were no country acts at Live Aid . . . so country is going to help our country while rockers help other countries."

At some point, apparently, Nelson and Young had a change of heart about rock musicians and invited Mellencamp on board; and he was happy to connect the country and folk-rock icons with modern rock bands. Mellencamp's only stipulation was that he didn't want any part in the money side of the festival, and that included accepting corporate sponsorships. He also wanted to keep ticket prices low for the average American. He was there to help spread a message, to evangelize the cause at the heart of Farm Aid.

With help from Illinois governor Jim Thompson, who coordinated the donation of the University of Illinois' Memorial Stadium for the concert, Nelson, Young, and Mellencamp, along with promoter Buddy Lee, who was also Nelson's agent, and some staffers, put together the first Farm Aid concert in six weeks. Many of their musical friends and peers composed the lineup, whose length was not unlike a rolling list of modern-day film credits.

To say that the first Farm Aid concert was a bargain would be a gross understatement. Tickets cost $17.50 (about $50 today), and the concert ran for fourteen hours, encompassing a who's who of the musical 1980s. Tom Petty and the Heartbreakers, Bob Dylan, Bonnie Raitt, X, Joe Ely, Lone Justice, Don Henley, and John Fogerty were among the heartland rock aligned to appear at the show, along with Mellencamp and Young. Country artists Nelson, Johnny Cash, Glen Campbell, Vince Gill, David Allen Coe, Merle Haggard, Waylon Jennings, Tanya Tucker, Loretta Lynn, Kenny Rogers, and Emmylou Harris performed in addition to storied songwriters such as Randy Newman, Roger Miller, Joni Mitchell, Arlo Guthrie, John Denver, the Beach Boys, and Jimmy Buffet. Billy Joel showed up, as did Carole King, Kris Kristofferson, Lou Reed, Roy Orbison, and many others. Promoter Lee said in interviews that he had to turn down fifty other musicians who wanted to perform, including Tammy Wynette, Charlie Rich, and Ted Nugent, because he'd already filled fourteen hours of music. Just two Black musicians, B. B. King and Charley Pride, the latter of whom performed via video, made the concert's lineup, which was a point of consternation in the press. "I spoke to a lot of Black artists, but those people have a lot of other causes," Mellencamp explained to a reporter.

Willie Nelson performs at the first annual Farm Aid benefit concert in Champaign, Illinois, in 1985.

PHOTO BY JOHN S. STEWART

"You have to remember that they've been fighting a battle for their whole history."

The new festival benefited from a spate of volunteers. Members of University of Illinois fraternities pitched in to help prepare the university's Memorial Stadium for the concert, including laying down layers of plastic, waterproof tarp, and plywood atop the stadium's artificial turf to help preserve it. Technical Theater Staging Inc., a Denver-based concert staging company, volunteered its services, and the festival used the same rotating stage, which was sixty feet in diameter, as the Live Aid concert in Philadelphia. "Our emphasis—and this is something that's very important to Willie—is on a grassroots approach," said Rick Worpel, the head of the staging company. "We don't want this to seem massive or grandiose. It's a rural, heartland issue and that's the feeling we want to have in the production." Two of Live Aid's production workers, John Baptiste and Morris Lyde, also volunteered to be on site during Farm Aid. Country singer Lynn organized a bus caravan from Nashville to Champaign, Illinois, led by her own two tour buses. All hotel rooms in Champaign and nearby Urbana sold-out, and so did all others within a one-hundred-mile radius. Artists were encouraged to stay in Chicago and fly in for their performances.

The event was captured by twelve cameras broadcasting to TNN, The Nashville Network, a former cable channel that aired country music videos, concerts, and other related content. Actors Jessica Lange, Sissy Spacek, and Morgan Fairchild signed on to perform in television segments about the problems in American farming, which were aired throughout the show. At-home viewers were encouraged to call 1–800-FARMAID to donate money to the cause, or mail in donations to a post office box in Champaign. Though Mellencamp didn't want to be involved in the money side of Farm Aid, Nelson received a lot of other advice about where it should go. Farmers suggested lobbying for farm-related legislation, and counseling and job retraining for those who were down-and-out. "Do not give the money to politicians," advised Nebraska governor Bob Kerrey, a former Republican who flipped to the Democratic party in 1978.

Though the event was largely met with enthusiasm for its mission and its noncommercial qualities, there were a few dissenting voices. There were others, such as Roger Miller, who openly admitted he didn't have a solution. "I'm a farm boy from Oklahoma. We musicians don't have all the answers to the farm problem. We're just trying to bring attention to it," he said. Many other musicians spoke in support of specific proposals. Some backed a farm reform bill sponsored by Senator Thomas Harkin of Iowa, which aimed to raise the prices of agricultural products and institute production controls. Mellencamp and Nelson testified before Congress in June 1987 in support of Senator Harkin's Family Farm bill. "When I am out on tour and I am talking to people, they are afraid," Mellencamp said. "Their vision of the future is: 'What is going to happen to my children in 20 years when, all of a sudden, three farmers are farming the State of Indiana and they also own all the food-processing plants!'"

Others felt the bill would hurt the farming community even more. Many criticized the Reagan administration's proposals that would cut farm subsidies to reduce the federal deficit. Such remarks were met by sarcasm from those who actually worked on farm-related matters. "I'll promise not to sing if they promise not to continue developing agricultural policy," said Larry Weiss, the head of the Illinois Department of Agriculture.

A New York–based concert promoter, Roger Abramson, claimed that the farm charity concert idea was stolen from him. Abramson said he originally planned to stage an event in Minneapolis with Bob Dylan and a group of country musicians, and had contacted Nelson's management, but received no response. To make amends, Farm Aid invited Bobbi Polzine, of a Minnesota-based farm action group called Groundswell, which would have been the beneficiary of Abramson's concert, to be the sole political figure to speak from its stage. "I guess they stole our idea," Polzine told a reporter, "but I'm grateful for the forum. I don't mind."

Newspaper and magazine reviewers, of which there were about 1,200 on site, noted that the crowd, which included many college students, seemed energized by the rock musicians present, and less so for the country artists. This was particularly true of those who emphasized a nationalist sentiment with unmistakably conservative overtones—as if to support the very leader at the center of the farming crisis. Merle Haggard, for example, performed "Amber Waves of Grain," a song that connotes racism and xenophobia through its anti-globalist lyrics decrying Japanese industry in America, and the sale of American crops to foreign countries.

After Tom Petty and the Heartbreakers finished its four-song set, consisting of its 1979 underdog anthem "Refugee," "Straight Into Darkness," which positions the absence of light as a form of anxiety, and covers of "Bye Bye Johnny" and "Don't Bring Me Down," Bob Dylan, who was a must at the concert given his comments at Live Aid, stepped onstage to join them. The two acts had been jamming together in Los Angeles at the behest of Elliot Roberts, the Asylum Records cofounder who also managed Dylan, Neil Young, and Joni Mitchell, and who was comanaging Petty and his band with Dimitriades. He'd connected the artistic dots between some of the Heartbreakers' members who played on Dylan's new album *Empire Burlesque*, and the possibility of a winning collaboration that could boost both acts. Though Farm Aid marked the first time that a large crowd absorbed the pairing in person, September 19, 1985, marked the new supergroup's first encounter with an audience. It was then that a small crew from ABC's *20/20* newsmagazine program filmed them practicing for its appearance at Farm Aid, which was used in an upcoming episode that aired on October 10. Correspondent Bob Brown became the first person to conduct an interview with Dylan on network television.

At Farm Aid, Dylan, Petty, and the Heartbreakers marked a different milestone in The Bard's career when they performed "Maggie's Farm," the blues-rock anthem rife with grievance, which had electrified the Newport Folk Festival twenty years earlier. The supergroup also rolled through three new songs. "Shake" was a twelve-bar blues romp Dylan rehearsed with the group in LA. The collective also performed "I'll Remember You" and "Trust Yourself," from *Empire Burlesque*. The studio version of the former featured Heartbreakers Mike Campbell on guitar and Howie Epstein on bass, while the latter included the keyboard work of Benmont Tench. This appearance also served as a kind of warm-up for the True Confessions tour that would kick off in February of 1986, featuring Bob Dylan backed by Tom Petty and the Heartbreakers. The polarizing collaboration played sixty dates in New Zealand, Australia, Japan, Canada, and the US, and carried on in 1987 as the Temples in Flames tour through Israel, Europe, and England. "I learned so much from Bob Dylan," Petty told *The Telegraph* in 2012. "He gave us a kind of courage that we never had, to learn something quickly and go out on stage and play it. You had to be pretty versatile because arrangements could change, keys might change, there's just no way of knowing exactly what he wants to do each night. You really learned the value of spontaneity, of how a moment that is real in a concert is worth so much more than one you plan out."

On account of *Scarecrow* and its warm reception from fans and the press, Mellencamp had plenty to work with in the Farm Aid setting. For his set, the Hoosier swooped onto the stage like a peregrine falcon and performed "Pink Houses" with Mick Jagger-esque dance moves. "I'm so proud of you people I can't even express it," he told the audience after peeling off his denim jacket—the same one Mellencamp wore in promotional photos, its back emblazoned with the words Seymour, Indiana, arced around a large Future Farmers of America patch. After thanking Neil Young and Willie Nelson, Mellencamp and his band—Mike Wanchic on guitar, Kenny Aronoff on drums, Toby Myers on bass, Larry Crane on guitar, and John Cascella on auxiliary instrumentation—gave a scorching performance of "Rain on the Scarecrow" and "Lonely Ol' Night." Bonnie Raitt sang background vocals. In the midst of his set, the firecracker frontman and Raitt also discussed the problems affecting farmers, to remind the audience of the reason everyone had come to town.

Raitt, heartland rock's most elegant and soulful monarch, dressed in all purple with a fabulous mullet, also performed a delightful solo set with Mellencamp's band, including two songs from 1982's underrated *Green Light*—"Can't Help Myself" and "Green Lights"—as well as her arresting cover of John Prine's "Angel from Montgomery." The Hoosiers also backed Creedence Clearwater Revival's John Fogerty, who'd just released *Centerfield*. Though the album was yet another example of a heartland rock progenitor being reanimated by the genre's height in the 1980s, it was this Farm Aid performance that tied the two decades together in an unmistakable way.

New Jersey quintet Bon Jovi gave one of the most unexpected performances at the inaugural Farm Aid. The group was still finding its sea legs after its second studio album, *7800° Fahrenheit*, underperformed commercially and was panned by many critics. For its set, the band stuck with its one recognizable hit, "Runaway," and a new song written specifically for the charity gig, titled "The Heart of America." Clothed in faded denim and black T-shirts, Bon Jovi's showing at Farm Aid was the greatest indicator of what may have happened had they followed the cues of heartland rock and their friend Bruce Springsteen, and not gone the way of Poison and Mötley Crüe. "Runaway," after all, is an anthemic rocker with an earworm chorus whose underdog narrative rings beyond its East Coast confines. "The Heart of America," written by Jon Bon Jovi and guitarist Richie Sambora, heralded hard work and family tradition in an almost roots-derived fashion. On stage that day, there were no wild costumes, vulgar posturing, or pyrotechnics; just five men who'd come up a difficult road and slotted in seamlessly among the country and rock acts that took to the stage that day. Just imagine if "Livin' on a Prayer," which details the hardships of a Jersey dock worker and his waitress girlfriend, had been refracted through *Exile on Main Street* and James Dean, instead of hair metal's sonic gloss and spandex.

Hard rock agitator Sammy Hagar provided the most obnoxious display of the evening. What was meant to be an announcement to the country became the thing that temporarily shut down the live television broadcast. Hagar had just signed on as the new singer of Van Halen, succeeding David Lee Roth, and the group was going to reveal it to America onstage after Hagar performed a few of his solo tunes.

Instead, Hagar declared, "This is for all you tractor-pulling mother-fuckers!" ahead of "I Can't Drive 55," and the cameras were immediately cut. What's worse is that Lone Justice, whose hype was strong but album sales were weak, was set to perform after him. Instead of a nationwide showcase for the gifted but commercially floundering band, its set became a Farm Aid-only gig. In interviews, Hagar has said that he believes Lone Justice's singer Maria McKee still resents him.

Though reports from the concert stated that Farm Aid hoped to raise $50 million dollars for its cause, it raked in somewhere between $7 million to $9 million through ticket sales and donations during and just after the concert. Those funds were deposited into the account of a nonprofit corporation set up in Illinois to handle the money, First National Bank of Champaign, Farm Aid, Inc., and were audited by the accounting firm Price Waterhouse. Nelson later explained that Farm Aid never intended to be the celebrity-driven financial powerhouse that Live Aid was; he was more interested in assembling a grassroots coterie of musicians from across the US, some of whom came from the punk world, like X and Lone Justice, and the hardscrabble corners of country music, and who were not commercial juggernauts. The idea was to act as a spotlight on the issue of the farming crisis, and serve as a de facto lobbying effort through such visibility.

Today, Farm Aid has produced forty shows and remains represented by Nelson, Young, and Mellencamp on its board, with the addition of jam band figurehead Dave Matthews, and neo country-rock outlaw Margo Price. The founding trio also performs each year at the festival's annual concert, which is no longer a fourteen-hour marathon. According to its website, Farm Aid has raised $80 million over the years "to promote a strong and resilient family farm system of agriculture." Mellencamp's relationship with the nonprofit has lasted longer than any of his marriages. On the couple of occasions that I've interviewed the singer, I've asked him about his sustained support of Farm Aid, and if the organization is really needed four decades later. Each time he has offered roughly the same retort: Are you still eating?

CHAPTER 7

THE WAY IT IS

I'm really glad I did it now, because it sold a lot of trucks to save a lot of jobs.

—BOB SEGER

On January 28, 1986, NASA's Space Shuttle *Challenger* exploded in the sky above Cape Canaveral, Florida. The tragedy occurred just seventy-three seconds after liftoff, and it killed all seven of its crew members: commander F. Richard Scobee, pilot Michael J. Smith, mission specialist Ronald McNair, mission specialist Ellison Onizuka, mission specialist Judith Resnik, payload specialist Gregory Jarvis, and Christa McAuliffe, a payload specialist and teacher at Concord High School in New Hampshire, who was chosen for the mission under NASA's Teacher In Space program, which had been announced by President Reagan in 1984. Thousands of Americans watched the launch and explosion in person. Estimates put home viewership of the *Challenger* disaster in the many millions—those school children and adults who watched the shuttle break apart in real time or via playback on network television. "Never before in 25 years of America in space, never in 25 launches of a space shuttle, had a life been lost. Today, that record went down in flames," CBS *Evening News'* Dan Rather said to his viewers hours after the disaster.

Though the disaster unfolded in mere seconds, it left a permanent mark. The United States had not experienced such a visceral tragedy and rupture in the nation's confidence since the Vietnam War. American exceptionalism had failed yet again, but this time its brutal images were broadcast from domestic shores. It had literally hit home.

As the nation grappled with the emotional and spiritual fallout, prayer circles, memorials, and fundraisers were held in communities across the nation. Tributes, speeches, and platitudes were offered by politicians, pastors, and other leaders. In his address to the nation, President Reagan offered no answers as to why the event occurred, but spun the shuttle's tragic end as an inevitable aspect of progress. He addressed the throngs of American children—many of whom watched the disaster unfold on box TVs that'd been placed on AV carts and wheeled into their classrooms—by saying that such painful things are "all part of the process of exploration and discovery." He concluded that the "future doesn't belong to the fainthearted; it belongs to the brave."

Some scientists took a more scathing stance. "For a successful technology, reality must take precedence over public relations, for Nature cannot be fooled," theoretical physicist Richard Feynman wrote in the appendix of the Rogers Commission's report on the disaster. It was a damning condemnation of the disconnect between NASA's executives and the warnings of its engineers. He was particularly outraged at the space administration's false safety assurances, which had been used in part to recruit McAuliffe. The report's revelation that the accident was avoidable, and the product of NASA's negligence, sowed confusion and chaos into the president's "progress" narrative, and into the hearts and minds of many Americans.

As the nation attempted to reconcile what had happened with its leaders' responses, network news inundated its viewers with footage of the explosion, effectively retraumatizing its survivors, particularly the crew's family members, repeatedly. Soon after, physical reminders of the *Challenger* and its crew were erected in the form of monuments, such as the inclusion of the astronauts' names on the Space Mirror Memorial at the Kennedy Space Center and a marker at Arlington National Cemetery. Countless statues, plaques, and other visible tokens were erected in towns across the country, and many schools, education programs, and libraries were renamed after McAuliffe.

In June 1986 the folk and country musician John Denver released the ballad "Flying for Me," dedicated to the *Challenger*'s crew members. As the son of an Air Force pilot, the singer-songwriter had long been fascinated with aviation. He became a private pilot as an adult, and sat on the board of the nonprofit National Space Society. NASA also recruited Denver to help create its ill-fated program that put everyday citizens in space, of which he took part. After going through several tests, Denver thought he would be the first participant, which would have put him on *Challenger*. In a cruel twist, Denver died a little more than ten years later, in October 1997, when he crashed his two-seater Rutan Long-EZ plane into Monterey Bay on the Central Coast of California.

After the *Challenger* disaster, America was at a spiritual crossroads. All space shuttles were grounded as further investigations took place, a move that signified uncertainty about the program's future and America's place at the forefront of progress. What had once been a cause for excitement and hope became a symbol of failure and trepidation. It took months for the remains of the shuttle and its crew to be collected, and each step toward that end was a stinging reminder of what had happened. Soon, a series of dark turns shrouded America in tumult. The Cold War continued to loom as President Reagan held talks with Soviet leader Mikhail Gorbachev in Iceland. Patrick Sherrill, a carrier for the United States Postal Service in Oklahoma, killed fourteen of his coworkers and injured six others, before killing himself, with three guns he packed into a mail bag. It was the twenty-sixth mass shooting of the decade, which in part inspired the phrase "going postal." In September, a Pan-Am flight from Bombay to New

York was hijacked, and twenty-one people died. About two months later, reporting detailed how senior US officials were secretly aiding the sales of arms to Iran, which was subject to an embargo at the time, a wide-reaching scandal known as the Iran-Contra affair.

The No. 1 albums of 1986 seemed to reflect the American populace's desire to escape its painful present. Madonna's *True Blue* called back to girl groups, Motown, and the purity and joy of young love. Janet Jackon's *Control* and Boston's *Third Stage* grappled with youth, autonomy, and maturation. Barbra Streisand offered an album of classic Broadway tunes, and Bruce Springsteen released a box set of live recordings that reminded fans of a blessed era prior to the national tragedy. The *Top Gun* soundtrack transported listeners to a slick tale of flight with a Hollywood ending. (Bryan Adams notably passed on its soundtrack, saying that the film glorified war.) Whitney Houston's record-breaking self-titled debut channeled all of America's most glorious and comforting singers into one unforgettable voice and album: the pop sophistication of Diana Ross, the playful R&B of Chakka Khan, and soul of Aretha Franklin.

Not every pop artist offered an escape. Jackson Browne, whose "Running on Empty" is literally about running out of fuel and figuratively about being out of step with the pace of modern life, and who helped set the tone for heartland rock, returned with eight tunes that bound the personal and the political. *Lives in the Balance*, released in February 1986, included three songs that were critical of the Reagan administration. "For America," a single threaded with Clarence Clemons-esque saxophone, is an unflinching critique of American apathy as well as a prayer for peace and clarity. Its title track, which criticizes the federal government's dishonesty amid the Iran-Contra affair, set the tone for one of the darkest episodes of the crime drama *Miami Vice*.

Heartland rock released in 1986 also offered a portal to a different time. Bob Dylan toured with Tom Petty and the Heartbreakers and released the gospel-inspired single "Band of the Hand" in the process. Bob Seger returned with chart-topping anthems rife with Midwestern grit and nostalgia. Singer-songwriter Steve Earle sprang out of Nashville as the physical embodiment of a post–Farm Aid alliance between country and heartland rock musicians, like the past and present joining hands in one steely Texan. Alternative and indie rock bands such as BoDeans, R.E.M., the Replacements, Lone Justice, and others made a greater splash, and a classically trained pianist from Virginia, Bruce Hornsby, broke through the charts with earthen heartland rock that summoned young love and issued a call for compassion.

★ ★ ★

By May 1986, Bob Seger's fortieth birthday had passed and he'd released four well-received albums with the Silver Bullet Band. His newest work, *Like a Rock*, released in 1986, took four years to make. That Seger sought to have a heavier hand in the album's production didn't help. "There was nobody to say 'no' to me and I ended up recording 25 songs in four different cities," he told the *Los Angeles Times* in 1986. Those songs were originally meant to compose two different albums, but as he'd done with *The Distance*, Seger made big cuts. He scrapped the first album, which had been scheduled for release in 1984, and just two songs made the cut for the album he released under the title *Like a Rock*.

This isn't to say that Seger idled in the four years since *The Distance* went to No. 5 on the Billboard pop albums chart. Of all of his heartland rock peers, Seger had found the most success with movie soundtracks. His songs had a way of reanimating in a way that few others did. His 1979 single "Old Time Rock & Roll" had been resurrected. This was after the song "Night Moves" was included on the platinum-certified soundtrack to the widely panned 1978 comedy-drama *FM*, and "Nine Tonight" appeared in the track listing of the beloved soundtrack to the John Travolta film *Urban Cowboy*. Seger also wrote "Livin' Inside My Heart" for the Brat Pack romantic comedy *About Last Night*, released in 1986. This is not to mention future soundtrack hits such as "Shakedown" from *Beverly Hills Cop II*, which became his only No. 1 hit, and "Against the Wind" being prominently featured in the 1994 Tom Hanks blockbuster *Forrest Gump*.

Like a Rock produced two thriving singles, and offered a gateway to young love and adult heartache. It offered the balm of Seger's voice to a hurting nation. Seger drew a full circle with its cover of "Fortunate Son," Creedence Clearwater Revival's sonic snarl about war, class, and privilege, which helped pave the way for the left-wing populism of heartland rock. "American Storm," a full-throated indictment of cocaine culture in the 1980s, was originally the title track of the 1986 album before Seger changed his mind. Bruce Springsteen had already released the biggest political hit of the decade with "Born in the U.S.A.," even if its meaning was widely misunderstood and misappropriated. Still, Seger didn't want to risk being accused of riding The Boss's coattails even more than he already had been. The song's power chord-and-piano intro also sounded a lot like "Born to Run."

Seger chose "Like a Rock" instead, a mid-tempo ballad that showcases his gift of melding evocative adolescent imagery with adult wisdom to proffer a relatable sense of nostalgia. Its central image—human resilience in the face of difficulty—fit the mood of America's collective grief. So many can see themselves in the carefree version of youth Seger describes in the song, and how such tender meat falls from the bone when placed in adulthood's pressure cooker. "The songs are based on things that are close to me, though not necessarily about me," Seger told *Creem* magazine in 1986. "I very rarely write about myself that much. I draw on my own experiences like anyone else, but I'm not like my songs at all." Though "Like a Rock" was partially autobiographical—drawn from the unraveling of a long-term relationship with his partner Jan Dinsmore, and Seger's belief that his late teens was the best and most easygoing time in his life—the song's lyrical hook may be transposed onto myriad other American biographies.

Though "Like a Rock" was a hit in its day, cradling a nation in mourning, it was more remarkable for its second act, which stretched far beyond the culture of music. Like Seger's "Old Time Rock & Roll," "Like a Rock" took on a life of its own after being placed in popular media, when it soundtracked a series of Chevrolet truck commercials for more than a decade.

The early '90s saw more Americans buying cars from manufacturers based overseas, like Toyota, Honda, and Subaru, but sales of larger vehicles such as trucks and SUVs remained steady among American automakers. Amid a short period of economic decline, from 1990 to 1991, these trends indicated what Chevrolet had long hoped to convey: that trucks were a rugged symbol of American inimitability, and the purchase of an American-made truck was an investment in America itself. It was the perfect opportunity to further transpose patriotism and capitalism.

Chevrolet had long sought music that amplified these themes, commissioning jingles such as "Baseball, Hot Dogs, Apple Pie, and Chevrolet," and "The Heartbeat of America" for its commercials. In the early '90s, General Motors executives tasked the Warren, Michigan-based advertising agency Campbell Ewald with developing "a campaign to communicate the truck's promise of durability in a meaningful, emotional way." Don Gould, an associate creative director at the agency, soon heard Seger's song, "Like a Rock," and decided that it embodied everything outlined in the automaker's brief: such as endurance, toughness, and heft. The singer's voice was also the sound of legions of working men who'd sit behind the wheel—road-worn and resilient, hardworking and impassioned.

The problem? Seger wasn't comfortable with being a promotional engine beyond his own albums and concert tickets. Seger refused Campbell Ewald's request for about ten months before he had yet another change of heart. As the story goes, one evening Seger was sitting in a nightclub in Royal Oak, Michigan, called the Jukebox, and a patron at the next table leaned over, punched Seger on the arm, and said something to the tune of, "When you gonna do something for the car companies in this town? They need your help." This simple query appealed to Seger's civic pride in a way no beer company could. He called his manager Andrews about the Chevy commercial the next day. "Detroit's down right now. If it'll help, let's do it," Seger argued, according to Andrews.

Of all the times Bob Seger fretted and changed his mind, this about-face made the most sense. He was a son of Michigan who'd worked in, and written songs about, its auto factories. Like his fellow Midwesterner John Mellencamp, Seger never really left his homeland, except for extended trips to Los Angeles and Muscle Shoals, Alabama, to make records. Beyond his music, Seger had the genuineness that advertisers eternally seek and rarely find.

Seger and Andrews initially offered Chevy a two-year license for "Like a Rock," and were so pleased with the results that the commercials ran for eleven more years. Though the motive of the spots was to sell vehicles, Chevy's "Like a Rock" commercials became a dominant hue in the tapestry of Americans' lives in the 1990s, marking the song as Seger's defining tune in the minds of many. The spots were notably played during major televised sporting events, including *Monday Night Football*, and iconic games, such as the 1992 NBA finals when Michael Jordan made six three-pointers in the first half of Game 1 against Portland, and then nonchalantly shrugged. They were so pervasive that a writer for *The New York Times* described how he "came to hate Bob Seger" while watching a college basketball game on TV. "Every 1.2 seconds, somebody would foul somebody else, the players would trot to the bench, and they—the great 'they' who run sports— would switch to a commercial for pickup trucks, featuring Seger singing 'Like a Rock.'" Today, Chevy's "Like a Rock" commercials are considered one of the most successful campaigns in the history of the auto industry.

In saying yes to Chevy, Seger also opened the door for future heartland rock anthems in auto commercials. The soundtrack of everyday Americans fortified the vehicles of everyday Americans. By 2005, Seger's Chevy truck ads were quietly phased out and replaced by new spots featuring "Our Country" by Mellencamp, yet another tune with patriotic overtones, even as the singer adamantly opposed President George W. Bush's administration and the war in Iraq. Their saturation on radio and television similarly drove sports fans and commentators to deride their ubiquity. Sportswriter-turned-media-mogul Bill Simmons famously created an entire movement in mocking the ads, prompting a wave of negative comments from his readers, such as a warning for Mellencamp to "go into the witness protection program" because the reader was "ready to snap and go OJ on him for ruining another postseason." Though executives told the press the Mellencamp spots were equally as successful as Seger's, sales of Chevy Silverado trucks were flat during the first couple of years that they ran.

Sixteen years later, America erupted in vexation when Bruce Springsteen starred in a sanctimonious Jeep commercial titled "The Middle," which ran during Super Bowl LV. If it was true to The Boss's legacy of humanism, and belief that Americans should be able to find some common ground regardless of background and political affiliation, it was received by many as tone-deaf. The spot ran in February 2021, amid an unprecedented global pandemic that had deepened already intense political divisions, particularly in the wake of the January 6 insurrection, which occurred after former president Donald Trump lost the November 2020 election but refused to concede. Jeep subsequently pulled the ads after learning that Springsteen had been arrested in Gateway National Recreation Area in New Jersey a few months prior, and had been charged with driving while intoxicated, reckless driving, and consuming alcohol in a closed area.

In the new millennium, heartland rock's children, such as Wilco, the Gaslight Anthem, and the War on Drugs, also lent their songs to car commercials, for companies including Volkswagen, Nissan, and GMC. Not everyone has buckled in for the ride, though. Tom Petty's team famously convinced a judge to issue a temporary restraining order that required B. F. Goodrich to pull its 1987 advertising campaign, which included an original song that sounded very similar to Petty tune "Mary's New Car." Petty had turned down the tire maker's request to use "Mary's New Car," making the company's copycat effort all the more glaring.

The Floridian famously declared that he would never put his songs in a commercial. He also insisted that he hadn't "gone corporate" when he and the Heartbreakers agreed to play the Super Bowl halftime show in 2008, coincidentally sponsored by another tire company,

Bridgestone. Springsteen and the E Street Band followed his lead and performed at America's biggest game the next year. Both groups stuck to the spirit of their established live shows and offered little more than a fleet of middle-aged men with their instruments, moated by fans, and charged by music's particular transcendence. Each was a cipher of heartland rock's enduring populist appeal. If they were safe bets in the wake of Justin Timberlake, Janet Jackson, and Nipplegate, they also fit like hand in glove as distinctly American institutions rife with the kind of regular-guy ascent that could be transmuted into national pride. They also provided the chance for fans to catch an arena gig by an arena band in an era of skyrocketing arena ticket prices. There were no backup dancers, wire flying, or giant gilded lions. No dynamite pyrotechnics or wild costumes. For these guys, as with legions of American dads, uncles, brothers, and neighbors, dressing up for the occasion meant wearing black denim instead of blue.

It's no stretch to imagine that such commercial appearances may

General Motors' Fleetwood plant in Detroit closed in 1987 and was demolished in 1992.
PHOTO BY JIM WEST

not have happened without Seger sticking his neck out for Detroit in the early '90s. Through a chance encounter in a local bar, he became the first of heartland rock's pillars to concede that one promotion may double as a kind of populist largesse. "I just felt like we should do something for the auto industry, which at that time, especially GM, was not doing well," Seger explained to a radio interviewer in 1994.

In music, first takes have long been associated with authenticity, an openhearted attempt to exert creative sequence to interior and exterior chaos, to channel something rather than rehearse and deploy it. There is the idea that recording such earnest spontaneity is comparable to catching lightning in a bottle. Seger, on the other hand, is a lingering reminder of the good that may come with second takes and better thoughts. There are undoubtedly times when a gut instinct is best; and there are blessed others when logic prevails.

★ ★ ★

Long before Bob Seger's "Like a Rock" became the soundtrack of Chevrolet, Chrysler chose the science-lab patriotism of Kenny Rogers for its car commercials. "The Pride is Back" featured The Gambler and a mysterious female rock singer named Nickie Ryder—later revealed as the Swedish belter Marie Fredriksson of Roxette—trading lyrical benchmarks of American exceptionalism to music that was genetically engineered to evoke Bruce Springsteen funneled through a dentist office's sound system. If it was a cynical attempt at harnessing both Reagan's new patriotism and heartland rock, it also reflected the reeling nature of major labels in Nashville in the mid '80s. By Reagan's second term in office, the "urban cowboy" trend was decidedly out, and country music executives were on the hunt for music that would appeal to traditional country music fans and the ever-elusive youth market. It was another mile marker in the music industry's quest for authenticity.

What they could not extract from Kenny Rogers, they found in a set of artists who had a loose outlaw sensibility with strong country and rock allegiances, such as Dwight Yoakam, Roseanne Cash, Vince

Gill, Marty Stuart, and a thirty-year-old Texan who'd been gigging in Nashville for about a decade, Steve Earle. Farm Aid had just demonstrated the compatibility of proletarian rock and classic country, and these artists existed in a notably contemporary plane between the two genres. Columbia Records signed Stuart and Cash. Reprise Records signed Yoakam in Southern California. RCA inked a deal with Gill. MCA's Nashville arm released Earle's debut studio album, *Guitar Town*. It also issued Rogers's Chrysler car commercial ditty.

Though most of these artists had enough widespread appeal to crack the Billboard 200, with Gill being the sole name relegated to the country charts, only Yoakam's and Earle's debut albums conveyed the palpable concern for the working class that had long been a throughline for Springsteen, Seger, and Mellencamp. Yoakam's brand of Bakersfield-inspired honky-tonk included contemporary voices, such as Lone Justice's Maria McKee on the song "Bury Me," and homages to the hard lives of Kentucky miners and townsfolk, the people and places of his childhood. Earle, on the other hand, spoke of the reflexive trek between South and North, along a "Hillbilly Highway" from hollers to the Rust Belt for industrial jobs, and then from the Rust Belt to Southern cities when those jobs ran out. These paths were familiar terrain in heartland rock.

Earle also made a habit of covering Springsteen songs such as "State Trooper," and has been open about just how much he was inspired by the singer, particularly when writing *Guitar Town*. As the story goes, one of Earle's friends bought him a ticket to see Bruce Springsteen and the E Street Band at Murphy Center in Murfreesboro, Tennessee, on the *Born in the U.S.A.* tour. "Bruce walked out that night and sang 'Born in the U.S.A.' right out of the box," Earle told the audience at a show in New York in 2016. "Three hours and fifteen minutes later, I walked out into the Tennessee night, and I knew exactly what to do."

His main takeaway was that he needed a song that could direct the entire course of the album, something close to home and his conscience. Earle wrote the song "Guitar Town" on a Japanese guitar he borrowed from his sister while visiting his parents for Christmas. In the ensuing months, he composed "Little Rock 'N' Roller" and "My Old Friend the Blues." His publisher Noel Fox then persuaded Tony Brown, vice president of A&R at MCA Nashville, to join Earle, his friend and fellow songwriter Jimbeau Hinson, and Fox on a songwriting retreat at a beach house in Alabama. After traveling down country roads from Tennessee, and many more in pursuit of his art and freedom, Earle solidified "Hillbilly Highway" and "Down the Road." He returned home from Alabama with a record deal.

Like the figures of heartland rock, Earle and Yoakam each wrote loosely from their own lives and communities, chronicling the pain and glory of everyday Americans whose lives on the margins proved worthy of such empathetic portraits. The difference between them lay in each artist's intent. Yoakam and his music were country not because he was born and raised in Kentucky, but because he loved Wynn Stewart, Merle Haggard, Buck Owens, and the Bakersfield Sound, and sought to refract that movement's country and rock influences through an '80s prism. He intentionally aimed to bring electric instruments and backbeats to modern listeners with his own Kentucky twist. The rock part of Yoakam was implied due to his Bakersfield associations, his electrifying performances, and the fact that he played Madame Wong's and toured with the likes of Midwestern posthardcore beloveds Hüsker Dü. Conversely, Earle was rock-forward, and slotted into the world of country music strictly on the basis of province. His rock music was also country music because he was a Texan living and working in Nashville. "It's country 'cause I talk like this," Earle explained in an MCA Records promotional bio released alongside *Guitar Town*. "And it's country because I write lyrics, and I tell stories, and I record in Nashville." Earle's country sound was as a river's white water, varying influences pushing in all directions, layers that swirled to create a dynamic flow. Yoakam was a good songwriter and also an astute stylist. Earle was just a good songwriter.

Earle's "Hillbilly Highway" was released on March 22, 1986, as the debut single from his debut LP, and served as his introduction to many, even though he'd been working long before the song hit the radio. In it, Earle describes a grandfather who was a miner and had traded the promise of black lung for the clamor of the Motor City before being forced down to Houston when the auto factories in Detroit stagnated. The song's final verse skips a generation to describe the life of its narrator, a young musician who quit school for a different kind of life and travels along those same highways. "It's autobiographical in the sense that it borrows things from everybody, from my family," Earle told a reporter for *Sounds* magazine in 1987. "My grandfather wasn't a miner, he was a farmer and my father's an air traffic controller and it's like I'm one generation removed from the farm."

Unlike many of heartland rock's figures, Earle grew up middle class near San Antonio and left behind a comfortable life to roll the dice on his art. He showed up in Nashville when outlaw country was a dominant force, and its picking parties ran the gamut from newbies like him to iconic songwriters such as John Prine and Waylon Jennings. Country artists who wrote their own songs were kings. That culture eventually gave way to cocaine and urban cowboys; upon the advent of so-called "new country," the label given to so many emerging artists in Nashville in the mid '80s, Earle was already a seasoned veteran. "I consider myself to be a straggler of the outlaw movement in the '70s more than a part of any new country," he said, "basically because it was a singer-songwriter movement."

Earle's facilities as a songwriter quickly earned him comparisons to Springsteen for his ability to strip America's most commonplace iconography to its marrow in order to recast its cars, guitars, laborers, losers, and lovers in a poetic and profound fashion. It would be easy to say that Earle benefited from The Boss's post *Born in the U.S.A.* break—in which Springsteen attempted to settle into family life, and then wrote a record about the hardships of love and marriage—but that would discount Earle's own way with summoning relatable underdogs. There's the band of merry misfits in "Guitar Town" who extol the self-actualizing nature of the open road and its baseborn landmarks, and the small-town gas station attendant-slash-philosopher of "Someday." "Goodbye's All We've Got Left" reduces one of life's messiest emotional catastrophes—a breakup—into a tidy and entirely devastating concession. There were the down-and-out characters of "Good Ol' Boy (Gettin' Tough)" and "My Old Friend the Blues," and the beleaguered hearts of "Fearless Heart" and "Little Rock 'N' Roller." Though Steve Earle's *Guitar Town* rang out from south of the Mason-Dixon line, its themes and characters carried across regions and ideologies. In amplifying lyrical sketches of people for whom success and prosperity was not a given, *Guitar Town* brought succor to their real-life counterparts in a time of national duress.

"In the end, you either cheer people up [with your songs] or help them exorcize some problems they have—and people need a bit of both right now," Earle told the *Los Angeles Times*. "The mood of the country as a whole is that things aren't as they are being advertised. Lots of people are going hungry. Even more have had to downscale their expectations. They are confused. They remember everything they heard about this country in school and they wonder what happened to it." It was as much a celebration of America's backbone as it was a critique of America's facade. The album was released amid a wave of xenophobia as Japanese industry spread across the heartland. Reagan imposed 100 percent tariffs on Japanese goods. He also enacted damage control amid the Iran-Contra affair, and abolished the FCC's Fairness Doctrine, which enabled the rise of rightwing media figures, such as Rush Limbaugh, who were no longer required to include opposing points of view or even to tell the truth. Earl's line about a "Jap guitar" in the title track, a "man from Iran" in "Good Ol' Boy (Gettin' Tough)," and other questionable phrases may be read as a survey of the day's nationalist sentiment.

The country music establishment paid little attention to *Guitar Town* upon its release, but rock critics such as Robert Christgau, Dave Marsh, and Robert Hilburn understood the relevance of Earle's blend of country and rock. And then, *Guitar Town* went to No. 1 on the Top Country Albums chart. Earle appeared on the Johnny Carson show, and earned two Grammy Award nominations for Best Male Country Vocal Performance and Best Country Song for "Guitar

Town." As the album introduced Earle as a serious and gifted writer and player, it also solidified themes that would appear throughout the songwriter's career, such as hard times, blue collars, alienation, heartache, and a steadfast hope that things would improve further down the road. Expanded reissues of the album have featured Earle's cover of "State Trooper."

On July 4, 1986, Earle took to the stage at the second annual Farm Aid festival in Manor, Texas, about twelve miles northeast of Austin, along with Joe Ely, Jason and the Scorchers, Roseanne Cash, Dwight Yoakam, and other artists blending country and rock. Earle's time on that stage looked as if he had returned to the notional place of his birth—in the Lone Star State and at the epicenter of two major American genres merging under the auspices of working-class advocacy. In its preview of the second Farm Aid, a writer for the *Austin American Statesman* described Earle as "one of the young Turks who are making some of the Nashville gray heads look anxiously over their shoulders." To wit: Though there were several repeat artists at the festival's sophomore affair, Kenny Rogers was notably absent.

★ ★ ★

Heartland rock has long had acute points of tension, many of them rooted in the fact that its artists are millionaires propped up by corporate industry, and its fans are regular people working for the man. This dichotomy has prompted important conversations around privilege, appropriation, and album, merch, and concert ticket prices. In 1981, Tom Petty had fought for the standard list price of $8.98 for an album; forty years later, when Bruce Springsteen announced a new tour with the E Street Band, and Ticketmaster's "dynamic pricing" structure rocketed the cost of a ticket up to $5,000, the musician shrugged it off. "Well, I'm old. I take a lot of things in stride," he said in an interview with *Rolling Stone*. "You don't like to be criticized. You certainly don't like to be the poster boy for high ticket prices. It's the last thing you prefer to be. But that's how it went."

A less obvious but no less important conflict that pulsates within the canon has long existed in the heartland itself: the corrosive relationship between manufacturing and the environment. Heartland rock as a rule isn't focused on solutions, and its artists have long chosen a mirror as its primary weapon, reflecting the people and places of America it views as overlooked, underestimated, and marginalized. In general, the genre focuses on the past in order to say something about the present—namely, that America has lost sight of its values, is too complicated, corrupt, and shortsighted. Heartland rock had very little interest in the future, and hoped instead to have a more immediate social impact.

In breaking from its hippie-era roots, heartland rock's voices have been able to circumvent such no-win situations, celebrating both America's workers and American industry as well as the country's natural wonders. Most of the genre's big names have sung of rivers, lakes, rain, fields, and flowers, and also manufacturing, farming, and gas-guzzling classic cars. In the 1980s, the genre's most evident environmental concern, parked at the intersection of industrialization and conservation, was about nuclear power, though Petty began speaking out in support of Greenpeace in 1989, and nearly every artist had a climate-change awakening in the new millennium. Today, however, such artists as John Mellencamp continue to travel on tour and in life by private jet.

As heartland rock and alternative rock became bedfellows, combining a roots-focused sound with leftist and antiestablishment attitudes and lyrics, R.E.M. became the first band to make a heartland rock album with unmistakable ecological themes. With *Lifes Rich Pageant*, the Athens, Georgia-based quartet of Bill Berry (drums), Peter Buck (guitar), Mike Mills (bass), and singer Michael Stipe looked to the future in order to say something about America's present. And the band did it at John Mellencamp's studio with John Mellencamp's producer.

For *Lifes Rich Pageant*, the group wanted a producer who could move them away from the muddy, murky, murmuring nature of their previous records into something more powerful and clear, particularly as they stirred in traditional instruments such as piano and banjo and pump organ. They also didn't trust record labels, and Don Gehman, who had a long association with the majors, and who'd been with Mellencamp since *American Fool*, wasn't a shoo-in.

Instead, the band invited him to a preproduction session in Athens, and hired Gehman after they came around to his style. "I think they were taken aback at the process that I worked in," he said in a 2011 interview on Sirius XM radio. "I didn't just record things. I liked to spend time on the arrangement and layer in the overdubs and comp the vocals—all this process which, to me, was normal record-making, they had never been through before. When they saw that kind of record-making process didn't take anything away, that it actually added another level of artistic expression, they were very excited by it. That's when they said, 'Let's go make a record.'"

Gehman was adept at layering instruments, and also narrowing in on two specific aspects of a band: the rhythm section and the vocals. This is why Kenny Aronoff's snare drum explodes like a string of firecrackers, and why John Mellencamp as a singer could transcend the pop music world at all. It is also why, for the first time, R.E.M. fans could hear and discern Michael Stipe's words, and why the songs of *Lifes Rich Pageant* seem boosted by a jolt of adrenaline. Though Berry was no Aronoff, his drumming had a reserved Charlie Watts-like quality in which he seemed to frame in around the guitarist, making the pronounced rhythm section of Berry and Mills a trellis for the wild branches of Buck and Stipe.

As fans truly heard the components of the band as a whole for the first time, it was quickly apparent that *Lifes Rich Pageant* was less interested in being something classicist or even tethered to the realm of traditional folk-rock. The album's opening track, "Begin the Begin," all but affirms this in its assertion that society needs a reset, to "begin again." R.E.M. envisioned and depicted a future world via traditional folk and rock instruments, like Tom Petty in the "You Got Lucky" video with a more campestral backdrop. It was akin to the visionary art of fellow Georgian Howard Finster, with whom Stipe collaborated on the cover of the band's second album, *Reckoning,* but in its case Mother Earth was the messiah and she was under threat. *Lifes Rich Pageant* was political and environmental. It was Sierra Club-core.

"Cuyahoga" from the album was released about a decade after the Federal Water Pollution Control Act of 1948 was completely rewritten and then amended to include the nation's first and most progressive environmental laws housed under the Clean Water Act. The song wasn't released as a single but quickly became one of the LP's signatures for its oblique references to the river in northeast Ohio that famously burned on multiple occasions, and the many Indigenous tribes that were evicted from their homelands along the river near the turn of the nineteenth century by the new United States military. Stipe sings from their perspective when he asserts that the riverland is "ours," and nods to the most left-wing populist folk song of all time, "This Land Is Your Land."

Bassist Mills explained that "place is very important to our music," with regard to the new album, and that the song was inspired by years of passing through Cleveland and then reading about the body of water. The Cuyahoga River was once America's most polluted, and its repeat fires in part prompted the formation of the Environmental Protection Agency, and federal criminal charges being filed against a number of US steel companies. "I think it's a little more topical this time," he added of the album and Stipe's lyrics. "I think what he's really saying is, 'Don't be apathetic. Just be aware of what's going on around you.'"

The periphrastic chorus of "Fall On Me" alludes to air pollution and acid rain, and "Hyena" swipes at the Reagan administration's defense buildup and choreographed bravado. "This is a song which is about the small underground rooms which you went into during wartime to protect your head from the big bad bombs," Stipe explained of "Underneath the Bunker" at a 1989 performance at the Pinkpop Festival in the Netherlands.

With a poet-jester's lyrical quality, nod to Woody Guthrie, clear-as-a-bell guitar jangle, and a rocker's edge, *Lifes Rich Pageant* placed a distinctive stamp on heartland rock's envelope without mail-

ing it too far from home. The album was released just days before
Bob Dylan and Tom Petty and the Heartbreakers concluded their
True Confessions Tour of 1986, and what R.E.M. offered seemed to
meld each artist's sensibilities into one disc of new songs from a fast-
emerging voice. It took those two pasts squarely into the present as a
way of predicting the future. If it was novel to make an overtly political
album with eco-conscious overtones with Mellencamp's guy in Mellencamp's studio in the middle of Indiana, the result was as clear and
cohesive as most any other project discharged from Belmont Mall.
This band of merry murmurers from Athens, Georgia, had stepped up
to the mic to lock in a series of pieces that formerly didn't fit together.
Their parts finally amounted to one clear unit. As Bob Dylan once
said of Tom Petty and the Heartbreakers, "This band is like talking
to one guy."

★ ★ ★

As the '80s shifted into its latter years, many of heartland rock's mon-
archs wrote, recorded, and recuperated. After completing the biggest
tour of his life in support of *Born in the U.S.A.*, Bruce Springsteen's
personal life was fraught enough that he began crafting an entire
album about it, turning from social concerns to the fiefdom of internal
angst. Tom Petty and the Heartbreakers toured with Bob Dylan until
August 6, 1986, returned to Los Angeles, and then began to translate
Dylan's looseness and the band's heightened capacity to operate as a
responsive unit in the studio. In September 1986, John Mellencamp
decamped to Belmont Mall with the whole of his *Scarecrow* touring
band to record a roots-focused song cycle centered around family, tradition, nostalgia, and dreams. Bonnie Raitt, who was dropped from
Warner Bros. as she was finishing *Tongue and Groove*, her follow-up
to 1983's *Green Light*, learned that the label had reversed course and
intended to release the album without her input. She spent much of
1986 battling with the major until they agreed to let her rerecord
about half of the album, which was released under the title *Nine Lives*
in November 1986. It received some of the worst reviews of her career.

In the absence of new and compelling work from nearly every major heartland rock artist except Bob Seger, bands from the alternative rock, indie rock, and regional rock worlds continued to cross over into the genre. Artists who'd sailed across eras and false starts also docked at heartland rock's port. The Replacements' fourth studio album *Tim* had received widespread year-end praise in December of 1985, and the band made its debut on national television about a month later, on January 18, 1986. Taking to the stage at *Saturday Night Live*, which had been designed to approximate a downtown Manhattan loft, the Replacements brought shambolic working-class anthems to a national audience, demonstrating the rise and popularity of a next generation of heartland rock-adjacent misfits. If the suits at its new label Sire expected anything but the Replacements' way of doing things, they were sorely mistaken, however. With the night's host, Harry Dean Stanton, each member of the band drank himself silly ahead of the appearance, and the group earned a lifetime ban from the show's producer Lorne Michaels after sloppy performances of "Bastards of Young" and "Kiss Me on the Bus," particularly due to Westerberg's profane cue to guitarist Bob Stinson during the former. "Come on, fucker," he said, on live television.

The Georgia Satellites, a four-piece bar band from Atlanta, touted a roughhewn arc from regional obscurity to chart-topping singles. Unlike many of the new-school acts whose heartland rock flourishes blended with a countercultural sensibility, the Georgia Satellites' artistic center was closer to a squalid roadhouse than a punk rock dive bar, and it name-checked the most mainstream of acts as its inspiration: Little Richard, the Beatles, the Rolling Stones, the Yardbirds, James Brown, and even John Mellencamp. Lead by singer-guitarist Dan Baird, and drenched in the undone blues-rock of *Exile on Main Street*, the Satellites rebuffed heartland rock's slick production for a sleazier quality, but had a chart-topping hit with the raw guitar-boogie of "Keep Your Hands to Yourself." On its self-titled debut, released in the fall of 1986, the group also sang of American industry, young love, and broken hearts, and constructed an implied bridge between the northern and southern heartlands, like Steve Earle. Its cover of Terry Anderson's "Battleship Chains" would also inspire a 1990 cover by the Hindu Love Gods, a one-off collaboration between Warren Zevon and members of R.E.M.

Tom Petty said that the Georgia Satellites' self-titled debut was "a Heartbreakers' fave rave," and that they loved the group as soon as they got their hands on the album, before the first single climbed the charts. Petty and his band also took the Satellites on the Rock 'n' Roll Caravan tour of 1987, along with the Del Fuegos, a heartland rock-adjacent alternative rock band from Boston. Warren Zanes, one of the band's founders, became Petty's biographer.

The Madison, Wisconsin–based band Fire Town, led by Butch Vig, who'd go on to produce Nirvana's *Nevermind*, The Smashing Pumpkins' *Siamese Dream*, and cofound the alternative rock band Garbage, released its major label debut on Atlantic Records in 1987. *In the Heart of the Heart Country* combined heartland rock's roots focus with Tom Petty's guitar jangle and a power pop edge. It garnered enough buzz for the group to record a second album, *The Good Life*, which tanked. Though the band lasted just a couple of years, Vig cites those sessions as critical to his education as a producer.

Across the pond, The The, a late '70s post-punk act helmed by singer-songwriter Matt Johnson, issued *Infected*, its second studio album. Its singles included "Heartland" and "Sweet Bird of Truth," and spoke to working-class issues of blind patriotism, prosperity, and war, over rock music that edged closer to the mainstream. The Kinks, who'd long sung of everyday life and people, and the pomposity of high society, released *Think Visual*, which stitched together powerful, piano-tinged rock arrangements with lyrics that were reminiscent, dissenting, and steeped in a working man's doldrums. "Working at the Factory," the album's lead, was tailor-made to slip onto heartland rock's dress form. Revolutionary folk-punk poet Billy Bragg also released his critically acclaimed third album, *Talking with the Taxman About Poetry*, which stretched-out his guy-with-a-guitar posture to include a host of guest musicians, including Johnny Marr of the Smiths and Kristy MacColl, who'd soon have a hit in "Fairytale of New York" with the Pogues. Its songs were unmistakable in their proletarian allegiance, with titles such as "There is Power in a Union" and "Help Save the Youth of America."

In Los Angeles, Lone Justice released its sophomore album *Shelter* in November of 1986, produced by Jimmy Iovine, Steven Van Zandt, and the band. It had also completed its first overseas tour. Though the album's title track, cowritten by McKee and Van Zandt, became the band's highest-charting single, the album received lukewarm reviews, many citing its lack of lyrical specificity—and its sales were again underwhelming. Though it had hype, connections, and obvious talent, the band couldn't seem to propel itself beyond its popularity in Southern California clubs.

Slash Records, the LA label that issued records by X, Los Lobos, the Knitters, and the Blasters, also released a couple of albums in 1986 by Midwestern rock acts that had heartland-rock potential. *The Blind Leading the Naked* by the Milwaukee, Wisconsin–based folk-punk act Violent Femmes was the group's most obvious attempt at commercial crossover. With songs that decried government corruption and war, and promoted friendship and faith, its themes landed within the heartland realm, but the band's leader Gordon Gano was too eccentric to ever be a mainstream rock star.

Another group from Wisconsin was a safer bet. BoDeans, from tiny Waukesha, about thirty minutes west of Milwaukee, gained popularity in the local bar scene in the early '80s and signed with Slash Records after submitting a demo tape to the label—a wholesome bar band-to-recording artist arc, similar to the Georgia Satellites. Its leaders and principal songwriters Kurt Neumann and Sam Llanas met in the late '70s in high school and began gigging in Milwaukee clubs in the early '80s, and each came from prototypical Midwestern origins. Neumann spent his childhood watching his parents wake at 6 a.m. to go to day jobs. Llanas, whose parents were from Mexico, recalled visiting his dad at a local factory that made steel castings, which he described as "dark and loud and dirty." After signing with Slash in

1985, the pair, along with bassist Bob Griffin and drummer Guy Hoffman, who'd go on to join the Violent Femmes in 1993, traveled to Hollywood to record its studio debut, which had a title akin to a neon sign advertising youth's most primary facets. As with a lot of heartland rock, it was borrowed from the Rolling Stones. *Love & Hope & Sex & Dreams* wasn't inspired by *Exile on Main Street*, however, but by "Shattered" from 1978's *Some Girls*, which nods to the street-rat observations of Lou Reed. In spite of the album's 1950s and '60s touchstones, such as its upbeat Buddy Holly jitters, and Everly Brothers–esque vocal harmonies, Neumann and Llanas name-checked influences as disparate as Yes, Tom Jones, Nancy Sinatra, and Tom Petty's *Damn the Torpedoes*. They also said they were moved by the live-rock harmonies of Bruce Springsteen and Steven Van Zandt. The group's most obvious reference was in the album's credits, however. There, every band member adopted the surname BoDean, like the members of the Ramones.

Released the first week in June 1986, BoDeans' first album was produced by T Bone Burnett, by now an established voice in country music who had a distinct sense of tone and atmosphere, and who aimed to capture an unadorned version of the band's live sound, as he'd often done with his own recordings. *Love & Hope & Sex & Dreams* was a simplistic but mighty rock suite that opened on a jangly tale of a down-and-out runaway and closed on a young man pining for his version of Tom Petty's American girl. In between lay everything promised in the title, a band fulfilling its mission statement in a direct and convincing way—lovelorn, earthen, and accessible.

Similar to Lone Justice, BoDeans garnered heavy buzz in its home areas, including Milwaukee and Chicago, but *Love & Hope & Sex & Dreams* peaked at No. 115 on the Billboard pop albums chart. A late October issue of *Billboard* magazine included a report from MTV that stated BoDeans' "She's a Runaway" video was in "light rotation," where it had been for at least four weeks, the network's lowest rating behind the "heavy," "active," "medium," and "breakout" categories. Though the band's song "Still the Night" appeared in *The Color of Money*, Martin Scorsese's 1986 follow-up to the pool hall drama *The Hustler* starring Paul Newman and Tom Cruise, it wasn't included on the film's soundtrack. Reports placed sales of *Love & Hope & Sex & Dreams* around one hundred thousand, about the same as the Replacements' *Tim*. It seemed both acts might go the way of Lone Justice except for the fact that the Replacements released three more studio albums, and the BoDeans recorded new material well into the new millennium in varying formations. Maria McKee's outfit, on the other hand, broke apart amid an earthquake of industry pressure.

She recalled that the band's 1986 overseas tour was its major fault line. According to McKee, "Ways to Be Wicked," one of the band's most popular singles, a song written by Tom Petty and Mike Campbell, contained a lyric that made her ill at ease. It also capped each of the song's three verses. During the band's first recording sessions with Jimmy Iovine, McKee asked the producer if he'd talk to its authors

Maria McKee of Lone Justice performs in Boston in 1985.
PHOTO BY ARTHUR D'AMARIO

about revising the phrase "stick it in." "Tom Petty basically says, 'fuck you,'" she told me. And so, she sang the phrase with evident discomfort, like a hostage forced to read a script on video.

About a year later, amid tour dates in England and Scotland, McKee, a young blond in her early twenties, was "sitting in a room with these middle aged, salty, British journalists, and that was always one of the key questions, that the song is very suggestive," she told me. "Then I go and play the first London show and there's a sea of boys holding their skateboards literally chanting, 'stick it in.'" Lone Justice began to fall apart before *Shelter* was even finished. Three of its members—Ryan Hedgecock, Don Heffington, and Tony Gilkyson—quit the band, leaving McKee and bassist Gregg Sutton to finish the album and tour with various session musicians. McKee dissolved the band permanently in 1988. "People wonder," she added, "why I'm a man-hating lesbian now in my golden years."

★ ★ ★

As countercultural pens marked up heartland rock's stylebook, the genre's best-selling breakthrough of 1986 began with a new age demo tape.

Singer, songwriter, and multi-instrumentalist Bruce Hornsby had been in Los Angeles vying for a major label record deal for nearly six years before Paul Atkinson, former rhythm guitarist of the Zombies, signed him to MCA after a short bidding war. Hornsby was a classically trained pianist, jazz devotee, and musician's musician, who'd been signed to a publishing deal with 20th Century Fox where he attempted to write pro-forma pop songs. He later played with Scottish pop singer Sheena Easton's touring band. Hornsby counted members of the Band and Michael McDonald among his friends and fans. Huey Lewis, who produced three tracks on Hornby's studio debut, called him "a male Rickie Lee Jones." Due to his affinity for ECM-style jazz-fusion, and totally unassuming demeanor, Warner Bros. had passed on his material and Fox eventually gave him the boot. In some interviews, Hornsby figured he was rejected seventy or so times by different music industry players. Instead, he played in small combos in LA clubs, but was dissatisfied with how those bands translated his songs.

"I decided for the first time ever to just make a demo tape where everything just came out of my head," he explained. "That was the first demo I made just on my own, thinking that no major label would have any interest in it because it sounded so uncommercial to me." He gave the loosely spiritual songs to Dawn Atkinson of Windham Hill Records, then vice president of A&R for the label, who he met while working on the soundtrack for a George Lucas animated film. Label head Will Ackerman called Hornsby soon after with an offer, but Hornsby's attorney advised against signing it. He sent the tape to a few major labels instead, and struck a deal with RCA.

On September 18, 1985, *The Virginia Gazette*, a newspaper in his hometown, Williamsburg, ran a full-page photo of Hornsby with a simple tagline: A star is signed.

Bruce Hornsby and the Range win Best New Artist at the 29th Annual Grammy Awards in 1987.

PHOTO COURTESY MEDIAPUNCH INC.

This is yet another example of how the heartland rock genre shifted into a vibes-based sound, rather than a rigid framework or narrative, after *Born in the U.S.A.* Bruce Hornsby and his band the Range had such broad appeal that their debut album played on pop, rock, adult contemporary, and new age radio in the late '80s, and earned the group a Grammy Award for Best New Artist.

Their origin story is the opposite of other major heartland acts— working-class misfits who eventually learned to navigate within a corporate system with the express purpose of reaching as many listeners as possible. Instead, Hornsby was a highly educated son of colonial Virginia who played by the rules until he just couldn't anymore. With *The Way It Is*, Hornsby found success by going against the way it was.

This is also true of the album's songs, which are punctuated by improvised chamber-jazz licks adjacent to Keith Jarrett, one of Hornby's musical heroes. It also folded in folk instruments, including hammered dulcimer, mandolin, violin, and accordion, the year before John Mellencamp's *The Lonesome Jubilee* hit record store shelves. Both translated as a Reagan-era version of the Band. Like Dire Straits' *Brothers in Arms*, the album was mixed and mastered with the CD in mind, and it became one of the highest selling on the format that year. If it was a sophisticated and slickly produced album, it also foretold the direction of heartland rock as its authors sought a more roots-focused sound. What truly made it a standout in the genre lies not in its instrumental compositions, however, but in its lyrics.

As a native of Williamsburg, Hornsby and his two brothers were privy to the area's universities, including the College of William & Mary, the second-oldest institution of higher learning in the country, and also the state's deeply rooted prejudices. Hornsby described the chatter he heard about the late civil rights activist Martin Luther King Jr. when he was growing up. "In my town he was a real *evil* man—just the vibe in the air that he was *terrible*. And if you grow up in that environment you can't help but be affected by it," he said. "Luckily,

I came from a family that guarded us against that conservatism, but sure, I grew up in the thick of all that bad feeling."

He also was inspired by the South's literary traditions, and has named the writers William Styron, Lee Smith, William Faulkner, and William Hoffman as influential on his first two albums with the Range. "All of those writers have a strong sense of place in their writing, and so I wanted to have that same sense of place in my lyric writing," Hornsby explained. "John Mellencamp wrote about Indiana. My old friend Bruce Springsteen has been the bard of New Jersey. This was my version of that in Tidewater Virginia." Like Mellencamp, Seger, Petty, Springsteen, and others, Hornsby never sought to excoriate the place that he called home. He even moved back to Williamsburg after eight trying years in Los Angeles. Instead, he sought to assign reason and progress to an otherwise overlooked area. He honored his roots while also testing them.

The nexus of these forces is most obvious in the album's biggest and most enduring hit. Hornsby's lyrics for "The Way It Is" specifically references two pieces of landmark legislation established in 1964, when he was about ten years old. The Civil Rights Act and the Economic Opportunity Act were both passed under the banner of affording equal protection and opportunity to Americans across races, sexes, religions, national origins, and classes, though their aims were met with great resistance, particularly in the South, where minds were set even as the country changed. Hornsby's narrator switches between these scenes in the song's verses: an older woman queuing for welfare, and a yuppy in a silk suit who castigates her for kicks; a young boy of color caught in the crosshairs of segregation, and a man who refuses him empathy; laws enacted to criminalize such acts, and the ruling class that refuses to adhere to them. Of its success, Hornsby said, "It was totally unexpected. A song about racism with not one but two improvised piano solos is not the standard formula for pop success."

Aside from that song's abolitionist sentiment, the album *The Way It Is* ticked off nearly every box required of the heartland rock category, often within the same song. The album's two other major hits,

"Mandolin Rain" and "Every Little Kiss," combined rural and work-ingman's landscapes with wistful reminiscence and young love. So did "The Long Race," "Down the Road Tonight," "The River Runs Low," and "The Red Plains." The album's instrumental makeup was unques-tionably rock music, even as Hornsby's bright, syncopated piano play-ing took the lead. There were gated drum sounds, and electric guitar. Hornsby's vocals, pleading in their most insistent moments, were a natural vehicle for anthemic choruses, rising in demonstration of his six-foot four-inch frame.

Like many of his peers in this period, Hornsby preferred to be cat-egorized as a social observer rather than a political songwriter. But unlike Mellencamp's "Pink Houses," "The Way It Is" was unmistakable in its antiracist posture. It couldn't be misconstrued or recontextual-ized to suit a different narrative—unless you are Tupac Shakur.

About a year after Shakur was assassinated in 1996, Hornsby received a cassette tape from the Shakur Foundation explaining that they'd found the rapper's interpretation of "The Way It Is" in his archives, and that they'd like to use the song as a single on a forthcom-ing greatest hits album. After being tweaked by Interscope Records— including a remix by Poke of the production duo Trackmasters, the removal of "R" rated language, and a hook sung by Kansas City R&B trio Talent—"Changes" was released in October of 1998, and became one of the most beloved rap songs of all time. It was similarly founded on protest, but sung from the perspective of the marginalized. It also made a call for unity. "I was sort of floored by his creativity. I thought he was so clever, and really profound, and deep," Hornsby said of Shakur, though he never got to meet him.

Though Tupac's rendering of "The Way It Is" remains music's best known and most iconic, even if some fans mutter "corny" under their breath when they hear it; other rappers have used the song as a basis for their art. E-40 of the Click sampled it in his 1996 single "Things'll Never Change." So did Snoop Dogg, in 2008, on "Can't Say Good-bye." Mase, Rhymefest, and even the British avant-garde pop act Art of Noise have also sampled "The Way It Is." Thirty-four years after its release, Chicago rapper Polo G used it most similarly to Shakur, in a conscience-stirring track titled "Wishing for a Hero," which includes Shakur and Hornsby in its writing credits. The same year, in the summer of 2020, "Changes" became the unofficial anthem of the Black Lives Matter movement when peaceful protesters amplified the song at worldwide demonstrations in the wake of George Floyd's murder by Minneapolis officer Derek Chauvin.

After his debut album hit No. 3 on the Billboard 200, and its three singles performed similarly as well, Bruce Hornsby made two more albums with the Range, and wrote and recorded with his peers and heroes. He produced Leon Russell's 1992 comeback album *Anything Can Happen*, and played piano on Bob Dylan's 1991 album *Under the Red Sky* and on Crosby, Stills & Nash's *Live It Up*, released in 1990. His piano brings radiant emotional color to Bonnie Raitt's "I Can't Make You Love Me," like bursts of gulal on Holi. Hornsby sang "Two Kinds of Love" with Stevie Nicks for her fourth solo album, and sang and played piano on Robbie Robertson's second solo album *Storyville*. He cowrote, coproduced, and played keys on "The End of the Innocence" with Don Henley; its David Fincher–directed music video, with nostalgia again drenched in black-and-white, visually protested Ronald Reagan and Oliver North, one of the architects of the Iran-Contra affair. From 1990 to 1992, Hornsby was also a touring member of the Grateful Dead. In 1993, he released "Talk of the Town," a song about America's first interracial marriage.

For all of his accolades, "Changes" remains Hornby's most visible and asked-about collaboration. He remains a vocal advocate of rap music. "He wanted to come down to Williamsburg and ask my permission in person, but as soon as I heard what he had done I told him to save the airfare. It's an amazing song," Hornsby said of Polo G. As for why so many Black artists have favored his 1986 hit: "I'd like to know," Hornsby said in 2020, "but I don't have any idea."

CHAPTER 8

1987

GROWING PAINS

It's horrible to think you've gotta be a miserable son of a bitch
to write a good song, but I guess that's kind of the way it works
sometimes.

—JOHN MELLENCAMP

With the Reagan presidency came a preoccupation with "family
values" as a marker for American society's well-being. In folksy
Christmastime radio addresses and other speeches, the president defined such values as faith, responsibility, and kindness, and
often returned to the idea that such virtue was in jeopardy due to dead-
beat dads, public assistance, and abortion. The overriding message was
that a person's obligation to American society was tied to a traditional
role within a nuclear family. It allowed Reagan to pummel Democrats
for eroding this moral code, as he saw it, and to vilify single mothers
on welfare, middle-class women who worked full-time, the LGBTQ
community, and divorcees. Never mind that Reagan's relationship with
his children was detached at best and he himself was divorced.

This obsession with family values made private life a political issue; related virtue signaling has been issued in each subsequent administration: from President Clinton's affair with Monica Lewinsky, to President Obama's support of gay marriage, and President Trump's history of sexual assault and infidelity. In 1987, heartland rock's progenitors, figureheads, and newcomers released hit albums about the issues of death, divorce, fatherhood, chosen family, and the immigrant experience. Contrary to the government's prevailing sentiment of the nuclear family as the antidote for societal ills, each of these artists positioned such issues as an opportunity for rebirth and to strip music back to its most elemental forms. Gone was the arena-ready bombast of heartland rockstars. What emerged instead were plaintive and mature meditations on family and perseverance, many incorporating folk instruments.

* * *

In director Sidney Lumet's 1960 drama *The Fugitive Kind*, cowritten by Tennessee Williams, Valentine "Snakeskin" Xavier, a guitar-wielding drifter played by Marlon Brando, states that humanity may be divided into two orders: those who buy and those who are bought. Talking with Lady Torrance, a troubled shop owner played by the Italian actor Anna Magnani, he pauses, averts his dark eyes, and then quickly adds a third category of people as a sociological caveat. There is also, he says, "a kind that don't belong no place at all." Then, in a magnificently executed monologue, Brando, his impassioned gaze piercing an unknown realm, describes a rare, light-blue bird. It doesn't have legs, and must spend its entire life in flight. Its tiny body has wings that stretch wide and slender, and it can fly so high that it is invisible to predators. "They sleep on the wind," he says, "and they only alight on this earth but one time—it's when they die."

If Williams's lines are a metaphor for an artist, thinker, or other nonconformist whose high-flown ambitions drown out society's doldrums, they also describe what happens when the basic requirements of the human condition insert themselves into an artist's life. We are wind-born until we decidedly aren't, and only death and destruction may tether us to the material world. In life, he says, there is a loss of innocence and order, and an inevitable education in adversity. It is a fact of life that everyone will eventually die, and life is short. Soar as high as you possibly can.

After a professional whirlwind in which an unknown Hoosier became one of America's most successful rock stars, John Mellencamp, the high-flying bird, finally alighted. "Everything in my secure little world has changed during the last year," he said just after the release of his ninth studio album, *The Lonesome Jubilee.* "It seems everybody I know is getting divorced. I'm sick of people dying around me . . . things are changing in my life around me, and I just don't like it." The last year had forced Mellencamp to grow up against his will, and the singer couldn't shake a looming sense of mortality. His fatalism was suffused throughout the new album, from cover to groove.

"Generations come and go but it makes no difference," states a verse from the book of Ecclesiastes that Mellencamp printed on the inside of the LP's gatefold jacket. "Everything is unutterably weary and tiresome. No matter how much we see, we are never satisfied. . . . So I saw that there is nothing better for men than that they should be happy in their work, for that is what they are here for, and no one can bring them back to life to enjoy what will be in the future, so let them enjoy it now."

Mellencamp's call for carpe diem can be traced to his uncle Joe, who died at fifty-seven from pancreatic cancer amid the making of *The Lonesome Jubilee.* The singer's grandfather Speck died not too long before that. And there was death of another kind, in which families and life partners irreparably break apart. For an artist whose identity was wrapped in the ethos of small-town life, watching its fabric rip apart was unsettling. It was perhaps worse than the crisis in farming that had invaded his homeland because its call was coming from inside the house. Mellencamp and his second wife Victoria would separate not too long after the album's release, in May of 1988.

Turning thirty-five after *The Lonesome Jubilee* was released on

August 24, 1987, also seemed to rattle the artist. Some of the album's songs hold a mirror to the listlessness that hovers within aging's specter. "Check It Out," with its opening lyric that recalls Allen Ginsberg's "Howl," describes how youthful hope and ingenuity unravels into a boring life of mortgages, children, repressed feelings, and stunted communication. "Cherry Bomb," like a lot of heartland rock songs, seems to view the past through rose-colored glasses until a closer inspection of its lyrics reveals that at a certain point, the song says, we stop improving and live in a suspended state, stuck in our ways and too stagnant for growth or enlightenment. The pair at the center of "The Real Life" have watched their lives slip through their hands, and desire a more meaningful existence. Many of this song's lyrics were spoken by Uncle Joe over dinner at Red Lobster in Bloomington before he died. "My whole life I've done what I'm supposed to do. Now I'd like to maybe do something for myself," he reportedly told his nephew, shortly after he'd divorced Mellencamp's Aunt Rose.

The singer has said that "Paper in Fire" concerns his family's history of "ingrained anger," a hotheadedness that burned its way into the singer's own psyche, but had significantly mellowed in the wake of marriage, children, divorce, and maturation. The song also conveys the singular dissatisfaction that simmers just below the surface of middle age and its routines. As with Mellencamp's 1985 single "Lonely Ol' Night," it includes a line from the film *Hud*. "We keep no check on our appetites," he sings in the third verse.

The sense of pride and agrarian resistance threaded throughout the lyrics of *Scarecrow* had matriculated into a palpable sense of resignation on *The Lonesome Jubilee*. If the former heralded the hard work of everyday Americans, the latter questioned who was really the boss. Though its dread was similar to that which underpinned Bruce Springsteen's *Nebraska*, Mellencamp's lyrical concerns stemmed from external, material problems and observations, rather than a spiritual crisis and depression. And unlike the skeletal echoes of Springsteen's solo instrumentation, *The Lonesome Jubilee* was layered with traditional folk instruments whose function was to inject a sense of place, a sense of history, and a sense of family into the album, a contrast to its lyrical concerns about societal ills.

Mellencamp had pivoted from cocksure youthful naivety to a mouthpiece for the weariness of adulthood, and this sentiment began to spill over into how he presented his music live. "I began to think, 'Who in the hell am I trying to kid here? Why would I ever even want to pretend to relate to a 13-year-old?'" he said in 1988. "I'm glad teenagers do come to the shows and buy the records, but the reality is I'd much rather relate to some people between 25 and 45. . . . I don't know how the Stones and the Who stood it a few years ago . . . playing to crowds that were [predominantly] teen-agers. In a strange way, it must have been kind of humiliating."

Mellencamp's sonic shift to a folk-rock sound began when he assembled the touring band for *Scarecrow*. It was then that he added Lisa Germano and John Cascella, whose instrumental contributions are inextricable from the new sound. The former played violin and the latter accordion, claves, penny whistle, keyboards, saxophone, and melodica on *The Lonesome Jubilee*, hastening each song's melody in place of an electric guitar. Pat Peterson, a soul and gospel singer from Texas who'd been a member of the Raelettes, Ray Charles's backing group, first worked with Mellencamp on the *American Fool* tour, and toured *Scarecrow* on backing vocals and percussion alongside Crystal Taliefero, a Gary, Indiana, native. Mellencamp's longtime friend and guitarist Larry Crane had a natural curiosity about folk instruments, and played steel guitars, mandolin, harmonica, autoharp, and banjo, while guitarist Mike Wanchic added dobro, banjo, and dulcimer to his album credits. Even drummer Kenny Aronoff expanded his reach to include hammered dulcimer, tambourine, vibraphone, and congas.

Mellencamp called his new sound "gypsy rock," something that bridged his childhood in the Nazarene church and his ancestral roots in Germany and the Netherlands to the modern world. In interviews each band member has remarked on the commands Mellencamp placed on them for the rendering of his most accomplished album. Their leader insisted that each member learn at least one folk instru-

John Mellencamp and Lisa Germano perform at the second Farm Aid benefit concert in 1986.

PHOTO BY BOB DAEMMRICH

ment during the break between the *Scarecrow* tour and *The Lonesome Jubilee* recording sessions. "This is the first record where I can say we had a vision and we connected with it," Mellencamp said shortly after the album was released.

They reunited at Belmont Mall with producer Don Gehman and a new recording and mixing engineer, David Leonard, who'd worked on Prince's *1999* and *Purple Rain*. The result was something that was and remains singular in the landscape of pop music. Held against the biggest albums of the year, such as Fleetwood Mac's *Tango in the Night*, Bon Jovi's *Slippery When Wet*, and Michael Jackson's *Bad*, Mellencamp's album was revolutionary for its refusal of 1980s production norms that prioritized sleek and thunderous precision. Instead, *The Lonesome Jubilee* sounded as if it grew organically from the farmland in which it was recorded—warm, fresh, and deliciously imperfect. For as resigned as the album's lyrics, and Mellencamp's mindset, seemed to be, *The Lonesome Jubilee* also provided a stage for the singer's growing expressions of protest.

"Down and Out in Paradise," the album's second track, was a naked plea for Reagan and his administration to do better for the American people. It was also an open expression of the singer's disbelief in the president's willingness to do so. The meditative "We Are the People" issues a warning to myopic political leaders, and a unifying message to Americans, in the vein of the famous Chilean protest song "¡El pueblo unido jamás será vencido!" (the people united will never be defeated). There were also the ways in which Mellencamp chose to visualize his songs. For the "Paper in Fire" music video, Mellencamp and his band traveled to Savannah, Georgia, and set up with a film crew outside a house on a dirt road in the middle of an impoverished Black community. The singer has explained that he knocked on doors to gain the neighbors' trust and permission, and invited them to participate. Many of them did, clapping and dancing along as Mellencamp and his band played the song in the street. The idea was to highlight inequity and demonstrate unity, even if it also comes across as exploitative. For the "Cherry Bomb" music video, Mellencamp depicted a young Black and white interracial couple slow-dancing near a jukebox, and in the music video for "Hard Times for an Honest Man," he sat on the steps of a former slave auction house, also in Savannah.

Though Mellencamp's well-meaning appearances in Georgia may have been the by-product of regional convenience—he and his family vacationed on Hilton Head Island in South Carolina—*The Lonesome Jubilee* and its imagery was also released as racially motivated violence in America's cities and on college campuses made headlines. A lot of it was centered in Georgia. Forsyth County, at the time a rural area about thirty miles northeast of Atlanta, was considered a sundown county and was 99 percent white. Virtually no Black person had lived there for seventy-five years after white mobs burned down Black churches and Black-owned businesses in 1912, and then racially motivated violence and prejudice persisted in its wake. In the earliest days of 1987, however, a small group of residents banded together to form a protest in conjunction with Martin Luther King Jr. Day, which they dubbed a "March Against Fear and Intimidation."

It drew about seventy-five participants, including white residents of Forsyth County, Atlanta residents, and national civil rights activists that arrived by bus. About four hundred counterprotesters also showed up, including leaders of the Ku Klux Klan and neo-Nazis, who overwhelmed police, shouted racist slurs, and threw rocks, bricks, and bottles. Hosea Williams, an Atlanta-based civil rights leader who helped organize the march, told *The New York Times* that Forsyth County was analogous to apartheid South Africa, and that white children as young as ten had yelled racial epithets and death threats at protesters. Mellencamp was similarly threatened by the Ku Klux Klan after he released the music video for "Cherry Bomb."

Seemingly undeterred, Williams and others organized a second demonstration in Forsyth County on January 24, 1987, calling it a "March for Brotherhood." National media turned its attention to the protest given the previous violence, and Forsyth County was flooded with twenty thousand demonstrators and one thousand white supremacists. Sixty-four people in total were arrested. Weeks after the march, on February 9, Oprah Winfrey taped the first out-of-town episode of her new talk show at a restaurant in Forsyth County. There, she interviewed white residents who espoused racist beliefs, and others who expressed solidarity with the protesters. After the interview, an Associated Press reporter asked Winfrey if she felt at ease in the area. "Not comfortable at all," she responded. "I'm leaving."

On April 22, the Supreme Court ruled in *McCleskey v. Kemp*, rejecting an appeal filed by attorneys for a Black man in Georgia, Warren McCleskey, which argued that the death penalty in the state discriminated on the basis of race, and violated his right to equal protection under the Fourteenth Amendment. McCleskey was sentenced to death after being convicted of killing a white police officer during an armed robbery. The court's decision came after a University of Iowa law professor conducted an extensive study of more than two thousand murder cases in Georgia, and found empirical evidence of systemic bias: that prosecutors were more likely to seek the death penalty, and juries were more likely to impose it, in cases involving white victims and Black defendants. In a highly controversial 5–4 decision, the court held that the study didn't provide substantial enough evidence to reverse McCleskey's conviction. In an opinion written by the conservative Justice Lewis Powell, the court stated that such disparities in sentencing were "an inevitable part of our criminal justice system," effectively condoning racism in American law. With its ruling in this case, the court could've struck down capital punishment in the state on the basis of racial discrimination, and paved the way for national challenges to the death penalty. Instead, it upheld the practice by one vote. Today, Congress has proposed more than a dozen laws that attempt to offset the ruling, but none of them have passed. Warren McCleskey was executed by electrocution in September 1991. The same year, and a couple after he had retired, Justice Powell's biographer asked him if, given the chance, he would change any vote he cast over the course of his career. "Yes," Powell told him. "*McCleskey v. Kemp*."

Outside of major demonstrations and legal injustices, many scholars and activists in the late '80s believed that the issues of racism that pervaded America at that time, including systemic racial inequality in housing, education, unemployment, and the law, were more subtle and less conducive to the media coverage and demonstrations of moral outrage that had occurred at the height of the civil rights movement. Instead, the Reagan administration's efforts to shore up negative popular opinion around marginalized communities—which became a defining characteristic of the former president's time in office—shifted national focus to the emergence of crack cocaine amid the so-called war on drugs, which disproportionately affected Black Americans. Conversely, little mention was made of the drug's powder version, which was widely used among white Americans. The subject of crack cocaine dominated news coverage in the summer of 1986 to the point that *Newsweek* magazine compared it to the Vietnam War, and *Time* magazine declared that it was the issue of the year. Terms such as "crack baby" and "crackhead" became common in the American vernacular, a reductive and dehumanizing slur aimed at the poor and disenfranchised, and especially Black people.

"What's really disgusting is just the lack of human dignity that people are allowed to have," Mellencamp said of American society shortly after he released *The Lonesome Jubilee* in 1987. "There's always something there to take that dignity away from you, be it the government or schools or churches or whatever." With the album, and its themes of injustice, complacency, and dashed dreams, he became an amplifier of issues facing overlooked Americans. Unlike with *Scarecrow*, Mellencamp seemed to speak alongside them, instead of just singing about them, because Mellencamp had made himself a character in the album's story. His narrator was one in an entire class of people who weren't powerful, but also weren't helpless. They were, as Brando said, "a kind that don't belong no place at all." For those suspended between life and prosperity, just getting by was miraculous. "The title refers to ordinary victories," Mellencamp explained, "the private ones that are usually very solitary."

★ ★ ★

In between the True Confessions and Temples in Flames tours with Bob Dylan, Tom Petty and the Heartbreakers recorded the band's seventh studio album. For the first time, Petty and Mike Campbell took total control of the creative reins, serving as both the album's songwriters and its producers. It was the first time the band worked without Jimmy Iovine since 1978's *You're Gonna Get It!* It was also the band's first album without any involvement with original bassist Ron Blair, who slowly slipped away from the brotherhood over a long series of months. Though his replacement Howie Epstein joined the Heartbreakers in 1982, Blair had stepped in for a spell on every album through *Southern Accents*.

Petty has long professed that the thing he liked the most about *Let Me Up (I've Had Enough)* is its title. If it's an open plea reflecting the Florida native's exhausted psyche as he was suspended between worlds, it's also one more tortured domino in heartland rock's line of play in 1987, as its figureheads released highly varied works indicative of great personal trials. Given the band's position as the backing

Tom Petty and
the Heartbreakers
back Bob Dylan
during the True
Confessions Tour
in 1986.
PHOTO COURTESY
MEDIAPUNCH INC.

ensemble for Bob Dylan, Tom Petty and the Heartbreakers couldn't
help but feel as if they were in a kind of limbo. Were they leaders or
supporters? Burnished studio perfectionists or a highly intuitive live
act capable of following one of music's most unpredictable players?
Did their work with Dylan afford them greater credibility among a
wider listenership, or were they cannibalizing their own career? Could
all of these things be true at the same time?

Many Dylanologists of the High Court of His Bobness regard this
period in his career as the worst. In its day, the media wasn't much
kinder when it came to the new supergroup's live shows. *The New York
Times*' critic called the show at Madison Square Garden "an oddly
paced, willful concert." A reviewer for *The Globe and Mail* set the bar
even lower. He pointed out a slew of blemishes at one of two shows in
Berkeley, California—Dylan forgot the words to many of his songs,
most of the songs sounded the same until the chorus, guitar attacks

fell flat—before conceding that these mistakes actually, somehow, made the concert good because Bob Dylan has never been perfect. In his memoir *Chronicles: Volume One*, Dylan himself said that, "Tom was at the top of his game and I was at the bottom of mine."

Touring as the I-beam for a spiraling icon is a precarious enough position. Add the tension of rebounding from an uneven and broadly misunderstood paean to the South, and find a band enclosed in a hissing pressure cooker. Would the lid pop open and reveal an enticing new album? Or would the whole thing explode?

As Petty has told it, *Let Me Up (I've Had Enough)* began as a Dylan album. Bob had booked studio time between the two legs of the tour to record with the Heartbreakers, but wasn't ready for it when the time came. Instead, Petty and his band began testing some things they'd written on the road, and also wrote new material on the fly in the studio. "The rules of the session were when the first guy gets there you roll tape until the last guy's gone," Petty explained. "So some of these songs were being written as the tape was running." The album's third track, "The Damage You've Done," is also a recording of the first time the band played the song together. It seemed the quintet had decided to lean into the touring version of itself, the group who could anticipate the movements of one of music's most erratic frontmen, the band who operated as if by psychic connection.

That was Petty's way of working on the album, anyway. Campbell, the prolific demo architect who fashioned "The Boys of Summer," brought in a number of fully realized songs, some with overdubs and everything. "My Life/Your World," "Runaway Trains," and "All Mixed Up" were the product of a solo mad scientist, not the communal spirit of the Dylan tours. This lent the album a dueling quality in which aleatoric energy wasn't exactly a throughline. "Jammin' Me," the album's big single, was a melding of the two worlds. Campbell wrote much of the music. Petty and Dylan collaborated on the lyrics in the earliest days of the session. Its themes reflect a growing concern among the two songwriters: the oversaturation of media and how it may be used for good or evil. The times were changing. Today, as headlines, advertisements, video games, social media, movies, television, and YouTube light up our phones, tablets, and watches, "Jammin' Me" stands out for its predictive qualities.

A 1987 issue of *Channels*, a trade magazine established by the pioneering television journalist Les Brown, who also cofounded the famous Gate of Horn folk music club in Chicago with Dylan's former manager Albert Grossman, called the year the "Second Age of Television." In an article titled "Five Tumultuous Years," Brown wrote that the years since 1982 were "the most turbulent in the history of media in America" and that 1987 was "a new time in which the networks are joined by cable, syndication, VCRs, fourth networks, pay-per-view operators, and marketers of backyard dishes in pursuit of the same audiences." He attributed these advances in technology as prompting the Reagan administration's deregulation of broadcast channels, whose licenses "came to be regarded as the equivalent of real estate." In this period, the Australian media mogul Rupert Murdoch entered the American market with his purchases of the 20th Century Fox and Metromedia TV stations. So did mighty financiers who previously had no interest in America media, such as Warren Buffett and Coca-Cola. VH1, which launched in 1985 as the softer sibling to MTV, sold along with all of MTV Networks to Viacom, which expanded the station's adult contemporary programming to include classic rock, Top 40, and '80s pop. The move, combined with VH1's more mature audience, greatly benefited those under the heartland rock umbrella as their videos now had two stations with two different audiences.

These changes in broadcasting were also met by the advent of personal computers, which Dylan and Petty reference in the song's lyrics. In "Jammin' Me," they also name-checked three celebrities who were, as the two musicians saw it, at the center of the era's exhausting and overwhelming media onslaught. Eddie Murphy was reportedly upset about his being included among that cohort. The song's video placed the band in relief from these sentiments. A cacophony of newspaper headlines, television sitcom and news clips, video games, and home computers flash in the background as the band plays the song on a soundstage.

Beyond "Jammin' Me" and its social criticisms, *Let Me Up (I've Had Enough)* contained the strongest-ever expressions of Petty's worldview, yet another extension of the album's fed-up sentiment. Most evident are the lyrical shots Petty fired at millionaires and America's ruling class, and the empathy he conveyed for working people upon whose necks their Italian loafers rested. Petty was exhausted by the media, but he also understood its fast-growing influence. In the run-up to recording his new album, he decided to use it. "Being a songwriter now in 1986 is a much more important job than it was in '76," he said. "I used to have an aversion to musicians giving their view on this and that but now there are so many things that are just black and white. A lot of kids and adults get their information now through the entertainment media, so without turning into an outright boor, you do have a certain responsibility."

★ ★ ★

Around the same time that Mellencamp and Petty displayed new, disaffected armatures, a rising roots-rock band from Los Angeles dared to ask, "Is this all there is?" Los Lobos sprung from the Los Angeles music scene surrounding Slash Records, which reared X, the Blasters, the BoDeans, Dream Syndicate, and others. Though geographically and spiritually aligned with these bands, Los Lobos were sophisticated players whose skills transcended the punk realm. They were also the only act from the scene to ascend the underground and highlight a specific, widely underrecognized contingent of working Americans in the 1980s: Hispanic immigrants, particularly those from Mexico.

By the fall of 1987, the nation's Hispanic population neared nineteen million, a figure that was 30 percent higher than the US Census Bureau's estimate from 1980. The bureau's study also found that the Hispanic community in America—which composed about 8 percent of the total population—was younger, poorer, and growing more rapidly than any other group. For his part, Ronald Reagan often demonstrated an appreciation of the community in California and beyond, citing their commitment to hard work, family, and God. The president often credited his 1980 win to Hispanic voters who joined the Republican party in the 1970s. In 1988, at the behest of Air Force Colonel Gil Coronado, a San Antonio native, Reagan expanded the country's celebration of Hispanic heritage from one week to one month, from September 15 to October 15. He also appointed Lauro Cavazos as secretary of education the same year, making the Texas native the first Hispanic person to serve in the United States Cabinet.

This doesn't mean Reagan's record reflects the spirit of these charismatic public displays, or that Hispanic people in America universally approved of the Gipper. In 1983, the League of United Latin American Citizens, which represented more than one hundred thousand Hispanic Americans, issued a report detailing how Reagan's domestic policies hurt the very people he praised in public. It charged that Reagan's administration appointed fewer Hispanic people to federal government positions than President Carter's. It also stated that Reagan cut funds for bilingual education programs and opposed civil rights legislation. The group was also concerned about Reagan's militaristic approach to problems in Central America.

Los Lobos' early albums were released amid a charged national climate in which saying and doing were very different things. The group (which translates to the Wolves in English) released its sophomore album, *By the Light of the Moon*, in January 1987. Its compositions featured a diverse array of folk instruments, such as accordion, bajo sexto, mandolin, harmonica, and the vihuela—a lute-like instrument that dates to the fifteenth century—that were threaded through cable-knit rock 'n' roll inspired by the 1950s and '60s. Similar to Mellencamp's *The Lonesome Jubilee*, for as many folk instruments the group wielded, the album's sound was clean and accessible; it was part punk and part roots, an '80s-era case study in the power of back to basics.

The album's lyrics formed compassionate and evocative vignettes of grief and inequity in America, with titles such as "Is This All There Is?," "The Mess We're In," and "The Hardest Time." Its lyrics were so stirring as to earn comparisons to Bruce Springsteen's *Nebraska*. As the major white figures of heartland rock sang for their regional corners in Michigan, Indiana, New Jersey, Florida, and Virginia, Los Lobos asserted that the everyday workers of Los Angeles' garment district, California's Central Valley farm workers, and others, counted among those Americans whose stories deserved a stage. These facets alone guided the band's ship to heartland rock's port, but there is one more gargantuan act in this period that also affords Los Lobos safe passage.

When heartland rock became the center of popular culture, its artists also sought to resuscitate the careers of their heroes and influences. Tom Petty produced an album for Del Shannon, *Drop Down and Get Me*, released in late 1981, and went on to form Traveling Wilburys, a heartland-rock-inspired band with Roy Orbison, George Harrison, Bob Dylan, and Jeff Lynne. Garage-rock belter Mitch Ryder released *Never Kick a Sleeping Dog* in 1983, an album produced by John Mellencamp. Bruce Springsteen worked with Gary U. S. Bonds, and his bandmate Steven Van Zandt collaborated with his favorite teenage group, the Rascals. Bruce Hornsby produced Leon Russell's 1992 comeback, *Anything Can Happen*. These efforts, however, are a drop in the ocean compared to Los Lobos' resuscitation of America's most influential Chicano rock 'n' roller.

A beloved fixture in Mexican American communities, Ritchie Valens was thrust into wider America's consciousness after the film *La Bamba* was released on July 24, 1987, and became a box office hit. With the biopic came its chart-topping soundtrack, consisting of six Valens songs covered by Los Lobos—including "Come On, Let's Go," "Donna," and "La Bamba"—and six more tunes performed by the likes of Bo Diddley and Brian Setzer. The collection went to No. 1 on the Billboard 200, and the Top 10 of charts around the world, including in Canada, France, Australia, Finland, Spain, and Norway. "La Bamba," the Mexican folk song Valens reimagined as a rock single in the late '50s, remains Los Lobos' most popular song, even though they didn't write it.

There is a good reason for that. Rather than perform the song by rote, mimicking Valens's original, Los Lobos added a new dimension to "La Bamba" via singer David Hidalgo's rich vocals—his voice kindling with evident passion—and the band's sharp instrumentation. "We love this stuff so much that we wanted to be very careful about how we presented it," Hidalgo said. "It wasn't just a matter of playing the songs note for note, there was a feeling there." As Springsteen, with his pulp-outsider style and classic-car enthusiasm, punched an Elvis-shaped hole in the atmosphere, Los Lobos cut a figure of a 1950s Chicano icon who actually wrote his own songs. There could have been many more of those songs, too, if Valens hadn't died in the same plane crash that killed Buddy Holly in 1959, when he was just seventeen years old.

Los Lobos' interest in Valens also didn't begin when the singer's estate requested the group for the film's soundtrack. It had recorded a cover of "Come On, Let's Go" for its debut single, released in 1983, and the group often performed Valens's "That's My Little Suzie" in concert. The song "La Bamba" had been in the band's repertoire for more than a decade. Its care for and deep familiarity with Valens and his music made Los Lobos' homage to "La Bamba" immortal, like a hydra whose cells continuously divide.

Los Lobos was formed by five musicians who'd met in high school in East Los Angeles, a neighborhood composed of generations of working-class Hispanic families, and the center of the Zoot Suit Riots of 1943. They began under the name Los Lobos del Este de Los Angeles in the early '70s. The group shortened its name and made its way to the roster of Slash/Warner Bros. in the early '80s after it created a suite of songs on the road. *How Will the Wolf Survive?*, its debut LP for the label released in 1984, was inspired by the plight of gray wolves in America—how they are hunted and pushed out amid rapid urbanization, and how that narrative seemed to parallel the band's own story of survival as it tried to launch in the music industry without betraying its culture. Vocalist and multi-instrumentalist Louie Perez explained that the album marked a shift in the band's consciousness. "We decided to take a responsible look at what we represented and where we came from as Mexican Americans," he said. "Was this band going to be a fun, sock-hop party band or actually show they're of reasonable intelligence and concern?"

Its songs such as "A Matter of Time" and "How Will the Wolf Survive?" portrayed immigrant life North of the border; how families necessarily break apart in pursuit of the American dream; and the identity crisis that can occur amid an honest attempt at a better life. Along the way, the band became a symbol of the prosperity so many seek but few achieve. They were "the group that vaulted out of the barrio into the big leagues," as one *Los Angeles Times* reporter wrote, a narrative similar to Seger, Mellencamp, Springsteen, Petty, and other artists from working-class origins in forgotten areas, but with the added hurdle of America's systemic prejudice and xenophobia. Nonetheless, Los Lobos' debut album was so well received that the group was named Best New Band in *Rolling Stone*'s 1984 critics' poll, and tied with Bruce Springsteen and the E Street Band for Band of the Year. It went on to perform with heartland rock's biggest names, such as Mellencamp and Petty.

Los Lobos sang of the same America as the rest of heartland rock's artists, the nation whose coffers hold possibility and disappointment in equal measure, but Los Lobos offered a crucial, underrepresented vantage point. This couldn't have been more clear than when the band performed at the second Farm Aid concert in 1986. Though organizers made a concerted effort to gather a more diverse lineup, artists of color remained scant. Rick James and Taj Mahal were the only two Black performers. Julio Iglesias and Los Lobos were the only musicians from Spanish-speaking communities. The issues in farming weren't new to the LA band, however. Los Lobos had long aligned itself with the struggle of Central Valley farmers in California, and even contributed to a 1977 charity compilation, "Si Se Puede!," which benefited Cesar Chavez's United Farm Workers of America.

For its set at Farm Aid, Los Lobos opened on what was perhaps its most popular song at the time, "Will the Wolf Survive?," whose music video depicts two young immigrants on a hard-won journey to life in America. It helped that Waylon Jennings had his own hit on the country charts with the tune in 1986, which helped resuscitate his stalled career. After a scorching version of the group's "Don't Worry Baby," an homage to 1950s rockabilly days of yore, Los Lobos closed with a new song. Stepping up to the microphone, singer-guitarist Cesar Rosas explained to the audience that the song was titled "One Night in America."

To a crowd of about forty thousand Americans, in front of a mural of an American flag, Los Lobos performed an early version of the song that became "One Time One Night." It's the lead track on the band's 1987 album *By the Light of the Moon*. It's also one of the group's most stirring and solemn, a tune whose buoyant instrumentation belies the gravity of its lyrics. As Hidalgo sang of gun violence, kidnapping, and other national ills, there was the sense that Los Lobos' central query had shifted. As a featured act at one of America's most popular music festivals, the question was no longer, "Will the wolf survive?" With this new song, about the struggles of everyday people, Los Lobos asked, "Who among you is listening?"

★ ★ ★

As heartland rock musicians turned pages in their careers, singer-songwriter John Hiatt's neared its death rattle. When he walked into Los Angeles' Ocean Way studios in February 1987, his future in the music industry was uncertain. Since 1970, Hiatt inhabited a range of musical roles—in-house songwriter for the Nashville record label Tree International, a sensitive country-rock solo artist, a transgressive new waver adored by critics—but none of them propelled him to commercial success. Along the way, Hiatt alienated an expanse of music industry figures, and was dropped by the record labels Epic, MCA, and Geffen. He'd also fallen into a bad way with alcoholism and drugs. That *Bring the Family*, released in May 1987, was made at all is a demonstration of the better angels of our nature; that it was Hiatt's seventh studio album and first commercial breakthrough is nothing short of miraculous.

The idea was to capture the soul of Hiatt's art without any studio trickery or bells and whistles. Gone were the overdubs, keyboards, and auxiliary players that had been added as the majors tried to break him into the charts. Instead, Hiatt chose a trio of trusted friends who happened to be exemplary musicians, and recorded the tracks mostly live on a shoestring budget.

Born in Indianapolis, Indiana, in 1952, Hiatt bore a few similarities to Mellencamp. The pair were eight months apart in age, and about fifty miles apart in geography. They grew up listening to the same rock 'n' roll, R&B, and soul music broadcast on AM radio stations in the 1960s. They both grew up rebellious, racing down roads to nowhere going thirty miles over the speed limit. The two men experienced the limitations of their surroundings, but respected the homes of their origins, and took a circuitous route to success.

The alignment between them mostly stops there. Mellencamp was plucked out of obscurity for his boyish good looks, and then started on a path to pop stardom, eventually becoming a good songwriter; Hiatt started off behind the scenes, writing songs for other artists. With his scouring pad vocals, and gaunt comportment, he was no leading man. By the time *Bring the Family* was released in 1987, Hiatt had the most success with other people singing his songs. Willie Nelson, Ruben Blades, Bruce Springsteen, and Bob Dylan performed "Across the Borderline," which Hiatt cowrote with guitar hero Ry Cooder and producer Jim Dickinson. Roseanne Cash took Hiatt's "It Hasn't Happened Yet" and "The Way We Make a Broken Heart" high atop the country music charts. Three Dog Night had a hit with Hiatt's "Sure as I'm Sittin' Here," and the Neville Brothers covered his song "Washable Ink."

If the common thread of heartland rock released in 1987 was a dismantling of the genre's perfectionist production values, revealing the core of each artist's essence, and laying bare their nerve endings to the scrutiny of music's listenership, then *Bring the Family* was a mirror image of Mellencamp's *The Lonesome Jubilee*. As the Bloomington native constructed a back-to-basics fatalistic epic from death and divorce, the man from Indianapolis fortified a new, more hopeful beginning on a foundation of resolve. The album's title is its most obvious indication: Hiatt no longer wanted to hide, and to experience small mercies amid the loneliness of pain. Now, he was part of a life-giving unit, along with his daughter Lilly and his new wife, Nancy. Now, wherever life took him, he wanted to bring his family. The cynical wit that dotted so many of the songwriter's earlier albums dissipated to reveal a man wholly content at the intersection of adulthood and responsibility. "It never worked for me," he said of the tortured artist tag that had been affixed to him by the media. "In fact, I found that I spent so much time torturing myself that I had precious little time to sit down and write about it."

Between the tragedy of his second marriage, and the joy of his third, Hiatt wrote the songs that composed *Bring the Family*. A small indie label in the UK, Demon Records, advanced Hiatt $20,00 to record it, and he called upon the mercy of his friends. He assembled Ry Cooder (electric guitar), who he met in Los Angeles when the guitarist covered Hiatt's "The Way We Make a Broken Heart" for his 1980 album *Borderline*. Session ace Jim Keltner (drums), who often collaborated with Cooder, came aboard at the same time. Hiatt knew he wanted Nick Lowe to play bass due to their work together on Hiatt's 1983 album *Riding with the King*.

The group, with Hiatt on acoustic guitar and piano, spent four fast days tucked into Ocean Way on Sunset Boulevard in Hollywood. They played mostly live. Stripping Hiatt's work down to its main ingredients had the effect of elevating its spirit. For the first time in a long time, Hiatt worked in the vein of his heroes, laying bare his rawest feelings. "The real artists, like Ry [Cooder] and Guy Clarke, they're unafraid of real displays of emotion, almost cliche," Hiatt told a Dutch documentarian in 1987, shortly after the release of his new album. With *Bring the Family*, he joined those ranks. Like most of the heartland rock of the time, the album was vulnerable and spare, a masterclass in songwriting whose aim was to present an unvarnished account of the artist's present truth.

Shortly after the release of *Bring the Family*, Hiatt and his studio coconspirators played a show together at the Roxy in Los Angeles as part of A&M Records' twenty-fifth anniversary celebration. The label had purchased the rights to the album after it was finished, and released it on May 29, 1987. It became Hiatt's first charting album, peaking at No. 107 on the Billboard 200.

Seated at a piano on the Roxy's spartan stage, Hiatt explained that as a child he was mesmerized by the R&B and gospel music he heard on the radio, broadcast by a charismatic disc jockey, Bill "Hossman" Allen, on station WLAC in Nashville. He told the audience that night that his mind was overwhelmed by these Black performers' ability to "get out" of themselves, and that he wrote his new single, "Have a Little Faith in Me," with the aim of channeling that same spirit. For its multidimensional portrayal of love, how its joy necessitates pain, "Have a Little Faith in Me" stands alongside soul music classics such as Ben E. King's "Stand by Me." It similarly became a staple of film soundtracks and television shows, and positioned Hiatt as a reverent figure in heartland rock, for whom Black music was aspirational and animating.

Hiatt had dipped his toe into heartland rock's scene-setting with his songs such as "You May Already Be a Winner" from *Riding with the King*. It depicted a down-on-their-luck married couple whose only hope are the sweepstakes letters that arrive in their mailbox. Outside of its overt sense of hope spurred by love and family, *Bring the Family* also addressed America's losers and underdogs, those for whom prosperity was coupled with hardship.

"Alone in the Dark" is a character study of a self-sabotaging alcoholic, no doubt drawn from Hiatt's own past, and "Lipstick Sunset" takes heartland rock's fondness for reminiscing about childhood romance down a dark path to a bitter end. "Your Dad Did" illustrates how the stoicism and absence of a clock-punching father perpetuates cycles of generational trauma.

Like Bonnie Raitt, Hiatt channeled the poetic torment of American blues traditions, its melisma and shuffles threaded throughout the new album's opening songs. These qualities are what drew the long-underestimated Raitt to Hiatt's "Thing Called Love," which she would cover on her 1989 breakthrough album *Nick of Time*. "I love the lyrics, I love the playfulness, I love the John Lee Hooker shuffle beat. Of all the songs I've played over the years, it's one of my absolute favorites," she told *Billboard* magazine in 2021.

The two musicians' similarities extended beyond a penetrating ability to channel the blues. They'd both been grinding in the music industry for nearly two decades. Both experienced career paths dotted with failure, hardship, and self-destruction before finally finding success. Both knew what it was like to be misunderstood, miscast, and underestimated by industry executives to the detriment of their artistry and livelihood. Both were musicians' musicians, adored by their peers long before the rest of the world caught on.

Their energies melded at Farm Aid. At the charity concert's fifth encore in 1990, Raitt and Hiatt performed "Thing Called Love," harmonizing on its chorus like two streams falling into a river. Backed by John Mellencamp's band—Kenny Aronoff (drums), Larry Crane (guitar), Toby Myers (bass)—Hiatt deferred to Raitt's extraordinary vocal prowess for most of the verses. Together, they conveyed the song's grit and sensuality, he the whiskey to her full-bodied wine.

If the performance was an indicator of Raitt's great ability to align herself with canonical songwriters, it was yet another example of why she was heartland rock's most valuable cipher, elegantly encoding songs to appeal to a wider and more diverse audience. Bonnie Raitt's support of an artist unfailingly boosted their profile, from her cover of John Prine's "Angel from Montgomery" to her appearance on Steven Van Zandt's "Sun City" and Bob Seger's "Makin Thunderbirds," and her repeated support of Farm Aid. When she released her cover of "Thing Called Love" in 1989, Hiatt's entire career was reenergized.

Such commiserating—between artists, between fans, and between artist and fan—has long been a goal for Hiatt, whose songs on *Bring the Family* double as a generous offering to sit in one's own truth. The quartet he assembled for *Bring the Family* stayed together in creative partnerships and as friends. In 1992, Hiatt, Lowe, Cooder, and Keltner released *Little Village*, the self-titled debut of the roots-rock band they formed a year earlier. Beyond that, the bonds he formed with his listeners helped him to feel less alone in the world. "Songwriting for me has always been a means of checking in with my own feelings," he said. "When people connect with these songs, what I get back is that they're saying, 'No you're not from another planet because I've felt that way, too.'"

* * *

In 1987, John Mellencamp, Tom Petty, Los Lobos, and John Hiatt released uncluttered albums forged with traditional rock and folk instruments. The same year, two heartland rock titans reemerged with similarly bare expressions of self and society. With *Tunnel of Love* and *Robbie Robertson*, Bruce Springsteen and Robertson, an artistic force behind the Band, shared timeless sentiments using contemporary tools. Both reflected the sonic shift in heartland rock that arrived with *Born in the U.S.A.*, incorporating synthesizers and pop sensibilities alongside guitars and drums. Each release marked an evident distancing from the work each artist had built his name upon, an unpeeling of the artichoke to reveal a new layer.

After at last finishing the *Born in the U.S.A.* tour, which spanned more than 150 dates, five countries, sixteen months, and five million fans, Springsteen retreated into what should have been rest. He had a new wife, the actress and model Julianne Philips, and lived a comfortable life. By now a multimillionaire, Springsteen endeavored to build a domestic version of himself, one with roots and a narrower focus. After years on the road without a permanent partner or place to call home, he longed to cut a new figure. Springsteen had written songs about men out on the road in search of themselves. Now, he wanted to focus on men inside the home, the responsibility and anxiety of it all.

Born in the U.S.A. had marked Springsteen at the apex of his artistry, celebrity, and influence. The beefed-up commando version of himself that he revealed on the tour stood as a physical manifestation of the commercial might of his best-selling album. His sleeveless button downs, bulging biceps, and gravel-coated vocals commanded entire stadiums. Springsteen had also become an outsized symbol of American exceptionalism. In this version, his creativity and moxie, his gargantuan presence and success, exemplified the age-old promises of the nation—its mythical bootstraps. This version of Springsteen was proof of the winning side of the American gamble. It was at the same time ephemeral. The end of the *Born in the U.S.A.* tour also marked the end of something he'd never be again.

As Springsteen stood at the finish line, peering out in search of a new beginning, Robertson pushed off the starting blocks. He'd stood in Springsteen's position more than a decade earlier, on November 25, 1976, when the Band bid farewell at the Winterland Ballroom in San Francisco in what became one of the most cherished concert films of all time, *The Last Waltz*. Since then, the guitarist, singer, and songwriter struggled to find his identity as a solo artist. Instead, he acted in the 1980 film *Carny* alongside Jodi Foster and Gary Busey, and worked with director Martin Scorsese on the music for *Raging Bull* and *The King of Comedy*. He walked away knowing that his time with the Band had come to its creative end, and he gave up the ghost.

It took about a decade for Robertson to release his first solo album. The process began in 1984 with a project he originally called *American Roulette*, which he envisioned as a film and maybe an album that explored the life of a burnt-out rock legend from the 1960s who had disappeared and whose son was trying to find him. Its narrative current flowed through the lineage of American mythology—Elvis Presley, Marylin Monroe, James Dean—and Robertson's belief that these stars didn't collapse into a black hole for no purpose. He felt that each icon left behind a valuable lesson. "You take a kid from driving a truck and you put him in this situation where his music and his image is all of a sudden controlling the world to a certain extent," Robertson explained. "Then he realizes he can't go out of the house for the next twenty five years. I don't think that's a real healthy existence."

America and its idols had long fascinated the Canadian who was born in Toronto to a mother of the Mohawk and Cayuga First Nations, and a wayward biological father who was American, Jewish, and a professional gambler. Robertson's own Indigenous heritage wasn't recognized by the Canadian government due to Canada's Indian Act of 1876, which determined that Robertson's mother lost her Indigenous status when she married a white man. But he spent his childhood visiting the nearby Six Nations of the Grand River reservation where his mother was born and where a lot of his extended family lived. Robertson first traveled to the United States illegally when he was seventeen years old to play in the Hawks, singer Ronnie Hawkins's backing band, and also study the South's music culture. He described stepping off a Greyhound bus in West Helena, Arkansas, on the Mississippi Delta. "It smelled different and moved different," he said. "The people talked and dressed different. And the air was filled with thick and funky music." The songwriter's aptitude for rolling handmade myths into his music was clear even then.

He soon used this inspiration for songs such as "The Night They Drove Old Dixie Down" and "Up on Cripple Creek" with the Band. In the process, he became a key progenitor for the heartland rock and Americana music genres. The collective of Canadian musicians—Robertson, Rick Danko, Garth Hudson, and Richard Manuel—and the American drummer Levon Helm, transmuted the lyrical themes and instruments of traditional American folk music, jazz, blues, and country into a singular style of 1960s rock 'n' roll, paving the way for albums by John Mellencamp, Bruce Hornsby, and others. Danko may have best summarized the symbiotic relationship between the Band and the heartland rock wave that followed when he described an interaction he had with Springsteen at the Rock & Roll Hall of Fame in Cleveland. The encounter occurred after the reformed Band, without Robertson, recorded a cover of Springsteen's "Atlantic City" for its 1993 album *Jericho*. "He jumped over about 20 people and gave me a big kiss on the cheek and said, 'Thanks so much for recording Atlantic City; I'm really proud,'" Danko said. "And I said, 'Isn't that one of our songs?'"

Robertson left the Band and never returned after he felt his creative engine blow out under the pressures of touring, fame, and drugs.

Of the decade it took to recuperate and release his new solo project, he told *Rolling Stone*, "I can't just make a record. I have to make a move." With *Tunnel of Love*, the same may be said of Bruce Springsteen. Though he once reveled in the success of *Born in the U.S.A.*, by the end of its tour he was "Bruced out." "You end up creating this sort of icon, and eventually it oppresses you," he said. For Springsteen's new work, he traveled back in time to pre-Bossmania, to "Stolen Car" from *The River*, whose main character faces "the angels and devils that will drive him toward his love and keep him from ever reaching her." Instead of searing social commentary misinterpreted as a jingoistic fight song, and tales of working class struggle in the factory and on the road, he turned his attention to the intimate spaces of home and heart. As Robertson returned to the stretch of American road he helped pave in the 1960s, one that Springsteen expanded into a four-lane highway in the '80s, The Boss parked his car in the garage and headed inside.

Robertson reconnected with his Indigenous heritage as he mined the American experience, and this soon took hold of the project's direction. Its presence is most obvious in songs such as "Broken Arrow," with lyrics woven with Indigenous symbolism, "Showdown at Big Sky," a plea to stop the nuclear arms race filtered through allusions to warring tribes, the rhythms of "Fallen Angel," a song inspired by his former bandmate Richard Manuel, who'd recently committed suicide, and "Hell's Half Acre," the story of a Native American sent to fight in Vietnam. The latter's humanistic scenes build upon the hypocrisy and despair Springsteen outlined in "Born in the U.S.A." by spotlighting a Möbius strip of exploitation. In writing about the real and imagined experiences of Indigenous people, Robertson was also sharing a part of himself. There was an intimacy to the album's tales because they had long lived inside of the singer through his mother and ancestors. "American Roulette" became a song on an album that he called by his own name.

Amplifying his Indigenous heritage was something he'd long sought to do, but Robertson "didn't feel right imposing this on The Band." Now that he no longer had a group to which he was responsible, it was only natural to express this long-simmering desire. As part of this process, he traveled to a reservation in New Mexico, where he shot the videos for "Showdown at Big Sky" and "Fallen Angel," and had what he described as a religious experience within the community. In observing and living among his extended Indigenous family, he also meditated upon the triviality of contemporary America's rat race to nowhere. Though his writing for *Robbie Robertson* was largely based on images he'd read about and observed, its making also prompted an internal awakening. As he weighed the measures of success in Reagan's America, Robertson realized how unbalanced the scale was.

In November 1987, President Reagan proclaimed the seven days around Thanksgiving "American Indian Week," stating that, "Native Americans' assistance made a significant difference for early settlers," a colonizer's perspective that ignored the waves of atrocities those settlers committed. His proclamation occurred more than a decade after the American Indian Movement (AIM) declared Thanksgiving day a National Day of Mourning. AIM also rallied against Columbus Day and the appropriation of Indigenous ceremonies such as sweat lodges and vision quests.

In March 1987, Bernie Sanders, then the mayor of Burlington, Vermont, hosted AIM leader Vernon Bellecourt, of the White Earth Band of Ojibwe in Minnesota, and a small council, in discussion. Sanders's questions covered the current state of the US-Indigenous relationship, and Bellecourt and AIM's work in Nicaragua amid the conflict between the left-wing Sandinista National Liberation Front and the US-backed Contras fighting them for control of the Nicaraguan government. Bellecourt drew parallels between the Indigenous people in the Central and North Americas and "how they evolve amid the revolutionary process." After pointing to several recent acts that encroach upon or illegally overtake tribal sovereign land in the United States, Bellecourt concluded that "the American war against the Indigenous people in the United States continues." "The people who first gave sanctuary to immigrants from all over the world who came here to flee from economic, spiritual, and political persecution in their own countries reversed their role almost immediately when the oppressed peoples of the world became the oppressor," Bellecourt said. "We as the original land holders, though we never thought we could own Mother Earth, should be doing quite well, but we're at the bottom of every economic indicator."

Bellecourt's statements arrived months before the US Supreme Court ruled that individual states could not regulate Native American gambling operations, which paved the way for the Indian Gaming Regulatory Act of 1988. Though the move helped expand access and growth for Native American casinos and other gambling operations, it did nothing to repair the systemic issues of sovereignty and equality that remained. Robertson remarked on these disparities about a decade later, in 1994, amid problems with federal encroachment on the Standing Rock reservation in the Dakotas. "All these years later and we're still fighting the same problem here," he said. "What is it going to take before people will have to respect, will have a way of honoring the original people in the way that they deserve to be honored and not say, 'You know what? Throw them a bone here. Give them a casino and maybe that'll shut them up for a while.'"

For his creative awakening, Springsteen stowed away at his home in Rumson, New Jersey. He and engineer Toby Scott built a home recording studio in an outbuilding near his garage, centered around a 24-track digital recorder Springsteen had purchased. On one end of the small room sat the large soundboard. The space's kitchen housed the tape deck. There were two microphones, some synthesizers, and no soundproofing. Springsteen often recorded with the windows open to the murmur of passing cars, the soundtrack of his life until it had been replaced by the roars of sold-out arenas.

For the making of *Tunnel of Love*, he also stepped into the domestic life of the album's central concern. During the couple of weeks that it took to create the core of the album, he woke up, worked out, and then demoed his new songs from about 1 to 6 p.m. He ate dinner each night with his wife. It was consistent but, for him, it wasn't natural. Springsteen was an obsessive, a night owl, and a loner. In an interview with VH1 that aired shortly after the album's release he said, "That was really hard to do. The minute she'd be away I'd go until midnight. Instantaneously I'd revert back to, 'Oh, what time is it?'" Such conflict paralleled the main character of the album's "Cautious Man," whose knuckles are tattooed with words "love" and "fear," and "Brilliant Disguise," an unlikely hit, whose narrative line bisects an identity crisis triggered by a relationship. With his new album, Springsteen seemed to offer himself as collateral for the shortcomings of men.

As The Boss shut out the world and leaned into a minimalist way of working, Robertson called in a fellow Canadian after meeting with a long list of potential producers. The making of *Robbie Robertson* was a protracted process that cost nearly $1 million, including the advance he received for signing with Geffen Records. For its most productive period, Robertson paired with Daniel Lanois, who'd most recently worked on Peter Gabriel's *So*. Roberton also flew in a sprawling cast of session players.

In 1987, in between sessions with Robetson, Lanois also coproduced U2's *The Joshua Tree* with English musical pioneer Brian Eno. The album marked the Irish group's turn toward American subjects, which helped transform them into international superstars. U2 had toured in the United States extensively in the first half of the 1980s, but *The Joshua Tree* marked the group's first earnest exploration of American roots music and the country's provincial experiences. As an extension of this newfound interest, the band attempted to work within traditional rock and blues-based song structures and draw on American iconography.

The Joshua Tree reflects the spirit of its mission's naivety. It is a highly tuneful tourist's diary set to modern rock music forged with cutting-edge tools. Taken as a whole, it's an incredibly pleasing pop-rock record. But there are too many synth layers, too much guitar shimmer, and too much lyrical ambiguity for it to be considered heartland rock. Not even "Heartland," which the band recorded around this time and released on its next album *Rattle & Hum*, may pass through the genre's gates. U2 was heartland rock-adjacent at a time when the movement was changing, and maybe that was a good thing for the band. *The Joshua Tree* was one of the best-selling albums of 1987, and it won the Grammy Award for Album of the Year. Its massive sound and slick veneer helped fill the arena-sized void left by Springsteen and Petty as they retreated to their quiet corners and released new albums that were markedly different from their previous work.

Lanois was a forward-thinking aesthete who sometimes framed music as "spiritual content." He was born and raised in the blue-collar enclave of Hamilton, Ontario, about forty miles southwest of Toronto, and got his start making demos for local country and bluegrass bands in a basement studio he'd built for $5,000. His folksy backstory approximated Robertson's, who'd also recently come to recognize the spiritual qualities of music.

"It's not a total coincidence that you run into an artist—there's usually some natural force that pushes you together," Lanois said. "Robbie is a very visual lyricist, which is the kind of person I gravitate towards. There's a professional relationship, but there's something beyond that. There are common ideas we share without having to talk about them." They developed an atmosphere around Robertson's roots-centric lyrics, adding layers of dreamy synthesizer and programmed drums alongside bass, traditional drums, and textural guitar. It approximates '80s era work by Sting, Peter Gabriel, and U2 with more socially conscious lyrics. Robertson also wove Indigenous rhythms into the tracks by playing cassettes of such music to the band he assembled for the sessions, with French session drummer Manu Katché supplying the groove. The idea was akin to Paul Simon's *Graceland* but with less overt appropriation. The elder's roots in the Band and interest in American roots music poked through the songs' titles and the mythical stories held within them, tales that also feel authentic, like much of the Band's work. Springsteen's *Tunnel of Love* was the inverse. His roots shown through in the album's instrumentation, a combination of blues, folk, and '60s rock music filtered through '80s production and its synthesizers.

Springsteen essentially made a solo album—the directness of

Nebraska filtered through the technological awakening of *Born in the U.S.A.*—and called on members of the E Street Band and his production team to polish the agate. Roy Bittan replaced Bruce's parts on "Brilliant Disguise" and "Tunnel of Love"; Max Weinberg drummed on three tracks and played percussion on five others. Springsteen kept a lot of Scott's drum machine programming. Clarence Clemons, Patti Scialfa, Danny Federici, Nils Lofgren, and Garry Tallent also contributed. Each member was brought in one-by-one to emphasize the intimate, solo quality of the album, instead of performing as a full band. Bob Clearmountain and Bob Ludwig mixed and mastered it. Notably absent was Steven Van Zandt, who remained focused on his own solo career, and who didn't particularly care for the album's direction. "I'm like, 'What the fuck is this?'" he told David Remnick of *The New Yorker*. "And Bruce is like, 'Well, what do you mean, it's the truth. It's just who I am, it's my life.' And I'm like, 'This is bullshit. People don't need you talking about your life. Nobody gives a shit about your life. They need you for their lives.'"

When Robertson reemerged with a contemporary vision in the Reagan era, he embraced a range of young new talent. He met Lanois in Ireland during a session for U2's *The Joshua Tree* and wrote and recorded "Sweet Fire of Love" and "Testimony" with the band. Peter Gabriel guested on keyboards and vocals on the album's opening track "Fallen Angel." Members of BoDeans supplied backing vocals on "Showdown at Big Sky," and appeared in its music video, and sang on "Somewhere Down the Crazy River" and "American Roulette." Maria McKee of Lone Justice also sang on the latter. Roberton called in Clearmountain, Springsteen's guy, to remix the album at the last minute.

Springsteen and Robertson released their new albums in October 1987, about three weeks apart from one another. Each marked a major return and were received as such. Robertson, however, was subject to the disappointment of critics and peers who'd hoped for another Americana-drenched album by the Band. These folks, like many of music's fans, preferred not to accept one of their heroes for his present-day vision. They didn't want to see him flanked by young people. Springsteen wasn't held to such scrutiny, and *Tunnel of Love* was largely well received in spite of its thematic pivot and new production style, though it sold a fraction of its predecessor.

The *Tunnel of Love* tour was also a major departure for Springsteen, filled with B-sides, album cuts, and emotional versions of his popular songs. As he shared an intimate part of himself, Springsteen also demonstrated a willingness to step into an uncertain future, where he was unafraid to speak his mind. At the tour's stop in Philadelphia, he reframed his own "Roulette" and its nuclear apocalypse paranoia as the byproduct of political leaders who "keep playing roulette with my life, roulette with my kids and wife." He also took aim at false prophets by declaring that the televangelist Pat Robertson, who was eyeing the Republican nomination for president, "can't save my soul; in fact, Pat Robertson can kiss my ass." His cover of Edwin Starr's "War" ended with the twelve-piece band repeatedly shouting the song's first two verses and Springsteen shouting back at them, "Absolutely nothing!" He performed "Born to Run" alone on an acoustic guitar because the song he'd written fifteen years earlier had come to mean something new to him. What was once about breaking free now symbolized his belief that freedom is impossible without people with whom to share that freedom. He described "Born to Run" as the companion he traveled with as he searched for such a community. With these admissions, Springsteen tore open his chest to reveal a different kind of bleeding heart. He also tore down the invincible version of himself, the rock-star facade he'd built during *Born in the U.S.A.*

After releasing *Robbie Robertson*, the musician continued to write songs reflecting his Indigenous heritage. In 1994 he issued *Music for the Native Americans*, the soundtrack of a three-part documentary series. Four years later came *Contact from the Underworld of Redboy*. For the album, Robertson combined music inspired by Aboriginal Canadian songs and chants with hip-hip, electronic, and rock sounds; its title contains an epithet directed at the musician when he was a boy. He worked on the 1998 documentary *Making a Noise: A Native American Journey with Robbie Robertson* and narrated a four-part PBS documentary, *Native America*, released in 2018. Robertson also supported the American Indian College Fund and helped expand a cultural center on Six Nations land in Brantford, Ontario. In 2017, the same year he was able to reinstate his Indigenous status in Canada, he received a Lifetime Achievement Award from the Six Nations.

About four decades after he began collaborating with Martin Scorsese, Robertson's work on film scores and soundtracks closed a full circle. In 2023, the director released *Killers of the Flower Moon*, a sweeping epic detailing the murders of Osage people in Oklahoma in the 1920s. Scorsese dedicated the film to his old friend Robbie Robertson: The former Band member composed the score for the film, but didn't live to see its release in the United States. He died on August 9, 2023.

Robertson earned his first Academy Award nomination for Best Original Score for his work on the film. "I wanted for him to go where I knew he wanted and needed to go: deep into his own heritage, his soul, and to put it out there," Scorsese said of their collaboration. "And that's what he did."

CHAPTER 9

TURNING THE TABLES

Well, who's making the rules? Who says it has to be done that way?

—LUCINDA WILLIAMS, 1988

T hough it often advocated on behalf of underdogs and the marginalized, heartland rock was largely a white, cisgender, heterosexual movement dominated by men. Throughout the 1980s, its artists and music fell comfortably within widely accepted categories, which made it appealing to mainstream audiences and listeners across social and political spectrums. Its pop-oriented accessibility also opened the door for misinterpretation as its earworm choruses, big riffs, and social and political messaging were remixed by the personal biases of its listeners. Today, such cognitive dissonance is most obvious via social media commenters who instruct the likes of Bruce Springsteen to "stick to music."

As the decade barreled toward its conclusion, the marginalized in American society made headlines. The student-lead Deaf President Now protests at Gallaudet University in Washington, DC, highlighted the pervasiveness of the problem of ableism. The private university, dedicated to the education of deaf and hard of hearing students, hired its first deaf president in 1988 in the wake of the student demonstrations. The fight began when the university's board of trustees announced that it had hired a new hearing president, rather than a deaf candidate, and the dissent marked a milestone in the rights of the deaf and hard of hearing in the United States.

More than a century after it became an enduring symbol of the labor movement in America, New York's Tompkins Square Park saw another major demonstration that included clashes with police and widespread police brutality. The 1988 Tompkins Square Park riot occurred August 6 and 7 after the city tried to enact a 1 a.m. curfew in the public park. An attempt to ward off unhoused individuals, squatters, and anarchist punks who'd taken up residence in the park following widespread gentrification in Alphabet City and the East Village, tensions escalated when police attacked residents inside and outside of the park, most of whom were protesting peacefully or were simply innocent bystanders. A year later, Lou Reed memorialized the riot in the song "Hold On" from his 1989 album *New York*.

The year also saw the emergence of Act Up—AIDS Coalition to Unlock Power—whose protesters shut down FDA headquarters in Maryland for one day in response to the agency's failure to approve medications to fight acquired immunodeficiency syndrome that was spreading throughout the country. More than one thousand members of the organization flooded the grounds of the FDA offices, holding signs that said "Federal Death Agency" and shouting chants such as "Hey, hey FDA, how many people have you killed today?" The NAMES Project AIDS Memorial Quilt also drew attention to the cause as many AIDS victims were barred from having funerals due to a widespread misunderstanding of the virus and how it spreads. In response, NAMES constructed the largest quilt on record from panels with the names of AIDS victims. Today, it stands as one of the largest pieces of community folk art in the world.

Ryan White, a teenager from Kokomo, Indiana, who was a hemophiliac, became the poster child for AIDS after he was barred from attending high school due to the condition being stigmatized and poorly understood by the American public, largely due to its association with gay men. White contracted the disease from a contaminated blood transfusion. Prominent heterosexual men such as basketball star Magic Johnson and tennis great Aurther Ashe also were diagnosed in the 1980s, and thousands from the gay community suffered without recognition from the federal government. It wasn't until actor Rock Hudson, a star of the Golden Age of Hollywood and a deeply closeted gay man, was diagnosed with AIDS, that President Ronald Reagan began to pay attention to the illness that was killing thousands of Americans. He publicly acknowledged the disease for the first time on September 17, 1985, during a press conference, shortly after Hudson announced his diagnosis to the world. This was six years after the Centers for Disease Control discovered the virus in the United States. In between those two milestones, Reagan's administration, including his press secretary Larry Speakes, joked about AIDS, calling it the "gay plague." According to the CDC, more than one hundred thousand Americans died from AIDS between 1981 and 1990.

As the AIDS crisis became top of mind for everyday Americans, especially on the first World AIDS Day, December 1 1988, few popular musicians spoke out about the issue. Pop star Madonna, a longtime ally of the LGBTQ community, was one of the first to take a stand when she released her album *Like a Prayer*. The album included an insert with a fact sheet about safe sex and AIDS, in which she noted that it was an "equal opportunity disease" and that "people with AIDS— regardless of their sexual orientation—deserve compassion and support." Elton John and George Michael, both gay men, were also at the forefront of musicians as advocates.

The first heartland rock star to take up the issue was Bruce Springsteen. In 1993, he released "Streets of Philadelphia" for director Jonathan Demme's film *Philadelphia*, in which Tom Hanks stars as Andrew Beckett, a gay man living with AIDS. The legal drama centers around Beckett's fight against his former employer, who fired him after discovering his status. Springsteen's song, a mid-tempo synth-rock ballad written from the perspective of Beckett and the thousands of other men who died from the virus, won the Oscar for Best Original Song. Demme explained in interviews that he called upon Springsteen because he wanted an artist who could reach as many people as possible, those in rural and Middle American corners, those in cities and suburbs.

"You do your best work and you hope that it pulls out the best in your audience and some piece of it spills over into the real world and into people's everyday lives. And it takes the edge off fear and allows us to recognize each other through our veil of differences," Springsteen said in his speech at the Academy's Sixty-Sixth Annual Ceremony. "I always thought that was one of the things popular art was supposed to be about, along with the merchandising and all the other stuff."

Springsteen was also at the center of the Human Rights Now concert series in 1988, organized by Amnesty International. He and the E Street Band performed at twenty dates around the world, events that aimed to raise awareness about human rights and their abuses. Attendees were encouraged to sign the Universal Declaration of Human Rights, a document authored by Eleanor Roosevelt and adopted by the United Nations General Assembly in 1948, which was passed out in native languages at each concert. Though Springsteen was the main event, he and his band were joined by other household names du jour, including Sting and Peter Gabriel. Senegalese musician Youssou N'Dour also headlined. So did a newcomer, Tracy Chapman, whose debut album garnered widespread critical acclaim and climbed album charts worldwide.

If an artist's duty is to reflect the times, then it follows that 1988 would see the greatest breakthrough in female musicians assuming command of a music genre formerly steered by men. This proved to be true as a trio of women charted the path for heartland rock's new form, integrating American tradition into singularly modern voices.

* * *

Tracy Chapman, a queer Black woman born in Cleveland, Ohio, who sprouted from the folk music scene at coffeehouses in and around Tufts University, is maybe the least obvious candidate for latter-day heartland rock star. But her self-titled debut album embraced the sounds and principles of heartland rock as it transmuted into a more mature, reflective, and instrumentally bare form. When viewed through the lens of time, Chapman may stand as a round fixture in the pegboard of the genre, even though heartland rock was strongly associated with white men in its day. Back then, the only analog rock critics managed to summon for Chapman was Joan Armatrading, another Black woman.

It's nearly impossible, however, to ignore how Chapman's musical DNA is linked to the likes of John Mellencamp. Listen to "Fast Car," the album's biggest single, which hit No. 6 on the Billboard Hot 100, for how it approximates the hardscrabble aspirations of "Jack & Diane" in a less horny and more literary sense. The song's main riff, which recalls that of Mellencamp's 1982 hit single, softens his brash electric guitar into a poignant canticle. In "Fast Car," Chapman similarly describes cycles of generational yearning, and how the pursuit of more may only lead to more of the same.

Chapman was also a less obvious voice and influence in heartland rock because she didn't adopt many of its cliches. She was reserved, and incredibly private. She didn't enjoy interviews and certainly didn't aspire to be on the cover of *Rolling Stone* or to be a star on MTV. She refused the motorcycles and Porsches and McMansions so many of the men adopted. Chapman wore mostly unassuming clothes and maintained an antimaterialism that separated her from the trappings of white male success.

In 1988, just after Mellencamp, Springsteen, and Petty had reentered the world of popular music with existential concerns and stripped-back instrumentation and production values, Chapman carried these elements to their logical next phase. She summoned heartland rock's roots in the leftist singer-songwriter music of Woody Guthrie and Bob Dylan, and paired it with highly developed social commentary about race, class, and inequality in America.

Chapman was influenced early on by her mother's roots in church as well as episodes of the television show *Hee-Haw*. She played the ukulele as a child, and her mother gave her an organ. Chapman switched to guitar in elementary school, which she found more interesting and challenging. As a student at Tufts University, she wrote songs that fell into two thematic categories: love and politics. Like most of heartland rock's cohort, she was an observer, reflecting the times through fictional and fictional-adjacent stories about everyday people. She wrote her first song, "Talking About a Revolution," a galvanizing hymn about poverty and moral revival, when she was sixteen years old.

"As a child, I always had a sense of social conditions and political situations. I think it had to do with the fact that my mother was always discussing things with my sister and me—also because I read a lot," she explained. "A lot of people in similar situations just have a sense that they're poor or disenfranchised, but they don't really think about what's created the situation or what factors don't allow them to control their lives." She received a scholarship to attend a private boarding school in Connecticut in high school due to her academic performance. This is where she first encountered singer-songwriters outside of John Denver—artists such as Dylan and Joni Mitchell—in which she heard something of herself and her perspective. Her desire to break out of the Tufts folk music scene was rooted in its homogeneity. "I want to reach beyond that," she said. "The folk circuit in Boston has mostly white performers and the clubs don't attract people from different neighborhoods. I'm hoping my record will touch a more diverse audience."

Like Dylan, Neil Young, and Tom Petty, Chapman signed with Elliot Roberts as her manager after she got her first record deal, with Elektra Records, and recorded *Tracy Chapman*. She was like those artists in that her music was arresting but not of its time. "It was exactly the same feeling when I first heard Joni Mitchell," Roberts said. "Every song was moving, every song meant something—it was all driven by passion. . . . It was totally not what's happening, but when you hear it, you go, 'That's it. That must be the new thing.'"

Tracy Chapman, with its quiet arrangements, and traditional rock instruments combined with folk flourishes such as hammered dulcimer, sitar, dobro, acoustic guitar, and big social commentary, hit No. 1 on the Billboard albums chart after it was released on April 5, 1988. She performed "Fast Car" at Nelson Mandela's seventieth birthday celebration at Wembley Stadium in London, fulfilling her mission to play to a more diverse audience. She also fulfilled one of John Mellencamp's ultimate desires: to be recognized by Prince. The Purple One covered "Fast Car" with Andy Allo of the New Power Generation in a home studio recording that was released as part of the singer's online archival "vault" series. He also channeled Chapman's quaking vocal style in his 1997 single "The Truth," a blues-drenched folk song that marked a departure from his more typical futuristic funk.

At Amnesty International's 1988 concert series Human Rights Now, Chapman stood alongside Springsteen and other powerful men as one of the era's most affecting and effective voices. During a

Tracy Chapman and Bruce Springsteen perform at Amnesty International's Human Rights Now concert in 1988.

PHOTO COURTESY MEDIAPUNCH INC.

cover of Bob Dylan's "Chimes of Freedom," Springsteen took the first verse and Chapman the second, as if passing the baton to his successor. They reunited sixteen years later at another charity concert, Vote for Change, which encouraged people in swing states to register to vote, and served as an implicit referendum on President George W. Bush and his administration. On stage in Orlando, Springsteen and Chapman sang the former's "My Hometown," a song about class struggle and the indelible links between industry and its surrounding communities.

Chapman's rise signaled modernity in a business that had long marginalized women and people of color. With female artists that emerged in the 1980s came the idea that women in music wasn't novel but a norm. "It's time to stop thinking of women in music as a trend," Bonnie Raitt declared in 1989. "I'm real encouraged by what's going on in music right now. Tracy Chapman was the most incredible thing that happened last year, and the young women singers who're coming up are fantastic, as is the return to music that goes beyond skimming the surface."

If Chapman was a nonobvious force in heartland rock in her day, an important marker of the genre and its artists' influence emerged thirty-five years later, one that solidified Chapman's status and made it more clear. In 2023, "Fast Car," long considered a lesbian power anthem and one of the most stirring and successful songs about class struggle in America, hit No. 2 on the Billboard Hot 100 singles chart, and went to No. 1 on the Adult Contemporary, Country Airplay, and Hot Country Songs charts. It also reached the top of Canada's country music chart. Thirty-five years after she first released the song, Chapman became the first Black person to have a No. 1 country single with a solo composition. She was also the first to win the Country Music Association Award for Song of the Year. This is because Luke Combs, a thirty-something white male heterosexual country singer from North Carolina, covered "Fast Car" and propelled Chapman's signature to renewed heights.

Combs released his twangy version on his fourth studio album, *Gettin' Old*. The singer had long covered the tune in concert because

"Fast Car" was one of the first songs he learned to play after he bonded with his dad over it when he was a child. In interviews, Combs held it up as the soundtrack of fond memories, and how music may serve as connective tissue and a family heirloom passed from one generation to the next. Until this point, legions of blockbuster country music stars had cited their love of Mellencamp, Springsteen, Seger, Raitt, and Petty. With his cover of "Fast Car," Combs became the first country star to herald Chapman in a very public and affecting way. His tribute had the effect of eclipsing all previous connections between heartland rock and modern country music. His "Fast Car" was a runaway success. It was also unprecedented.

Given the country music world's legacy of discrimination and gatekeeping, it took the allyship of a powerful young white man for Chapman to achieve something she may have never been afforded on her own. There is little evidence to disprove this. Taken another way, Combs's "Fast Car" is a testament to the younger generations of country musicians who want to change the genre's track record—if by no other means than the adoration and amplification of artists that the industry has marginalized by default. Combs's particular age and perspective formed the valve through which "Fast Car" could be poured into country music radio, streaming, and mainstream fans in the new millennium. Most importantly, the song's success in the new millennium is a testament to Chapman's singular artistry and ability to crystallize the trials of the working class in such a relatable, moving, and enduring way. In the 1980s she set out to reach a wider listenership. In the 2020s, she continued to do just that.

Chapman appeared with Combs at the Recording Academy's sixty-sixth awards ceremony on February 4, 2024, where the latter's cover of "Fast Car" was nominated for a Grammy for Best Country Solo Performance. Together they performed the song that brought each of them widespread acclaim, she with an acoustic guitar and he with in-ear monitors, trading verses and summoning the spirit of the Springsteen-Chapman collabs of yore. Flanked by pedal steel guitar and fiddle, the spare country flourishes Combs had added in his version, the two exchanged glowing looks that radiated warmth and gratitude. Pop star Taylor Swift, who won two of her fourteen total Grammys that year, stood up in the audience as if by amazement, belting out the song's lyrics for all to see.

★ ★ ★

As Tracy Chapman topped the charts with her staggering debut, another queer female musician who spent time performing in Boston made her way into the scene. Melissa Etheridge was born and raised in a small town in Kansas, a place fueled by the prison industrial complex. Leavenworth, which has a population that hovers around thirty-five thousand, is located on the banks of the Missouri River near Kansas City, and is surrounded by correctional facilities: a US federal penitentiary, two disciplinary barracks and a regional correctional facility at Ft. Leavenworth, and the nearby Lansing Correctional Facility.

For many young people, growing up in a small Midwestern town can be constraining at best. Imagine how much more acute it must feel when the town is surrounded by actual prisons? "The Federal Penitentiary had a dome, so it always looked like the Capitol Building as far as I was concerned," Etheridge wrote of her childhood. The proximity of these facilities, and her neighbors who worked in them, had the effect of normalizing what would be abnormal in most other communities.

Etheridge became enamored with music at a young age through discovering the Beatles and listening to AM radio and her parents' records. She began playing guitar when she was eight years old, and was twelve when she started performing in local groups at bars, and at dances, retirement homes, and prisons in variety shows. Bruce Springsteen was an early influence. By the time she was eighteen, she knew that being a musician was the only thing she'd ever want to do. She was accepted into the prestigious Berklee College of Music in Boston, and moved to the East Coast. She lasted three semesters, and played in area restaurants in her free time, singing Barry Manilow medleys at haunts like Ken's Steakhouse. Not exactly a pinnacle of artistic expression. She then dropped out, moved to Kansas City for a little while, and then headed to Los Angeles to try to forge a career.

In the time that Etheridge was born, raised, and inched toward adulthood, the prison population in America more than doubled. This was especially true under the Reagan administration and its war on drugs that disproportionately targeted Black communities. When Reagan took office in 1980, 329,000 Americans were serving sentences in prisons across the nation. When he left office on January 20, 1989, there were more than 600,000—a dramatic increase that inspired the term "mass incarceration." Soon, America held the dishonorable distinction of being No. 1 in the world when it comes to jailing its citizens.

The US prison population increased by 7.4 percent in 1988 alone, which created a demand for more than 800 new prison beds per week. Most jurisdictions operated above their reported capacity, and many state inmates were held in local jails due to overcrowding in state-level prisons. Between 1986 and 1996, the number of women incarcerated for drug offenses increased by 888 percent; most of them from impoverished backgrounds. On November 18, President Reagan signed the Anti Drug Abuse Act of 1988 with remarks lauding First Lady Nancy Reagan's work in the administration's crusade for a drug-free America. "This bill helps us close rank on those who continue to provide drugs," the president explained of the legislation. "Arrests, convictions, and prison sentences of sellers and abusers are rising to record levels."

In 1970, when Etheridge was eight years old and beginning to play guitar, Johnny Cash made a stop at the Leavenworth Federal Penitentiary. He was there to perform for 1,200 inmates, just as he'd done during his famous concert at Folsom State Prison in California two years earlier. "This is the same show we did for President Nixon, but we're going to try a little harder here," he told the crowd of onlookers. "I thought, 'Prisons must be a place to find entertainment!' You know, a goal of mine was to perform at a prison," Etheridge explained years later. As a teenager she learned that few musicians actually toured prisons, as Cash had, and she felt a strange honor when the variety shows she was part of played each penitentiary within range of her hometown.

In the '80s, Etheridge got a foothold in the Los Angeles music scene by playing at area lesbian bars, where everyone knew she was gay. A bootleg recording from 1983 captured her cover of John Mellencamp's "Pink Houses." A couple of years later, she was discovered by a manager at a bar in Pasadena, California, and signed by Chris Blackwell of Island Records months later. By then, Leavenworth was but a memory for the singer, and becoming a rock star was a real possibility. Her debut self-titled album was released in May 1988 and its singles, "Like the Way I Do" and "Bring Me Some Water," were inspired by hot-burning relationships, their kindling and extinguishing, and the passions, jealousies, and infidelities that burn within them. Like all of the biggest names in heartland rock, Etheridge seemed to channel the voices of the radical '60s as a kind of lineage through which she was formed. She became known as the next Janis Joplin, and a belter in the school of Tina Turner. She was also a skilled guitar player, wielding the instrument with the power of a gale force wind.

Melissa Etheridge was also uninhibited in its queerness. Though Etheridge herself didn't publicly come out until 1993, a scan of the lyrics reveals no mention of men and their pronouns, and frequent references to female lovers. As she earned comparisons to historical female rock belters, Etheridge was also embraced by male heartland rock figures. Her first major tour was as the opening act for Bruce Hornsby and the Range. "Bring Me Some Water" fell into heavy rotation on Cleveland's WMMS, the same station that helped launch Bruce Springsteen in the 1970s. The station was so integral to the dissemination of her first single that Etheridge stuck a WMMS sticker on her guitar case.

Melissa Etheridge is steeped in tales of love and betrayal, but its sixth song called back to the singer's formative years in Kansas. Her debut was undoubtedly of the "I'm on Fire" school of Bruce Springsteen, but "The Late September Dogs" intimated where she fit among the next wave of heartland rock. In interviews from the time of the album's release, Etheridge cited it as her favorite song on the album. It's also the song that most clearly evinced Springsteen's *Nebraska* in its ghostly emoting about Middle American landscapes and the poetry the area conjures. Its central theme is about growing up, and saying goodbye. Writing it, she has said, offered a "moment of acceptance, releasing things I held on so tightly to." In this spare meditation, the howl of a nearby canine is a welcome companion when faced with intense loneliness, menacing changes, or both.

Etheridge's heartland rock strands wove into a fat braid as the years wore on. Her second album, *Brave and Crazy*, released the following year, was even sharper in its imagistic yearning, recounting vast landscapes and open roads and the hearts that travel across them. "All American Girl," from her 1993 blockbuster album *Yes I Am*, traces directly to Tom Petty in its guitar tones and paean to young women raised on promises, the seekers who desire more than life has given them. In 1995, she released the song "Nowhere to Go," which describes two lovers packing up some cheap wine, and steering a Chevrolet past a Wal-Mart and a prison to an empty boxcar where they can be alone. Four years later, she remixed John Mellencamp's tale of rural plight with her own "Scarecrow," which told the story of Matthew Shepard, a twenty-one-year-old student at the University of Wyoming who was kidnapped, tortured, and murdered for being gay. Six years later, on a greatest hits compilation titled *The Road Less Traveled*, Etheridge released the only cover she ever included on one of her albums: her version of Tom Petty and the Heartbreakers' "Refugee."

Unlike Tracy Chapman, whose private life has largely stayed that way, Etheridge has been outspoken about her identity. She came out when such a move was still considered career suicide. "I'm proud to have been a lesbian all my life," she told a roaring crowd as she hugged the singer K. D. Lang at the Triangle Ball, an LGBTQ-focused event that was part of President Bill Clinton's inaugural celebration. Seven years later, she spoke out against California's Proposition 22, which banned state recognition of same-sex marriages. Photos from her 2014 wedding to the actor Linda Wallem were splashed all over magazines.

Melissa Etheridge performing just before her breakthrough album *Yes I Am* was released.

PHOTO COURTESY ZUMA PRESS, INC.

In 2023, a theater production, "My Window," about her life and music, ran on Broadway.

If 1988 was the Year of the Woman in heartland rock, Etheridge stood out for her sheer ferocity, and that reputation grew as time went on. Like Janis Joplin, she didn't differentiate between male and female energies, and she was in fact ready for that binary to disappear altogether when it came to the evaluation of art within gendered categories. "I think this will be the year that everyone is talking about gender and that maybe it will break down the male/female categories from here on," she said shortly after her debut album was released. Her voice was more raspy and powerful than Bob Seger's. Her guitar playing stood alongside Mike Campbell. Her energy and endurance on stage rivaled Springsteen and Mellencamp. Chris Blackwell, head of her label Island Records, said in a 1988 interview that he believed that Etheridge was actually going to be the contemporary analog to Springsteen.

The Boss has long highlighted the ties between industry and its neighboring communities, but his songs such as "Factory," "Badlands," "My Hometown," and "Youngstown" largely narrate the struggles of blue-collar men, and how their livelihoods and sense of masculinity suffer from unemployment, exploitation, and the aftereffects of war. If Etheridge was carrying Springsteen's torch throughout her career, it was in honor of queer and incarcerated women who shaped her in obvious and implied ways. Writing about the first time she performed at a women's prison as a child, Etheridge said, "I remember standing on stage, staring out at the inmates, and thinking, 'What are all these men doing in a women's prison?' It took a while for me to realize that they were women. And once I had that realization, I was curious about them. Interested. Not on a conscious level, of course, but there was something going on in that prison that fascinated me." Near the mid '90s, after she'd won Grammys and topped charts, Etheridge began speaking about her desire to perform concerts at women's prisons. "I'm trying to get something together with some women performers I know to go to this women's prison in Virginia," she told *The Kansas City Star* in 1994. "It has a woman warden, all women staff, and it's the oldest women's prison." In 2015, she performed to thousands of women at the Ohio Reformatory for Women near Columbus.

Her desire to aid incarcerated women culminated in 2024 with the release of *I'm Not Broken*, a streaming docuseries in which Etheridge writes a new song inspired by five incarcerated women in Topeka, Kansas. The singer communicated with the women through writing letters, and then debuted the song during a concert she performed for all women imprisoned at the Topeka Correctional Facility—elder butch women with tattoos and buzzcuts, Gen X and Millennial women with wrinkles and French braids, young women who didn't know anything about Etheridge and her music. Throughout the two-part series, Etheridge discusses her son's death from an opioid overdose, and, with the five women with whom she corresponded, explores the cycles of trauma and incarceration associated with addiction. It is an uplifting if glossy portrayal of life in prison, institutions that have long been rife with negligence, abuses of power, and overcrowding.

"Growing up in Leavenworth, the prison loomed. You could see it right from my backyard," Etheridge explains in the doc. With *I'm Not Broken*, Etheridge completed the circle from her childhood visions of Johnny Cash and his prison concerts to a present-day reality where her fame and advocacy could spotlight a population that is often left behind.

★ ★ ★

When Springsteen and Mellencamp released their ascetic, blues-indebted tributes to life's great trials in 1987, Lucinda Williams had already lived alongside the actual blues. The Louisiana-born singer and songwriter was afforded a more worldly and literary upbringing than those two men, due to her father's position in academia and her parents' general bohemian outlook; like the icons of heartland rock, however, she also experienced her fair share of family dysfunction—divorce, mental illness, and alcoholism. Williams's distinctive singing voice was long a proper vehicle for such tormented sentiments, its fictile drawl like a soul-cleansing drag through the mud. Williams's career infancy was marked by the sounds and themes that Mellencamp adopted later in his career, such as traditional folk instruments and the stricken howls of country blues traditions. For as long as *The Lonesome Jubilee* has been heralded as the gate that flung open to welcome the Americana genre, Williams has been obscured as its rightful architect, and the kind of artist Mellencamp strove to be.

By the time she was a teenager, Williams's father taught in the MFA program at the University of Arkansas, and his home became the hub of literary debauchery in the 1970s. Its party reputation was so infamous that the likes of Charles Bukowski joined in on the drinking, drugs, and sex when he was in town. Williams set out on her own in her late teens, moving to New Orleans where her mother lived. She began performing in a local club, and enduring a lingering guilt born of a Christian upbringing that kicked against her desire to embrace the blues tradition's acceptance of the whole of one's life, its light and shadow sides. As she became enamored with Black musicians such as Memphis Minnie and Nina Simone, she endeavored a path that was circuitous, and rife with false starts and unending desire.

Ramblin' On My Mind, Williams's first album released in 1979, was a collection of blues and classic country cover songs by artists such as Hank Williams, Robert Johnson, and Sleepy John Estes. It was born of her time as an acoustic guitar toting singer-songwriter playing Southern clubs, a chanteuse of the wandering order. *Happy Woman Blues*, released in 1980, was composed of eleven originals that fused country, folk, and traditional blues sounds and sentiments with rock 'n' roll energy. It was closer to what she actually wanted to be—a rock musician in the Southern literary tradition. Both were released through the traditionalist label Smithsonian Folkways, and were steeped in the kind of earthbound trials that would come to mark pretty-boy heartland rockers' latter-day careers. Williams amplified her love of Black bluesmen long before John Mellencamp's smoking had pummeled his voice into a graveled snarl in the new millennium, and he began releasing albums filled with slide guitar and Delta-born truisms. Williams's first two albums were critically acclaimed but sold little.

In 1983 she traveled to New York to record demos. The hope was to create something that expressed her breadth of musical capabilities, and that would venture her first two folk-steeped albums into something like a career. She was tired of holding down jobs at book stores and restaurants as she wrote, recorded, and released albums. Contrary to most apocryphal origin stories in which down-and-out white songwriters are lifted up by some form of benevolent white patron—a manager, a family friend, a record scout who happened to wander into the shack where they sang—Williams was aided by a local enthusiast of a different stripe.

She befriended Hobart Taylor as a performer in Houston in the early '80s, when unknowns such as Lyle Lovett and Nanci Griffith were kicking around area dives. The son of a long line of Black family farmers in Texas, of the few who managed to hold onto their land, Taylor inherited a considerable sum when his father died, and he used $25,000 of it to fund Williams's recording session. He also became her manager. The money allowed her to hire such luminaries as T Bone Burnett and David Mansfield to play on the sessions, but record companies told her she was too rock for country and too country for rock. So she did what anyone in such a position would. She moved to Los Angeles, with the help of Taylor, the only place at the time where those two genres mingled in a prevalent way.

In the City of Angels, she trod many of the same paths as those forging the cowpunk scene, plus Dwight Yoakam and the coterie of jangle-pop musicians known at the paisley underground. She even recorded more demos, with Yoakam's longtime producer and guitarist Pete Anderson, which she scrapped in the end because she thought they were overproduced. Williams worked local clubs such as the legendary honky-tonk the Palomino, Al's Bar, and Raji's, an enigma in Hollywood that fused Middle Eastern culture with underground rock bands. In the process, she was passed on by a host of record labels. Columbia Records ultimately offered Williams a development deal, much as her friend and manager Taylor had. She took their $30,000 and got to work. In the end, however, Columbia was yet another echo in the chamber of industry men who were uncomfortable with the fact that Williams's art was difficult to position. The label's Los Angeles arm explained that she was too country for the rock world, and the label's Nashville office offered the inverse.

"Rough Trade caught me just before I headed off into the hills," she told a reporter for England's *New Musical Express* shortly after the release of *Lucinda Williams*, her debut for the label, released late in 1988. The punk rock label founded in 1976 by an English record store nerd seemed an unlikely fit for Williams's wayward Southern apologism, but luckily for the singer-songwriter, they signed her with an equally punk rock approach, immediately and without an in-person audition. "Now, that's unheard of in LA," she said. "I'd sent off so many demo tapes and listened to so many A&R men asking

me for yet another demo tape, that I'd reached the end of the line."
Williams had more in common with John Mellencamp than may be
understood: *American Fool* was also released by a British label, Riva
Records, after most other American record labels failed to see Mellencamp's promise.

After a long line of A&R men couldn't typecast her art, *Lucinda
Williams* offered an antidote to that line of thinking. Williams had long
sought to be a literary rock artist, even as she was starting off as an
acoustic guitar-wielding singer-songwriter in New Orleans dives. Dylan
had gone electric, and the Pretenders and its husky-voiced front woman
had become a mainstream success. Williams had long sensed there was
a way to amalgamate those postures. With *Lucinda Williams*, she'd
finally done it, and on the same record label as the Smiths, Cabaret Vol-
taire, and Stiff Little Fingers. "At the heart of what I do is rock 'n' roll and
punk," she later reflected. "Hank Williams was a punk, but I have just as
much in common with Shane MacGowan of the Pogues."

Lucinda Williams, a rock album with distinct country and blues
flavors, wove seamlessly into heartland rock's striving narratives; but
Williams singularly lined them with an unmistakable sense of female
desire in a kind of spiritual invocation. In "The Night's Too Long,"
we meet Sylvia, a waitress in Texas, who is unabashed in her hunger
for a faster way of life, one with better clothes and sexier men. "I Just
Wanted to See You So Bad" and "Passionate Kisses" were similarly
bare in their thirst, with female narrators who insisted upon the things
that they deserve: a comfortable bed, alone time, creative freedom, a
killer band, good sex, the autonomy to drive her car down a highway
in the middle of the night if she so desired. In "Change the Locks," she
flipped that script. Here we find the narrator protecting herself by any
means possible, demonstrating her right to say no to the thing that no
longer served her. Through the album sprouts heartland rock's favored
imagery: open roads and fields, underdogs who strive for more, the
small towns and small-town people who dot our everyday lives. It was
a work so indicative of what the singer had long envisioned that she
released it under her own name.

The album was placed at No. 16 on the Village Voice year-end Pazz & Jop critics poll, with Robert Christgau writing that Williams is "so at home in blues and country that she won't abide a rock and roll pigeonhole, and she can make a winner out of any song that spurns the cliches she's too avid and sensible to resort to. Why any record man would want to order her around I can only guess. Maybe because she seems just an inch's compromise away from a hit. But that inch is why this rock and roll traditionalist still sounds fresh." In its review of the album, *Rolling Stone* remarked that Williams's raw recording style "lets you hear plenty of human frailties. If that means an occasional tentative vocal or an awkwardly blunt line, it also helps reinforce the feeling that you're listening to a singer who is simply telling you the truth about herself."

In the Year of the Woman—a double-edged sword—much was made of the fact that Williams had forged a career largely on her own terms. News coverage from the time focused on the fact that she produced her own record, had spent much of her life touring, led bands filled with men, and was a woman. Williams, they seemed to say, was an exception to Reagan's prevailing narrative that women belong in the home, as if she was a rare coin or mythical creature, or someone who should care about the president's prescriptions. "They make such a big deal out of it," she told one interviewer with an audible sigh.

The album garnered enough attention that the major labels that once shunned Williams returned to bend a knee. But it would take another decade for her to find mainstream success. In 1998, at age forty-five, she released *Car Wheels on a Gravel Road*, coproduced by Steve Earle, his right-hand man Ray Kennedy, and Roy Bittan of the E Street Band. This marked her true commercial breakthrough, winning her a Grammy and the top position on many year-end polls. In the immediate wake of this album's success, Williams reissued her 1988 gem, *Lucinda Williams*, with bonus tracks. She wanted to make sure her new listeners knew where her vision was first realized.

The following year Tom Petty, one of her idols, someone she'd long considered spiritual kin, invited Williams to open dates with him and the Heartbreakers, on a tour in support of the band's final collaboration with producer Rick Rubin, *Echo*. He'd covered Williams's "Change the Locks" on the 1996 album *Songs and Music from She's the One*. As his single, it reached No. 20 on the Mainstream Rock Songs chart. Though the collaboration was a thrill, Petty's audiences weren't always friendly or even patient. Aware of this trend after a few of the shows, Petty walked on stage with Williams and insisted that his fans listen to her. "It just blew my mind, but that gives you an idea of the kind of person he was," she said. That was also the start of a growing friendship. Petty invited Williams to be part of his ASCAP Songwriters Hall of Fame induction and the celebration of Petty being named MusiCare's Person of the Year.

In 2003, Mellencamp showed the world just how much he admired Williams. For his last album with Columbia Records, one of the labels that told Williams she was too country for rock and too rock for country, he covered "Lafayette" from her album *Happy Woman Blues*. *Trouble No More*, Mellencamp's covers album of traditional blues songs, was the result of months of study, with the singer collaborating with the Smithsonian and Columbia's catalog division to release it. With his CD changer loaded with historical recordings, he happened upon Williams's tune on a compilation. "And thank God we recorded that song," he said. "It was the only light-hearted song on the whole record." She played Farm Aid the following year, and opened the Hoosier's North American tour in 2008.

Williams met Bruce Springsteen backstage in Los Angeles during his 2005 *Devils & Dust* tour, and the pair traded compliments, remarking on one another's bravery. Nearly twenty years later, Springsteen and his wife Patti Scialfa provided backing vocals on the lead single, "New York Comeback," from Williams's fifteenth studio album, as well as on its title track. *Stories from a Rock N Roll Heart*, released in 2023, calls directly to the young woman who was far ahead of the folkie-chanteuse the music industry made her out to be in the early '80s. Williams wanted to be a rock 'n' roller long before she was allowed to be one. Decades later, she towered among them, a goddess among men.

* * *

By the time George H. W. Bush won the 1988 presidential election against Democratic nominee Michael Dukakis, Bonnie Raitt had gotten sober. Her album *Nine Lives* had been a commercial failure, peaking at No. 115 on the Billboard 200; but it did earn her a Grammy Award nomination for her performance of "No Way to Treat a Lady," written by Bryan Adams and Jim Vallance. With the song, Raitt was added to the list of hopefuls in the Best Rock Vocal Performance, Female category. She lost to Tina Turner. Worse was that Raitt was no longer represented by a record label. Warner Bros. had dropped her.

What seemed like rock bottom actually had a silver lining. In December 1986, shortly after her thirty-seventh birthday, Raitt headlined the Beverly Theater in Los Angeles in support of *Nine Lives*. As it turned out, one of her biggest fans was in the audience. "Prince called me up and said, 'Hey you know you weren't treated right, come on over to Paisley Park, let's make a record together,'" Raitt recalled. He also offered her the opportunity to be an artist on his record label, Paisley Park Records, which was distributed by Warner Bros.

Prince sent his private limo for Raitt soon after, which was filled with purple baubles and lighting. They agreed to collaborate on a new album in which their styles would meld—Raitt's blues-fortified guitar scorchers and Prince's visionary electronic funk. Raitt was to travel to Paisley Park in January 1987, but a skiing accident that injured her finger compelled a delay. It also forced her to slow down and reflect on her life. "For a long time I had this rock and roll mama persona," she said. "But as I got older, drugs and alcohol weren't working—they beat you up too much." She was overweight and unhappy and longed for a change. With the help of Alcoholics Anonymous and a few supportive friends, she quit drinking, and began exercising. In April, she flew to Minneapolis.

The basic tracks for most of the songs were done by the time she arrived. Prince had written some songs with her in mind, but she had the space to make updates or change their key as needed. She spent one day working directly with him and another with her guitar and Prince's engineer. After the short visit, the plan was to reconvene in July after the Purple One's European tour. But that window overlapped with Raitt's touring schedule, and then Prince's tour went longer than he expected it to. Their project simply fizzled out.

Raitt had flown to meet Prince pleased that she'd lost twenty pounds. Had their collaboration been fruitful, she would've been more confident than ever to appear in a music video with the petite pop star. Instead, she took her new conviction on the road, playing a series of stripped-back acoustic sets and charity concerts. Raitt was one of few American artists chosen to play a festival in the Soviet Union aimed at promoting a cultural exchange between the two countries. She also appeared at a benefit for refugees from El Salvador in Oakland, California, alongside Boz Scaggs, Jerry Garcia and Bob Weir of the Grateful Dead, and others.

In September 1987 she sang as a backing vocalist at "Roy Orbison and Friends: A Black and White Night." It was the icon's first televised performance since his meteoric comeback spurred by Van Halen's cover of "Oh, Pretty Woman," and the use of his song "In Dreams" in David Lynch's film *Blue Velvet*. Raitt sang alongside K. D. Lang, Jackson Browne, and others, while Bruce Springsteen, Tom Waits, Elvis Costello, J. D. Souther, and T Bone Burnett each performed with Orbison as a sort of collective. Many consider the special, which originally aired on the Cinemax cable network, the greatest ad hoc collaborative performance since *The Last Waltz*.

If Raitt was reeling, it wasn't evident to the outside world. Her spare touring setup, composed of Johnny Lee Schell on bass and electric guitar, and herself on acoustic guitar, received positive reviews and drew the attention of Don Was, a fledgling producer and cofounder of the eccentric art-funk band Was (Not Was). He suggested she make an album closer to the bone, something simpler that harkened to her earlier career, much like the sound she'd been touring. After working together on a series of children's songs for various productions, the pair clicked and agreed to forge ahead as a team. They recorded a couple of demos at Was's home studio and, soon after, Raitt's new manager Danny Goldberg helped her land a new deal with Capitol Records. It seemed Raitt had far more than nine lives. She reentered the recording studio with Was in the fall of 1988.

Her collaboration with Prince was never properly released, but the curious may find one track on YouTube. The Minnesotan originally wrote "I Need a Man" for a girl group he called the Hookers, which never materialized. On Raitt's version, recorded on April 3, 1987, her honeyed if hesitant vocal coats the song's thumping bass, trumpet and saxophone stabs, and gated drum sound. Ultimately, the collaboration doesn't translate as two worlds melding into a seamless new sound. What it sounds like is Bonnie Raitt singing Prince's libidinous lyrics over Prince's pop-funk composition.

As that recording lay fallow, Prince's estate released his solo version in 2020, on the super-deluxe reissue of his album *Sign o' the Times*. About a woman who openly desires hot sex over money and fame, the second verse of "I Need a Man" describes the status symbols that are unimportant to its narrator. She rebuffs fancy cars like a Mercedes Benz, and also the idea that money can stand in for masculinity. She describes how little this man's powerful friends mean to her: specifically, Bruce Springsteen.

CHAPTER 10

THE STORM AHEAD

We got a kinder, gentler machine gun hand.

—NEIL YOUNG

George H. W. Bush was inaugurated as the forty-first president of the United States on January 20, 1989. After serving two terms as Reagan's vice president, the Republican defeated his Democratic challenger Michael Dukakis, then the governor of Massachusetts, winning both the electoral college and the popular vote. NBC News anchor Tom Brokaw called it one of the "longest, bloodiest presidential campaigns that anyone can remember."

The anchor's comment arrived in the wake of what is widely viewed as the first modern-day negative campaign, orchestrated by the political operative Lee Atwater, a dark political force in the 1980s. He once called his fight against Dukakis as Bush's campaign manager an effort to "strip the bark off the little bastard." In July 1988, Dukakis led Bush by about 17 points. Less than four months later, he lost to the former vice president 54 to 46 percent.

The nominee began his turnaround by giving a fiery speech at the

Republican National Convention that August. In it he referred to himself as someone "who believes it is a scandal to give a weekend furlough to a hardened, first-degree killer who hasn't even served enough time to be eligible for parole." Then Republicans hammered Dukakis, who'd supported such a program, with the story of Willie Horton, a Black man who raped a white woman from Maryland and stabbed her boyfriend while on a furlough from a Massachusetts prison. The strategy began with Atwater, who said that he was going to make Horton "a household name" and also make him Dukakis's "running mate." Atwater also sought to frame Dukakis, the son of working-class Greek immigrants, as weak. At Atwater's suggestion, President Reagan called the governor an "invalid." The Republican operative also seeded questions about Dukakis's mental health in the press.

The Bush campaign ran advertisements decrying prison furlough programs, which were meant to help ease an inmate's transition into society, but became a hotly debated subject. A Republican political action committee made the boldest appeal to racist fears about crime with a thirty-second political ad it called "Weekend Passes." It focused solely on Horton by displaying a photo of him glowering with narration that described his heinous crimes against the Maryland couple. Political analysts said that the Bush campaign's strategy evoked racist stereotypes, stoked division, and disenfranchised Black Americans. The civil rights leader Jesse Jackson, who had campaigned for the Democratic nomination in 1988, and was endorsed by Bonnie Raitt and Bob Seger, criticized its dog whistles. "There are those who use these signals to reinforce the worst fears of people," he said. "That is beneath the dignity of a presidential campaign in our country."

Today, the name Willie Horton is shorthand for racist campaign tactics that have become only more sinister in the new millennium. Atwater's work on the Bush campaign became so notorious that in 1991, shortly before he died from a brain tumor, he apologized to Dukakis for its "naked cruelty." If the Bush presidential run marked a grim turn in American politics, one it would never really recover from, it also had a way of foreshadowing the underlying sentiment of American popular culture in the early 1990s. Soon, the earnest left-wing populism of 1980s rock stars would cede to postures of despair, angst, and outright nihilism in popular culture and beyond. Bush would lead America into the Gulf War in Iraq in August 1990. Pessimism would become fashionable.

In 1989, after "The Boys of Summer" became a hit, Don Henley grew a little ponytail and released a fitting introduction to the new American order. The Eagles drummer cowrote and coproduced "The End of the Innocence" with Bruce Hornsby, whose radiant piano playing throughout the song is unmistakable. Henley was the first big name to contact Hornsby after his 1986 album with the Range took off, and the pair's collaboration ensued much as "The Boys of Summer" had. Hornsby gave Henley some music he'd written and filed away. Henley responded to it immediately and quickly summoned lyrics that surveyed childhood nostalgia and the difficulty of grown-up life. The collaboration became the title track of Henley's third solo album, and it won Henley a Grammy for Best Rock Vocal Performance, Male.

Henley's new song was particularly biting in its portrayal of opportunistic politicians and their henchmen, and he ensured that message was abundantly clear in its accompanying music video. Directed by David Fincher years before he helmed *Alien 3*, "The End of the Innocence" video includes a series of images of Ronald Reagan campaign posters, and footage of Oliver North's congressional testimony related to the Iran-Contra affair. All of this is corrupt, is what Henley wanted America to know, as Bush promised to continue Reagan's policies.

His new album also featured a familiar cast, including Stan Lynch of the Heartbreakers, who received three cowriting credits, including the album's second single, "The Last Worthless Evening." Heartbreaker Mike Campbell returned to collaborate with Henley and J. D. Souther on "The Heart of the Matter," the album's third single. Though it became the best-selling solo album of Henley's career, and peaked at No. 8 on the Billboard albums chart, *The End of the Innocence* lost Album of the Year Grammy to Bonnie Raitt. For his part,

Tom Petty earned two nominations in the same category for his work released in 1989, but also lost to the woman who'd long struggled to find respectable support in the industry.

★ ★ ★

Sudden changes in life, work, and country can feel like a storm whose whims are impossible to withstand. For Tom Petty, an actual storm hit at a tender point in his life, and changed the course of his career. On October 15, 1987, when he was on tour with Bob Dylan and playing Wembley Stadium in London, a wave cyclone struck the United Kingdom in an unexpected weather event known as the Great Storm. Petty soon took it for a sign for what followed: a series of fortuitous introductions and fast friendships. As these events unfolded, he stepped away from the band he'd known for most of his life. Then, in 1989, he released two of the best albums he ever would, aided by some of his old friends in the Heartbreakers, but largely without their input.

One of those new albums began with a feverish writing streak and Jeff Lynne of the English progressive-pop act Electric Light Orchestra. The pair didn't know they were neighbors until they ran into one another at a stoplight on Thanksgiving, and then again at a chic LA restaurant. Soon, they were collaborating on "Yer So Bad" and "Free Fallin'," two singles from Petty's first solo album, *Full Moon Fever.*

The move came as a shock. Petty was a man who'd long positioned himself within the communal energy of a band. He was a leader who steered his merry men from Florida's southern wilds to the world's biggest stages, and to exit this kind of social banditry was to be an entirely new person nearly twenty years into his career. For anyone paying close-enough attention, however, the writing was on the wall. For years Petty had been working to push his art further and inject a new energy into the Heartbreakers' dynamic. *Southern Accents, Let Me Up (I've Had Enough),* and the group's tours with Dylan were evidence of that. And there is perhaps no better excuse to start over than an arsonist burning down his house, which happened in May 1987, followed by the freak storm during a concert that happened about six months later. His foundation had been shattered. In a deck of rock 'n' roll tarot, Petty had pulled the Tower card.

He and Lynne knew "Free Fallin'" was special and soon headed to Mike Campbell's home studio in Los Angeles to record it over the Christmas holiday of 1987. The place was so small that they kept the console and related equipment in a bedroom, and performed in the garage. It wasn't unlike Springsteen's setup for *Tunnel of Love*. Phil Jones, a friend who'd appeared on Heartbreakers albums and 1981 tour, played drums while Lynne played bass. The ad hoc crew then tracked "Yer So Bad." Petty and Lynne quickly wrote "I Won't Back Down," which became the lead single on his solo debut, in a teensy booth in Campbell's studio. George Harrison, who Petty had connected with during the stormy show in London, and who'd worked with Lynne on his 1987 album *Cloud Nine*, stopped by to help them record it, and added acoustic guitar and vocals. Petty added the same, and Campbell played electric guitar. It all rolled out like a burst of magic.

The collaboration was so unexpected and easygoing that Petty convinced Lynne to stay on for a whole record, and they worked at breakneck speed, with the pair of them, plus Campbell, writing and recording the rest of its songs in mere weeks. The only thing Petty had pre-written was its ninth track, "The Apartment Song." The blonde bandleader originally planned to call his new work "Songs From the Garage," but decided it was too good for such an unassuming title. He landed on *Full Moon Fever* as a nod to the creative charge he felt during its making, among new friends and colleagues.

Petty's journey near the end of the 1980s didn't stop at one record. In a plot twist that is all but inconceivable, the same winter break saw Roy Orbison joining up with the new Petty-Lynne-Harrison crew. The rock 'n' roll icon moved to Malibu in 1986 as he mounted a career comeback, and was happy to fall in with the younger crowd of successful musicians. Petty, Lynne, and Orbison wrote the latter's 1989 hit "You Got It" during one of their first encounters, and similarly recorded the tune at Mike Campbell's house. George Harrison provided backing vocals and acoustic guitar uncredited. Phil Jones played drums.

The idea for a supergroup began when Harrison conceived of a band called the Traveling Wilburys during his sessions with Lynne, who supported his idea. At the root of the project lay a desire to be in a band, something Harrison hadn't done since the Beatles broke up in 1970. Contrary to that group's tensions, however, the former Beatle wanted to focus on joy, fun, and camaraderie. He wanted to write good songs and summon excellent performances in a no-pressure environment and for the sake of making art. The group materialized after *Full Moon Fever* was nearly finished, in April 1988. Under the guise of creating a B-side for Harrison's *Cloud Nine* single "This Is Love," Harrison, Lynne, Petty, and Orbison gathered at Bob Dylan's studio in Malibu, and wrote "Handle with Care" by strumming acoustic guitars together and riffing on verses over dinner. Dylan became its fifth member in the process. When the song was finished, Warner Bros. thought it had too much potential for the purposes of a European B-side. Instead, the label offered the group a recording contract.

Bob Dylan, George Harrison, Jeff Lynne, Roy Orbison, and Tom Petty walk into a studio. . . . It may sound like the start of a groan-inducing joke, but what the quintet produced at Dave Stewart's home recording studio in Encino, California, became a No. 3 charting album in the US and Top 10 in eight international markets. *Traveling Wilburys Vol. 1* asserted the five men's powers individually and as a group in a decade that saw each of them stumble, return, or stumble when returning. Though billed as a collaborative effort, the songwriting and the producing processes were led by Harrison and Lynne, who had originally discussed and approved of the concept. Consensus designated what made it into the album, however, including a cheeky set of liner notes that lay out the apocryphal origins of the mythical Wilburys: a fixed people who began to take short walks after realizing their civilization could not survive by standing completely still.

By nature of its personnel, the songs hit heartland rock's mark at the intersection of roots and pop, past and present, with lyrics that surveyed the down-and-out, life's everyday mercies, and the invigorating effects of friendships and community. With Orbison, Dylan, and Harrison on board, the Traveling Wilburys also fulfilled heartland rock's mission of highlighting its influences. "Tweeter and the Monkey Man," written and sung by Dylan with assists from Petty, Harrison and Lynne, translates as a mischievous lampoon of Bruce Springsteen—who was often called the new Dylan. Set in New Jersey, the singer sounds by turns defiant and omniscient, referencing a stolen car, mansion on the hill, state trooper, factory, river, and Thunder Road, as if to remind listeners who the real bard is in the most punk-ass way possible. "Not Alone Anymore," sung by Roy Orbison, brings the vocalist and his '60s sound squarely into the present, with orchestral flourishes and themes of loneliness. It also served as a theme song for the five frontmen who found a renewed sense of self as a group. *Rolling Stone* called the album a "low-key masterpiece."

The group's music video for "Handle with Care," the album's lead single and opening track, was a pinnacle of wholesome VH1-core. In it the five men huddle around a vintage microphone with their guitars—Orbison in dark glasses, and Petty in a top hat—signifying PG-rated campfire camaraderie. For "End of the Line," they ride in a box car with their instruments as Anywhere, USA, rolls by through a window. The camera closes in on each singer as they take a verse or chorus. A rocking chair holding an acoustic guitar is a gentle stand-in for Orbison, who died of a heart attack shortly before the band shot the video. The Traveling Wilburys' implied bridge between the 1960s and the 1980s welcomed multiple generations of listeners. Some could remember the Beatles on Ed Sullivan and Dylan going electric at Newport. Others had heard these stories from their parents and were approaching the age in which such music becomes appealing. The band's music and imagery was entirely palatable and a safe bet for family gatherings, Christmas gifts, and rock and pop radio. The Traveling Wilburys were the music equivalent of a flannel shirt in fall. For Petty the project was a joyous distraction from the fact that RCA had rejected *Full Moon Fever*. With "Free Fallin'," "I Won't Back Down," "Love Is a Long Road," and "Runnin' Down a Dream" to choose from, the suits claimed they didn't hear a hit. They also thought its nine-song run time was too short to constitute an entire album. Petty was dumbfounded, but in the ensuing months he made a few efforts to expand the track listing. He and Campbell cut "Alright for Now," and Petty recorded a fairly rote cover of the Byrds' "Feel a Whole Lot Better." He, Campbell, and Lynne fattened it up to twelve songs total. Petty then resubmitted it to RCA and, to his surprise, management had changed. The new leadership loved it, and the Floridian had his first solo album.

Though it marked a departure from the spirit of live performance he typically recorded with his band, all of the Heartbreakers save for Stan Lynch are credited on the album, even if they weren't particularly happy with the turn of events. Four Wilburys also appear. Roy Orbison sings backing vocals on the album's worst song, "Zombie Zoo." Del Shannon is credited with making "barnyard noises" during an interlude in which Petty cheekily instructs those listening on LP or cassette tape to turn over their media. While many reviews from the time remark upon its Wilburys-esque qualities, largely due to Lynne's distinctively crisp sound as a producer, and the way he tends to fill a track with overdubbed layers, *Full Moon Fever* was actually finished first, though it wasn't released until April 1989. It received some of the best reviews of Petty's career. It's also the album that caught the ear of a rising young producer, Rick Rubin, who'd recently moved to Los Angeles. Five years later, Petty would release his solo second album, *Wildflowers*, produced by Rubin, Petty, and Campbell.

A couple of months after *Traveling Wilburys Vol. 1* was released, and before Petty dropped *Full Moon Fever*, Virgin Records issued the single "You Got It," cowritten by Orbison, Petty, and Lynne. The song had become the lead single for Orbison's posthumously released album, *Mystery Girl*, which was yet another huge success and the highest-charting album of his entire career. It also gave Tom Petty and his new friends another Top 10 hit. The Petty-Lynne connection proved so fruitful that the pair continued on for the frontman's next album with the Heartbreakers, *Into the Great Wide Open*, released in 1991.

If there was anything to critique about Tom Petty until that point, it's that he had been a reliable vehicle for a hit single, but hadn't truly created an album that was compelling front-to-back. *Damn the Torpedoes* was the closest he'd come in the late '70s. Springsteen, Seger, and even Mellencamp had become the kind of artists to make such holistic statements, but Petty, though he tried with *Southern Accents*, had not. The *Full Moon Fever* era changed that, and situated Petty as the triumphant end cap to the Reagan era, and the most successful of the heartland rock coterie in the 1990s.

★ ★ ★

John Mellencamp rounded out the 1980s by navigating news coverage that often had little to do with the striking album he released in 1989. *Big Daddy*, his tenth full-length work, is a continuation of *The Lonesome Jubilee* in its mature lyrical themes and use of folk instruments. For the album, Mellencamp parted ways with his longtime producer Don Gehman, saying he felt like *The Lonesome Jubilee* was over-arranged for the folk sound he desired. Instead, Mellencamp wrote its songs on an acoustic guitar and presented them to the band on the day they were recorded as a nod to the spontaneity of his heroes Woody Guthrie and Keith Richards. "I'm not convinced he can add two and two," he said of the latter. "But those records feel great." *Big Daddy* also contains some of Mellencamp's most unequivocal protests—against Ronald Reagan, racism, and his own foolish behavior.

For a guy who had made it against most expectations—who was rich, writing and recording songs he believed in, and living in a fifty-eight-acre estate overlooking Lake Monroe in his beloved Indiana—one would assume he was in high spirits. But the opposite was true. Mellencamp, a rock star who was just shy of forty, was in fact miserable.

He and his second wife had separated a year prior, and were headed toward divorce after news of Mellencamp's philandering made rounds in tabloid newspapers. The music journalist Anthony DeCurtis profiled Mellencamp in June 1989 for *Rolling Stone*, and described an emotionally charged scene in which hope and abdication clashed with one another like enemy kingdoms. Standing in Mellencamp's home outside of Bloomington, he watched the singer stare through a window at his estranged wife as she pulled into his driveway and walked toward the front door. Mellencamp had a gift for her—a painting by a young artist he'd purchased in Chicago.

"Vicky looks sad, determined and mildly careworn," DeCurtis wrote. "Mellencamp's natural energy and charm are blunted by his desire not to assume too much from the fact of her presence. The playful domestic joke of the sweatshirt Vicky is wearing—THOROUGHBRED SPENDING TEAM, it reads—is almost heartbreaking in this context." Less than a month later, she filed for divorce, seeking child support and full custody of their two young daughters. Four days prior to the filing, the singer had become a grandfather, when his oldest daughter, from his first marriage, gave birth.

Though Mellencamp mostly declined to comment on the events, newspapers across the country closely followed the proceedings. The Associated Press even questioned the judge who oversaw the case. Anthony J. Metz told the AP that "it may be interesting in the aspect that I may learn a little bit about an industry that I don't know too much about—the music industry. But basically, it is still a divorce." The news organization syndicated a blurb to newspapers across the country with the headline "Mellencamp's No Different."

Going through a divorce he didn't want but couldn't avoid by nature of his conduct was one reason to meditate on his life. The state of popular culture in the late 1980s, its corporate sponsors, and general intersections with commerce, was another. His turn toward folk-rock aside, Mellencamp had long stood out among the cohort of '80s rock stars and the '60s era musicians who influenced them for his refusal of corporate sponsorship. He held out on this point well into the new millennium until 2023, when the genial cable television station Turner Classic Movies sponsored his "Live and In Person" tour. "I don't have anything against corporations, but how could I stand on stage and talk about something they might be doing if I've got a big corporate banner hanging over my head?" he said. "I also don't like the idea that you go backstage after the show and shake some big shot's hand." As Michael Jackson became synonymous with Pepsi, Ray Charles partnered with Maxwell House coffee, and even the Beatles' music began appearing in advertisements for cars and sneakers (Jackson owned the rights to most of their songs), Mellencamp refused such commercial partnerships until he took over for Bob Seger with Chevy in 2006. He also stopped closing his concerts with a medley of '60s era songs because he felt that too many of its artists were selling out.

As he watched his musical heroes accept money from big brands, Mellencamp also bemoaned how some were being left in the shadows. "Don't we respect anything?" he told DeCurtis. "Don't we respect what James Brown gave us?" Brown was arrested in September 1988 after leading police on a high-speed chase through South Carolina and Georgia after they arrived on the scene of him acting erratically with a shotgun at an insurance company near his office. A judge sentenced him to six years in South Carolina's State Park Correctional Center regardless, on weapons and traffic charges. "I just can't believe that there hasn't been ninety million letters written to the governor of South Carolina saying, 'You should pardon this guy,'" Mellencamp concluded. "I mean, they're gonna pardon Ollie North!"

Mellencamp reiterated this sentiment in May 1989 when he participated in a campaign to save Chess Studios in Chicago. Chuck Berry, Bo Diddley, Muddy Waters, Howlin' Wolf, the Rolling Stones, and others had tracked some of their classic songs at Chess Records' recording studio, located at 2120 S. Michigan Avenue, and the singer sought to have it preserved as a landmark. To raise awareness, Mellencamp and his band recorded a ninety-minute live performance that aired on Westwood One radio networks, the largest system of radio stations in the country. A year later, the Commission on Chicago Landmarks designated its status, which also saved it from the rapid commercial development that has since swept through the city; today it also houses Willie Dixon's Blues Heaven Foundation.

When Mellencamp released *Big Daddy* on May 9, 1989, it came with the caveat that he wouldn't tour behind the album. He'd said all he needed to with songs such as "Jackie Brown," one of his finest compositions, that tells the story of an impoverished and disenfranchised Black man symbolic of so many who are victims of America's ugly truths. "Country Gentleman" is an unblinking indictment of Ronald Reagan, who Mellencamp frames as uncaring about the poor because his main priority is to prop up his rich friends. The singer also turns the crosshairs on himself with "Void In My Heart" and "Big Daddy of Them All," two songs about a man who has it all yet remains unfulfilled, troubled, and at the mercy of his own poor choices.

Instead of hitting the road, Mellencamp worked overtime in the studio. In the years between making *Big Daddy* and his first release of the 1990s, the singer built out an art studio on his Indiana property. He filled it with art books and supplies, and began developing a style of oil painting drawn from the moody palettes of Dutch masters and German Expressionism. He drove to Chicago four times to stare at Renoir's "Two Sisters (On the Terrace)," a nineteenth century oil-on-canvas painting on display at the Art Institute. The first time he encountered it he cried. He constructed a world drawn from history as a way to bow out of the present. Soon, Mellencamp would make headlines for selling his own paintings to the tune of $15,000.

Lou Reed memorialized the rock star's new persona in the song "Last Great American Whale," a treatise on animal cruelty, environmental destruction, and gun violence. Released on his album *New York* in 1989, he refers to Mellencamp as his "painter friend Donald" in the song, and then quotes his friend's coarse maxim—about sticking a fork in something—in its last line. The pair became friends when Reed played Farm Aid in 1985 and then returned two years later. Ahead of his 1987 performance, the New Yorker stopped in Bloomington to rehearse with Mellencamp's band before heading to Lincoln, Nebraska, for the festival.

The visit was memorialized when Reed, Mellencamp, his band, and John Prine made a surprise appearance at the tiny Bluebird Nightclub in Bloomington. Billed as the Ragin' Texans, Mellencamp and company took to the stage for a Farm Aid warm-up gig. After performing "Small Town," "Paper In Fire," and other tunes with his *The Lonesome Jubilee* era band, Reed walked on stage and the group, with Mellencamp, performed "New Sensations," "Walk on the Wild Side," "Sweet Jane" and "I Love You, Suzanne." Prine, who sometimes stayed with Mellencamp to write songs or amid marital troubles, stepped out from the wings to join them near the end of the set.

The stunning assembly in the small college town made the rounds on bootleg cassettes and VHS tapes for years. These dubs stood as evidence of a seemingly mythical time when these three very different artists could and did converge—when country music, mainstream rock, and counterculture mingled under the auspices of charity and resistance. *New York*, billed as a back-to-basics return for Reed, earned some of the best reviews of his solo career. Mellencamp likened it to the '60s era works he long emulated, the raw sound of the Rolling Stones. Of the album, he said, "It sounds like it was produced by an eighth grader, but I like it."

★ ★ ★

"I could never get over this as long as I live," Bonnie Raitt declared after jazz legend Ella Fitzgerald announced that she'd won Album of the Year. Standing on stage at the Recording Academy's thirty-second annual ceremony clutching a small gold gramophone, Raitt appeared overwhelmed but resolute in her words: "It means so much to the kind of music that I do. It means those of us who love R&B are gonna get a chance again."

Her message was heartfelt but lacked a necessary caveat. With the win, Raitt became the first woman to do what men long had: draw from 1950s and '60s soul, rock 'n' roll, and R&B traditions, and receive widespread acclaim and major awards. More notably, she was the only heartland rock artist to win the Recording Academy's top honors.

In winning the Grammy for Album of the Year, Raitt achieved something *Born in the U.S.A.*, *Against the Wind*, *American Fool*, and *Full Moon Fever* hadn't. Raitt had fought for success even longer than Bob Seger, and by essence denoted Maya Angelou's assertion that each

Bonnie Raitt embraces one of her idols, John Lee Hooker, at the 32nd
Annual Grammy Awards in 1990.

PHOTO COURTESY MEDIAPUNCH INC.

time a woman stands up for herself, she stands up for all women. "I'm
here to champion women who aren't ridiculously gorgeous, which is
another reason that it's so great that I won the Grammys," she said in
1990. "I'm a heroine to a lot of women who are overweight, divorced
and angry, women who are drinking too much wine at night, listening to blues songs and thinking that they're never going to get a
chance." By her example, other mature female recording artists were
also afforded the same level of recognition by the Recording Academy.
Allison Krauss and the Chicks followed in her footsteps in the new
millennium, receiving Album of the Year awards when they were in
their late thirties.

"I was virtually unemployable six months earlier," Don Was, Raitt's
new and relatively untested producer explained. After tracking a few
children's songs together for varying projects, Raitt opted to remain

with Was because she sensed he understood her vision. She wanted to return to the bare essence of her earliest work, like 1972's *Give It Up*, to play guitar and have minimal production. The pair demoed and recorded *Nick of Time* in a few weeks.

Raitt took up space in an underexplored delta between youth and elder. As a long-active recording and touring artist, she was an enigma in an industry that favored new voices and triumphant comebacks. Though she'd finally arrived with *Nick of Time*, she'd actually never left the industry. The new album was remarkable for the fact of Raitt's perseverance and also for its narrative throughline. As with Mellencamp's *The Lonesome Jubilee* and Springsteen's *Tunnel of Love*, Raitt was nearing middle age. Having exited through the bright end of sobriety's long tunnel, however, she was more comfortable with change and with herself than those men. The album's laid-back, unselfconscious grooves meet lyrics that reflect the specific period of time in which many women find an antidote to the poisons stirred into us since childhood—gender roles, pay gaps, beauty standards—but also face some of life's most existential questions, such as whether to get married and have children.

It tracks that the first original song Raitt had written in seven years was about perimenopause. "I'd changed quite a bit in those intervening years," Raitt said. "In the process of cleaning up I discovered a whole new person inside myself—a person who I thought might have something to say—so I wrote 'Nick of Time' about a friend of mine who was going through the situation in the song. The question of whether or not to have kids touches all women my age." The album's title track also contains a verse in which Raitt examines her aging parents. She ponders how their minds and bodies are changing, and how it's difficult to reconcile that she will one day be in their place. Paired with the image of a middle-age woman torn over whether to have a child or keep her relationship, *Nick of Time* is unquestionably an album for adults, one whose mainstream sound and themes were relatable but also stood out from the catalogs of men who'd written about cars, women, and self-determination. Though her music was for the Everyman, it was specifically music for every woman, written to the tune of Raitt's contention that so-called women's music is "rhythm and grief."

The album's title track is set to the tune of a biological clock, and it's also true that it arrived at a time of intense transition and uncertainty for Raitt. The high stakes at this point in her career were unmistakable, especially with the involvement of a new label.

Faced with the hurdle of the album's mature themes in the age of Madonna and Debbie Gibson, as well as her underdog status in the industry, Capitol, like Warner Bros. before it, did little to assure her success. The A&R executive who'd signed her had trouble convincing the label's marketing department to promote Raitt—it also had big releases from Tina Turner, Carole King, and adult contemporary giant Richard Marx that year. Instead, Capitol took out ads in music magazines. According to Raitt's producer Was, the pair tempered their expectations, assuming *Nick of Time* would sell around 150,000 copies, nothing crazy but enough to make another album. Though *Nick of Time* had a slow build, by April 1990, worldwide sales exceeded two million.

The album's first single, Raitt's cover of John Hiatt's "Thing Called Love," undoubtedly aided its rise. Driven by the voice of a self-assured woman who knows what she wants, this sentiment extends to its music video starring Raitt's friend Dennis Quaid, dressed in saddle shoes, faded jeans, and a sleeveless Sun Records T-shirt. Filmed in a room meant to approximate a roadhouse—similar to her video for "Keep This Heart in Mind"—Raitt and Quaid lock eyes from across the room as she and her band play on stage. It ends with the actor drawn to a table near her as if by magnetic force, singing along and saluting Raitt's slide guitar solo, as all men should.

As was customary, Raitt undertook a massive North American tour behind *Nick of Time* with British folk-rock icon Richard Thompson as her opener. Throughout its sixty-eight dates, and in interviews, Raitt spoke fondly of other female musicians who were blazing a trail around the same time: Melissa Etheridge, Tracy Chapman, Suzanne Vega, and the mighty singer Phoebe Snow who'd returned to pop music after an eight-year break. By framing these women as mirrors of her own success, she demanded that women in music were not a category, not an alien "other" to the men that still dominated the business of rock and pop music. On stage at the Vic Theater in Chicago, emanating the power and sexual swagger of bluesmen before her, Raitt capped her femme forward banter with a hope many women long held. "Maybe," she said, "Joni Mitchell will have another hit."

★ ★ ★

There are precious few times in life when we flick on the television, watch something in real time, and understand that the world will never be the same. In music, these moments are attributed to Elvis and the Beatles on Ed Sullivan, Queen at Live Aid, and Michael Jackson moonwalking during Motown 25.

But there is another key event that stands as point of no return, when mainstream rock music of the 1980s was swallowed by a truculent beast. On September 30, 1989, Neil Young made his debut on *Saturday Night Live* in support of his newest album, *Freedom*, which projected both his acoustic pensiveness and electric guitar assaults. As a progenitor and ally of the heartland rock movement, Young capping the '80s with his best album in a decade was akin to an elder returning from war. He'd been on the front lines and had ideas about where the world was headed. *Freedom* was a troubled soundtrack for an American society caught in a period of extreme transition.

With Crazy Horse guitarist Frank Sampedro, drummer Steve Jordan, and multi-instrumentalist Charley Drayton on bass, Young gave an unprecedented televised performance that projected the brute force to which heartland rock and its alt-rock cousins had pointed but never truly unleashed, no matter how hard Kenny Aronoff thumped his snare drum. There were no synthesizers or blue-collar cool denim. No hope-laden diatribes about working-class solidarity. There were only equal parts antipathy and dread emanating from a gang of men who looked as if they would slash your tires. There was before Neil Young performed "Rockin' in the Free World" on *Saturday Night Live* . . . and then there was after.

For the song, which bookends *Freedom* in acoustic and electric versions—much like "My My Hey Hey" on *Rust Never Sleeps*—Young channeled the post-hippie earnestness of heartland rock into lyrics that unspool like a list of casualties, and paired them with chanty guitar aggression in a post-Vietnam take on "Search and Destroy." Some of its lyrics criticized the Bush administration and the president's call for America to become a "kinder, gentler nation" just before he readied its military for war.

On stage at 30 Rockefeller Plaza that night, the forty-three-year-old snarled, prowled, and raised his fist like a dissident bull rider. Young had a track record of finishing idealistic and self-indulgent decades with lyrical anguish and guitar brutality, but in the fall of 1989 there was little hope that anything he said would make a difference. Less than a year later the United States led an aggressive military buildup as part of the Gulf War, and homelessness, drug abuse, and racial tensions rose. "Rockin' in the Free World" held a mirror to society like much of heartland rock, but its surface was warped as to properly reflect the nation's psyche. This, combined with Young's image of an unkept howler in a black leather jacket, ripped T-shirt, and patched-up jeans, indicated where the culture was headed—to the anti-fashion thrift-store vestments of grunge.

Young on *SNL* marked the penultimate statement of a decade soon to pass, but it was underpinned by a youth-oriented ecosystem that helped extend its scope. Bob Mould of influential post-hardcore band Hüsker Dü released his solo debut, *Workbook*, which married the emotional intensity of his underground roots with an accessible soft-alt palette and became a staple of MTV. The Mekons' *Rock N Roll* took the scrappy English band's love-hate relationship with America and its traditions to one of its most tuneful forms released by a major label. *Don't Tell a Soul* saw the Replacements' first appearance on the

Billboard Hot 100 singles chart with "I'll Be You." All of this signified a bridge between eras that pointed staunchly toward the future.

1989 also saw the release of *The Bridge*, an eleven-song compilation of influential and marginal alternative rock acts paying tribute to Neil Young. Dinosaur Jr., Sonic Youth, Nick Cave, The Flaming Lips, Soul Asylum, and others each chose a Young song and refracted it through their own cracked prism, beaming it to the future place askew with layers of distortion. Pixies' version of "Winterlong" sounds as if it belongs in the film *Singles*, director Cameron Crowe's ode to grunge released in 1992—whose soundtrack includes two songs by the Replacements' Paul Westerberg.

Beyond its position as both cultural end and beginning, "Rockin' in the Free World" became one in an entire series of heartland rock songs used to soundtrack a range of messaging. It played over the title credits of documentarian Michael Moore's skewering of corporate media and George W. Bush, the 2004 film *Fahrenheit 9/11*. Both Bernie Sanders and Donald Trump have used the song at events. In 2024, US secretary of state Anthony Blinken played it with a Ukrainian punk band at a bar in Kyiv amid the country's war with Russia. The same year, "Rockin' in the Free World" filled the United Center after vice presidential nominee Tim Walz gave the final speech at the Democratic National Convention. Walz, the governor of Minnesota who grew up in a three thousand-resident city in Nebraska, also made good use of John Mellencamp's "Small Town" as he campaigned.

Like "Born in the U.S.A," and "Pink Houses," Young's 1989 anthem may be easily retrofitted to suit a listener's purpose on account of its vaguely jingoistic and entirely hooky chorus. What it actually probed, at the end of the Reagan era, was the country's entire foundation. "The chorus cuts both ways," Young explained shortly after he released *Freedom*. "It's true—keep on rockin' in the free world, that's what we Americans want to do," he said, "to keep on doing what we're doing and moving forward." "But then," he added, "how free is the free world anyway?"

AFTERWORD

This is the key to the engine.

—BRIAN FALLON
DISCUSSING BRUCE SPRINGSTEEN

The top albums of 1990 made heartland rock's roots-driven earnestness seem old-fashioned, a distant phenomenon frozen in amber, the soundtrack of an America that no longer existed. Bonnie Raitt's *Nick of Time* dominated the Billboard 200 for three weeks in April, but novelty pop acts, including Milli Vanilli, MC Hammer, Vanilla Ice, Paula Abdul, and New Kids on the Block commanded radio and the pop charts as the country was drawn into the Gulf War and an early '90s recession. Bubblegum-pop and its teen-focused marketing machine had captivated America. Mainstream rock's meat and potatoes were leftovers in the fridge hoping to be reheated.

The threadbare earnestness of heartland rock was especially threatened when a trio from Seattle hit No. 1 on the Billboard 200. Nirvana's *Nevermind* replaced Michael Jackson's *Dangerous* in the top spot on January 11, 1992, and brought with it a moody wave of disaffected grunge, alternative, punk, and college-rock bands whose messaging was rooted in anger, weirdness, and antiestablishment viewpoints. Flannel shirts replaced American flags; angst pummeled sincerity into submission. Studio perfectionism, Yamaha synthesizers, and gated drums sounds were passe. Heartland rock became the music of dads.

Though rock music such as grunge and alternative, and later rap metal and nu metal, became pop phenomena, none of the music within these genres was created with a mainstream adult audience in mind. Such music appealed specifically to youth suspended in an era of war, police brutality, homophobia, AIDS, domestic terrorism, rapid technological change, and school shootings, because it reflected their feelings of helplessness, hopelessness, and apathy. No one under the age of thirty wanted back-to-basics rock music from middle-aged white men extolling America's promise. Kids desired the outsider anthems of creeps, losers, and criminals so much that artists such as Radiohead, Beck, and Fiona Apple became the mainstream. Adding insult to injury, in 1993, a pre-fame Beck released his version of a heartland rock song, "Heartland Feeling," which clearly is satire.

With their wealth, fame, estates, and private jets, most of heartland rock's figureheads were also so far removed from the lives of the people in their songs that John Mellencamp all but declared himself a sellout. "You know, I have become a cliché and I can admit that to myself now, I am a rock cliché," he said in 1991. "I have fallen to every cliché a rock guy's supposed to do. I do have a Porsche. My girlfriend is a model. I couldn't admit that would ever happen to me, but guess what, it did."

Springsteen and Mellencamp each released a No. 1 hit song in the '90s, and Tom Petty had created three, but "Human Touch," "What If I Came Knocking," "Learning to Fly," "Mary Jane's Last Dance," and "You Don't Know How It Feels" were all relegated to the top spot on *Billboard*'s Mainstream Rock chart—a seat at the grown-ups' table far from the tastes and influence of the pop music world.

Many of heartland rock's major artists came together for John Prine's 1991 album *The Missing Years*, which garnered the singer-songwriter's first Grammy Award. On the album Prine performed "Take a Look at My Heart," cowritten with Mellencamp, with backing vocals by no less than Springsteen. Bonnie Raitt and Tom Petty and Heartbreakers' Mike Campbell, Benmont Tench, and Howie Epstein also appeared. It was produced by Epstein, a longtime Prine fan who gathered the high-profile ensemble.

Mellencamp also cast Prine in *Falling From Grace*, the 1992 film he directed and starred in, about a down-and-out country singer who returns to his small Indiana hometown after finding fame and fortune in Los Angeles. Its soundtrack also featured an exclusive version of Prine's song "All the Best," fleshed out and popularized on *The Missing Years*, but played in a stripped-back format for Mellencamp's movie. Two years later, Springsteen won an Oscar for "Streets of Philadelphia," which went to No. 9 on the Billboard Hot 100.

Despite these valiant efforts, after the scare of Y2K, mainstream rock all but issued its death rattle. The rise of pop stars, including Britney Spears, Christina Aguilera, Beyonce, Pink, and Rihanna, and the 808s, high hats, and Autotune of rap and hip-hop, permanently altered the prevailing sounds of popular music. Amid the cultural shift, heartland rock—its synthesizers, gated drum sounds, and populist lyrical screeds—became the soundtrack of boomer parents. The term "dad rock" was written into the lexicon of popular culture.

It wasn't until September 11, 2001, when terrorist attacks on the World Trade Center and the Pentagon killed almost three thousand Americans, that heartland rock returned as a comforting balm. The national tragedy and subsequent mourning ignited a wave of patriotism the likes of which had not been seen since Reagan's second term as president. In its wake, Bruce Springsteen released *The Rising*, a series of reflections on the attacks and their aftermath, which became his sixth No. 1 album and first since *Tunnel of Love* in 1987. Springsteen has said that he got to work on it after a fan spotted him in traffic, rolled down their car window, and shouted, "We need ya!"

Heartland rock and its allies also called upon their mid-'80s benefit concert roots in the wake of the tragedy. Springsteen, Tom Petty and the Heartbreakers, Neil Young, and Willie Nelson performed at

"America: A Tribute to Heroes" organized by the actor Geroge Cloo-
ney, and John Mellencamp played the Paul McCartney–led benefit The
Concert for New York City. Jon Bon Jovi appeared at both concerts.

By now, Petty's "I Won't Back Down" and its lyrical defiance had
become one of his most celebrated songs. Like "Born in the U.S.A." and
"Pink Houses," it also was a favorite of politicians seeking to inject a
working-class subtext into their campaign stops. At Petty's behest, the
singer's publisher, Randall Wixen, issued a cease-and-desist to George
W. Bush in February 2000 for its use of the song at his campaign
events. Twenty years later, Petty's family issued the same request to
Donald Trump's campaign. In between, it became an unofficial American anthem after the September 11 attacks. Johnny Cash's emotionally bare cover of the song, released on his *American III: Solitary Man*
album produced by Rick Rubin, only bolstered its greatness.

Toward the end of George W. Bush's presidency, a crop of bands
from the East Coast and Midwest, all of whom trumpeted a love of
Bruce Springsteen, Tom Petty, the Replacements, Lucinda Williams,
Bob Seger, Steve Earle, and others, began sprouting from underground rock's fertile soil. Early examples include the Philadelphia collective Marah, whose 2000 album *Kids in Philly*, released by Earle on
his now-defunct E-Squared Records label, was praised for its lyrical
sincerity and sonorous rumblings. The band used folk instruments,
like John Mellencamp, blues guitar, like Bonnie Raitt and Lucinda
Williams, and epic full-band arrangements dotted by a host of auxiliary instruments, like Bruce Springsteen, to seamless and compelling
effect. Critics couldn't help but admire the group's unabashed sonic
looting. The album remains a cult favorite most often celebrated in
Philadelphia. In 2003, the Ohio-born singer-songwriter Jason Molina,
who loved Bob Seger, released his full-band magnum opus, *The Mag-
nolia Electric Co.* Its stirring Midwestern fatalism, and evocative Rust
Belt imagery, endures as one of counterculture's most celebrated and
defining heartland-rock offerings.

Successive years saw the indie heartland-rock revivalist trend
break through in a notable way. The Hold Steady, formed in Brook-

lyn in 2003 and fronted by a singer-songwriter from Minneapolis, was quickly recognized for its narrative storytelling largely centered in the Midwest and its stripped-back heartland-rock influences. After garnering buzz from publications such as the *Village Voice*, the group received near-universal acclaim with the release of *Boys and Girls in America* in 2006, an album about the everyday American youth experience that panned out enough to allow listeners to fill in the details with scenes from their own lives. Its music was layered and raucous like the E Street Band. Bonus tracks on a Japanese edition of the album includes a cover of Bob Seger's "Against the Wind." Amid the group's rise, the band's frontman Craig Finn met with Springsteen, who often takes note of bands, such as Marah, who were making good work in his image. "Meeting your heroes, there's such an opportunity for them to disappoint you, because they can't live up to all the things you've hung on them," Finn said. "The good news is if your hero is Bruce Springsteen, he doesn't disappoint."

2008 saw the release of *The '59 Sound* by The Gaslight Anthem, a quartet from New Brunswick, New Jersey, lead by the singer-songwriter Brian Fallon, which melds punk-rock vigor with heartland rock's back-to-basics sound and lyrical accessibility. Springsteen also took note of the group and appeared with them at England's Glastonbury music festival and Hyde Park in London in 2009. Another highly literate rock band, Titus Andronicus from Glen Rock, New Jersey, released *The Monitor* in 2010. It's an album in which the Civil War is a recurring theme, and Bruce Springsteen's name and lyrics are referenced. It melds the lyrical depth of the Hold Steady and Springsteen with the boisterous energy of the Replacements. All of these bands embrace John Mellencamp's penchant for fist-pumping choruses.

The explosion of heartland rock-inspired bands in the 2000s proved that the sound's resurgence among independent musicians is here to stay. Philadelphia's the War on Drugs wove the synthesizers of *Born in the U.S.A*, *Brothers in Arms*, and *Robbie Robertson* into its distinctly blue-collar, road-hazy sonic palette. Its leader, Adam Granduciel, was raised on a diet of heartland rock and made no bones about his love of those records in the late aughts, when the genre was still largely derided as "dad rock," and as the band began to garner national attention for its breakthrough album *Wagonwheel Blues*. Springsteen now cites the group as one of his favorites. The Canadians of Japandroids issued *Evil's Sway* in 2012, which sounded like Tom Petty's "American Girl" shot through a cannon. Sam Fender, a beloved thirty-year-old English singer-songwriter, has long trumpeted his love of Springsteen and *Born to Run*—so much so that Springsteen had him open a couple of his Italian tour dates in 2023.

Ryan Adams finally covered "Summer of '69" in concert in 2015, igniting a wave of media coverage. Things didn't work out quite so well for fellow singer-songwriter Will Scheff of Okkervil River, who covered Don Henley's "The End of the Innocence" a year prior and received a cease-and-desist from its author. Indiana pop-punk band the Ataris had better luck with their cover of "The Boys of Summer" in 2003. The Ohio-born singer-songwriter Lydia Loveless, Katie Crutchfield of Waxahatchee, who lives in Kansas, and neo country-rock outlaw Margo Price continue heartland rock's spirit through distinctly female and gender-fluid perspectives. The Drive-By Truckers, Phosphorescent, and Jason Isbell create left-of-center Southern-steeped heartland rock in the spirit of Earle and Williams.

And this is nothing to say of the legions of new country musicians who've cited Mellencamp, Petty, Springsteen, Seger, and others as influences. Rapper-turned-country star Jelly Roll says Seger's "Against the Wind" is his favorite song, and he's covered it numerous times in concert. Zach Bryan, one of the most popular names in contemporary country music, appeared with Springsteen on the cover of *Rolling Stone* in November 2024. Today, artists such as Keith Urban, Mel McDaniel, Emmylou Harris, Jason Aldean, Kenney Chesney, Luke Bryan, Luke Combs, Trisha Yearwood, Little Big Town, Miranda Lambert, Darius Rucker, and many others have covered songs by Mellencamp, Springsteen, and Seger. In 2024, a Tom Petty tribute album titled *Petty Country: A Country Music Celebration of Tom Petty* was released featuring performances by country artists including Dolly Parton and Chris Stapleton.

If the primary tenet of heartland rock was to honor the grit and ingenuity of rock 'n' roll's icons, folk music's radicals, and the working class, through the modern perspectives and gear of a new generation, it follows that future generations of songwriters from humble beginnings and outsider vantage points will continue its mission. This is particularly true as the genre becomes its own kind of historical originator. The legacy of heartland rock is that of against-all-odds moxie and outrageously commercial omnipresence—how low class and high tech may meet to amplify a vast and crucial 99 percent, which is under attack in a post-Reagan world. Heartland rock's story is of a distinct place in time when America was in the midst of rapid and unsettling technological, social, and political change. In the hands of contemporary musicians, its legacy is also still unfolding. As in a religion or a democracy, the words of the poet and playwright Oscar Wilde apply: The one duty we owe to history is to rewrite it.

ACKNOWLEDGMENTS

This book wouldn't exist had I not grown up in the Midwest, about two hours south of John Mellencamp. So I must first thank the state of Indiana and the Hoosiers who raised me—those family and friends who showed me hard work, possibility, and the art of survival. I'm eternally grateful for my father, Randy Moore; my sister, Meredith Kasenow; and my friends (Kendra, Nicole, Brit, Becca, Alea, Shannon, Rachel, Katie, and many others) who supported me amid my work on this book, and amid the intense personal changes I navigated as I was finishing it. I'm very thankful for my agent, Alice Speilburg, who took me on as a baby author more than a decade ago. Thanks to Matt Weiland, Yumiko Gonzalez Rios, and the good folks at W. W. Norton for believing in this book, and for taking good care of it and me along the way. I'm grateful for my former colleagues at the University of Southern California for their support and for being a consistent source of inspiration. Thanks also to the gifted editors I've worked with throughout my career—those minds of surgical precision who've made me a sharper writer and thinker. Journalism, independent thought, and liberty in general is under siege in this country, and I'm thankful for my friends, colleagues, fellow writers, and other artists and changemakers who persist in the face of such hardship.

APPENDIX

150 ESSENTIAL HEARTLAND ROCK SONGS

BRUCE SPRINGSTEEN

"Born to Run"

"Thunder Road"

"Factory"

"The Promised Land"

"The River"

"Out in the Street"

"Hungry Heart"

"Atlantic City"

"Highway Patrolman"

"Born in the USA"

"Darlington County"

"I'm on Fire"

"Working on the Highway"

"Downbound Train"

"I'm Goin Down"

"Glory Days"

"My Hometown"

"Tougher Than the Rest"

"Brilliant Disguise"

"One Step Up"

"Streets of Philadelphia"

"The Rising"

BOB SEGER & THE SILVER BULLET BAND

"Turn the Page"

"Beautiful Loser"

"Hollywood Nights"

"Old Time Rock & Roll"

"Rock and Roll
  Never Forgets"

"Night Moves"

"Mainstreet"

"Still the Same"

"Feel Like a Number"

"Against the Wind"

"Long Twin Silver Line"

"Fire Lake"

"You'll Accomp'ny Me"

"Roll Me Away"

"Even Now"

"Makin' Thunderbirds"

"Like A Rock"

"American Storm"

TOM PETTY AND THE HEARTBREAKERS

"American Girl"

"Refugee"

"Here Comes My Girl"

"Even the Losers"

"The Waiting"

"Nightwatchman"

"One Story Town"

"Rebels"

"Southern Accents"

"Don't Come Around Here
  No More"

"Jammin' Me"

"Learning to Fly"

"Into the Great Wide Open"

"Mary Jane's Last Dance"

TOM PETTY SOLO

"Free Fallin'"

"I Won't Back Down"

"Runnin' Down a Dream"

"Wildflowers"

"You Don't Know
  How It Feels"

"Time to Move On"

JOHN MELLENCAMP

"Cheap Shot"

"Jack & Diane"

"Hurts So Good"

"Crumblin' Down"

"Pink Houses"

"Authority Song"

"Rain on the Scarecrow"

"Small Town"

"Lonely Ol' Night"

"Minutes to Memories"

"R.O.C.K. in the U.S.A. (A Salute to '60s Rock)"

"Paper in Fire"

"Check It Out"

"Cherry Bomb"

"Country Gentleman"

"Jackie Brown"

"Our Country"

"Longest Days"

JACKSON BROWNE

"Running on Empty"

BONNIE RAITT

"Keep This Heart in Mind"

"I Can't Help Myself"

"Me and the Boys"

"Nick of Time"

"The Thing Called Love"

SOUTHSIDE JOHNNY AND THE ASBURY JUKES

"I Don't Want to Go Home"

BRUCE HORNSBY AND THE RANGE

"The Way It Is"

"Mandolin Rain"

"Every Little Kiss"

"The Valley Road"

"The Show Goes On"

"Across the River"

IRON CITY HOUSE ROCKERS

"Junior's Bar"   "Friday Night"

MICHAEL STANLEY BAND

"My Town"   "He Can't Love You"

LUCINDA WILLIAMS

"The Night's Too Long"   "Six Blocks Away"

"I Just Wanted To See   "Right In Time"
You So Bad"
                                        "Car Wheels on a
"Changed the Locks"   Gravel Road"

MELISSA ETHERIDGE

"The Late September Dogs"   "Scarecrow"

BRYAN ADAMS

"Summer of '69"

DON HENLEY

"The Boys of Summer"   "The End of the Innocence"

WILLIE NILE

"Vagabond Moon"

DIRE STRAITS

"Walk of Life"   "Money for Nothing"

X

"The New World"

LOS LOBOS

"Will the Wolf Survive?"   "One Time One Night"

STEVE EARL

"Guitar Town"   "Hillbilly Highway"

LONE JUSTICE

"Ways to be Wicked"   "Shelter"

JOHN FOGERTY

"Centerfield"   "Rock and Roll Girls"

ROBBIE ROBERTSON

"Broken Arrow"   "Showdown at Big Sky"

NEIL YOUNG

"Motor City"   "Rockin' in the Free World"

JOHN HIATT

"Have a Little Faith in Me"

BOB DYLAN

"Union Sundown"

TRAVELING WILBURYS

"End of the Line"   "Handle with Care"

LOU REED

"Hold On"

GARLAND JEFFREYS

"American Boy & Girl"

THE BLASTERS

"Bus Station"

THE REPLACEMENTS

"Waitress in the Sky"   "Alex Chilton"

"Bastards of Young"

R.E.M.

"Driver 8"   "Cuyahoga"

FIRE TOWN

"Carry the Torch"

BODEANS

"She's a Runaway"

TOM COCHRANE & RED RIDER

"The Boy Inside the Man"

THE HOOTERS

"And We Danced"

JOHN PRINE

"Storm Windows"

TRACY CHAPMAN

"Fast Car"

THE WAR ON DRUGS

"Pain"   "Red Eyes"

THE GASLIGHT ANTHEM

"The '59 Sound"

MARAH

"Round Eye Blues"

TITUS ANDRONICUS

"A More Perfect Union"

THE HOLD STEADY

"Stuck Between Stations"

SONGS: OHIA

"Farewell Transmission"

PHOSPHORESCENT

"Song for Zula"

LYDIA LOVELESS

"Chris Isaak"

MARGO PRICE

"Heart of America"

WAXAHATCHEE

"Right Back to It"

NOTES

INTRODUCTION

5 **"longing for the way things used to be"**: Silas House, "Letter from Home," *Bitter Southerner*, July 8, 2025.

CHAPTER 1: 1980

10 **"Seger spent the past year"**: Dave Marsh, "Bob Seger: Against the Wind," *Rolling Stone*, May 15, 1980.

10 **"This is a true story"**: Dave DiMartino, "Safe at Home or Against the Wind: Bob Seger Bops Horizontally," *Creem*, September 1980.

12 **"to make sure I had that big stack"**: Gary Graff, "Bob Seger's More of a Family Man Than a Music Man," *Seattle Times*, October 21, 1994.

12 **"It's a matter of the best songs"**: DiMartino, "Safe at Home or Against the Wind."

14 **"I had never even seen Springsteen"**: David Fricke, "John Cougar Mellencamp: The Comeback Kid," *Rolling Stone*, January 31, 1986.

16 **"Eddie's music sounds good"**: Janet Maslin, "Eddie and the Cruisers," *New York Times*, September 23, 1983.

17 **"most exciting debut"**: Robert Palmer, "Willie Nile Sings Rock and Folk," *New York Times*, July 29, 1978.

17 **"My advice to people"**: Jonathan Takiff, "Live This Week," *Philadelphia Daily News*, May 16, 1980.

17 **"Even the heavy rain"**: Mark Mittan, "Michael Stanley Roars Back Home," *Akron Beacon Journal*, August 12, 1980.

18 **"blend of the Bruce Springsteen"**: Steve Ravago, "Del Mar Track Is the Place to Be This Saturday," *Daily Times-Advocate*, November 27, 1980.

18 **"strongest album an American band"**: Greil Marcus, "Love's So Tough," *Rolling Stone*, September 6, 1979.

19 **"Everyone was laid off"**: Jon Conroy, "A Conversation with Joe Grushecky," *LA Weekly*, December 3, 1981.

19 **"Springsteen may have popularized"**: Conroy, "A Conversation with Joe Grushecky."

19 **"While you are waiting"**: Al Freeders, "Mini Record Reviews," *Dayton Daily News*, October 7, 1979.

20 **"It's like a joke on America"**: "John Mellencamp—Interview 1980," Streamed by Reelin' in the Years Archive, Youtube, 15:28, https://www.youtube.com/watch?v=8d_YwGixibY.

21 **3.2 million more Americans**: "Money Income and Poverty Status of Families and Persons in the United States: 1980 (Advance Data from the March 1980 CPS)," United States Census Bureau report, August 1981, https://www.census.gov/library/publications/1981/demo/p60-127.html.

22 **"Someone once said"**: Rich Harrington, "John Cougar Mellencamp: No Longer the Rebel Without a Cause," *Washington Post*, March 1, 1986.

22 **"There's a certain type of woman"**: "John Mellencamp—Interview 1980."

22 **"write about something that matters to people"**: Gene Sculatti, "John Cougar: No Wonder He's Feeling So Up," *Los Angeles Herald Examiner*, August 7, 1982.

23 **"In places like Youngstown, Ohio"**: "American Bandstand 1980—Interview with John Cougar Mellencamp," streamed by Awards Show Network, YouTube, 3:10, https://www.youtube.com/watch?v=p8R0vc-Jm3M.

24 **"I don't know what you guys think"**: Bruce Springsteen, *The Ties That Bind: The River Collection*, Columbia Records 88875164672, CD Box Set.

26 **"Mike [Campbell] and I discussed"**: Max Bell, "Call Tom Petty the New Springsteen and He'll Cut You," *New Musical Express*, March 1, 1980.

27 **"I was interested in what it meant to be"**: Bruce Springsteen, *Born to Run* (Simon & Schuster, 2016), 216.

27 **"When I did *The River*"**: Dave DiMartino, "Bruce Springsteen Takes It to the River: So Don't Call Him 'Boss', OK?," *Creem*, January 1981.

28 **"You should see Springsteen"**: Dave DiMartino, "Bruce Springsteen Takes It to the River."

29 **"by continuing to root his"**: Robert Cristgau, "Bruce Springsteen: The River," *Village Voice*, 1980.

29 **"It is an almost certain bet"**: Greil Marcus, "Bruce Springsteen: The Man Who Would Save Rock and Roll," *New West*, February 1981.

CHAPTER 2: 1981

32 **"just about one of the most beautiful"**: Bruce Springsteen, "Bruce Springsteen and the E Street Band Live 1975–1985," Columbia, 1986, compact disc.

32 **"give voice to the stories"**: Springsteen, *Born to Run*, 292.

34 **"[Mueller] was sort of viewed"**: Marie Cocco, "Vietnam Veterans Find a Collective Voice," *Newsday*, November 11, 1981.

35 **"Vietnam turned this"**: Bruce Springsteen, "Bruce Springsteen and the E Street Band: Los Angeles Memorial Coliseum Sept 27, 1985," nugs.net, compact disc.

35 **"staggering amount of money"**: Marc Leepson, "Saved By the Boss: How Bruce Springsteen Rescued Vietnam Veterans of America—And the Vietnam Veterans Movement," *VVA Veteran Online* (March/April 2016).

35 **"Had Bruce not come"**: Bobby Muller, interview by Stephen McKiernan, July 8, 2019, transcribed by Benjamin Mehdi So, Digital Collections, Binghamton University SUNY Libraries.

36 **"I'm going to bring out"**: Gil Kaufman, "Bruce Springsteen Returns to Stage for Stand Up for Heroes Benefit, Tells Dirty Jokes and Performs with John Mellencamp," *Billboard*, November 7, 2023.

36 **"I would laughingly say"**: Warren Zanes, *Petty: The Biography* (Henry Holt, 2015), 153.

37 **"just how a rock star should"**: "Style of the Stars '81," *People*, September 21, 1981.

38 **"You know, when you're broke"**: Dave Marsh, "Tom Petty," *Musician*, July 1981.

38 **"Tom Petty just wants to"**: Jon Marlowe, "Tom Petty: Emotions in the Dark," *Miami News*, March 2, 1983.

38 **"If you think they're booing you"**: Peter Bogdanovich, dir. *Runnin' Down a Dream: Tom Petty and the Heartbreakers*, The Bigger Picture, March 3, 2008.

38 **"I'm just amazed that"**: Marsh, "Tom Petty."

39 **"originally wanted more"**: "Inside Track," *Billboard*, October 13, 1979.

39 **"We were pretty well beat up"**: Tom Petty interview with John Tobler, Rock's Backpages audio, 1989.

39 **The dispute played out**: Springsteen, *Born to Run*, 257–59.

40 **"reached the stage where"**: Bell, "Call Tom Petty the New Springsteen and He'll Cut You."

41 **"There is no security"**: Tom Petty interview with John Tobler.

42 **"I wanted to write anthems"**: Bell, "Call Tom Petty the New Springsteen and He'll Cut You."

43 **Reagan's firing of**: Rakesh Kohchar and Stella Sechopulous, "How the American Middle Class Has Changed in the Last Five Decades," Pew Research Center, April 20, 2022.

44 **"firing of the air traffic controllers"**: Alan Greenspan, "The Reagan Legacy" (speech), Ronald Reagan Library, Simi Valley, CA, April 9, 2003, posted on Board of Governors of the Federal Reserve Board website.

44 **"it's as easy to praise"**: Wayne Robins, "Music: Tom Petty and the Heartbreakers," *Newsday*, August 8, 1981.

44 **"I think the press had a lot"**: Blair Jackson, "Just a Popular Rock N Roll Band," *Trouser Press*, August 1981.

44 **"We got a lot of letters"**: Jackson, "Just a Popular Rock N Roll Band."

45 **"I . . . want people to"**: Bell, "Call Tom Petty the New Springsteen and He'll Cut You."

46 **"If anyone wants to"**: Richard Cook, "Neil Young: When a Dinosaur Cuts Off Its Tail?" *New Musical Express*, October 9, 1982.

46 **"I stand behind Reagan"**: Adam Sweeting, "Neil Young: Legend of a Loner," *Melody Maker*, September 7, 1985.

48 **"trigger-happy cowboy"**: "Neil Young Is Backing Reagan," *Lincoln Journal Star*, October 12, 1984.

48 **"You can't always support"**: "Neil Young Is Backing Reagan."

49 **"We're having our equipment"**: Sweeting, "Neil Young: Legend of a Loner."

49 **"that had to come"**: Sweeting, "Neil Young: Legend of a Loner."

50 **"Unlike style, which for me"**: John Mellencamp, "John Mellencamp's Style Diary," *Rolling Stone*, September 16, 1999.

52 **"We had the well tested"**: "Mellencamp was in the Pink but House Was Red Alert," *Tallahassee Democrat*, June 25, 1984.

53 **"There seem to be a lot"**: David Bowie, "David Bowie Criticizes MTV for Not Playing Videos by Black Artists," interview by Mark Goodman, *MTV News*, 1983, https://www.youtube.com/watch?v=XZGiVzIr8Qg.

54 **"I made my own decisions"**: Timothy White, "The Fire This Time," *Rolling Stone*, May 1, 1980.

CHAPTER 3: 1982

56 **"We see a couple of good things"**: "Woodstock II: Promoter Can Hardly Wait for US Festival," *Camarillo Star*, August 29, 1982.

57 **One executive claimed:** Cade Metz, "Tech Time Warp of the Week: The Commodore 64–1983," *Wired*, March 15, 2013.

57 **"I think they've gotta be careful":** Bud Scoppa, "Tom Petty's Year (or Two) of Living Dangerously," *Record*, August 1985.

59 **"He came out and":** Chase Kamp, "Gregg Turkington on Punk in Tempe, the '80s, and a Band as Good as Black Flag," *Phoenix New Times*, December 7, 2012.

61 **In 2009, Mellencamp explained:** "John Mellencamp, The Modern Mortal." Interview by Terry Gross. *Fresh Air*, NPR, March 31, 2009.

62 **"He says I discovered it":** Erin Osmond original interview with Steve Berkowitz.

62 **According to Booker:** Aubrey Woods, "Co-founders of Iconic Band Remember Its Early Days," *Seymour Tribune*, December 12, 2022.

63 **"The interesting thing about":** Doug Richardson, "He Started in a Band with John Mellencamp in Small Town Indiana. One Stayed, the Other Left," *Indianapolis Star*, April 27, 2023.

64 **"It was at that point":** John Mellencamp. "John Mellencamp Performs at the White House: 3 of 11," The Obama White House, White House Celebration of Music from the Civil Rights Movement, 2010, https://www.youtube.com/watch?v=Jn0 Ne813QUU.

64 **"I think John Cougar":** Bill Holdship, "John Cougar: Pink Houses in the Midwest," *Creem*, January 1984.

64 **"Can you imagine if":** Timothy White, "John Mellencamp's Heartland," *Penthouse*, August 1985.

64 **"I always thought we were":** James Henke, "Bonnie Raitt: The Rolling Stone Interview," *Rolling Stone*, May 3, 1990.

66 **"I finally got the right band":** Steven X Rea, "Bonnie Raitt Lightens Up," *High Fidelity*, June 1982.

67 **"push her into the star spotlight":** David Letterman, "Late Night with David Letterman," CBS, April 27, 1982, Youtube video, 16:12, https://www.youtube.com/watch?v=4QMbSSIo5ik.

67 **"Why can't Bonnie Raitt":** Don Shewey, "Green Light," *Rolling Stone*, April 15, 1982.

67 **"There were inklings of":** Rea, "Bonnie Raitt Lightens Up."

68 **"Music is probably the one real magic":** Neil McCormick, "Tom Petty: A Rock Star for the Ages," *Telegraph*, June 2012.

69 **"I have a habit of going headfirst":** Dave Zimmer, "The US Festival: A Celebration of Music, Technology, and People," *BAM*, August 13, 1982.

69 **"the hookup alternated":** "The US Festival Successfully Managed a Satellite Link With . . . ," United Press International, September 5, 1982.

72 **"Even though some of":** David Gans, "Tom Petty: Hot Spell," *Hit Parader*, April 1983.

72 **"I can't stand synthesizers":** "Sounding Good: Key Man," *Rolling Stone*, July 10, 1980.

73 **Reportedly, Michael Jackson:** Craig Marks and Rob Tannenbaum, *I Want My MTV* (Penguin, 2011), 106.

73 **"As I saw it":** Zanes, *Petty: The Biography*, 180.

74 **"There are two parts":** "Bruce Springsteen Knows About Loneliness and Fandom: He Took on Both at TIFF," *Toronto Star*, September 3, 2019.

74 **He was also on the brink:** Springsteen, *Born to Run*, 309.

75 **"felt as conspicuous":** Springsteen, *Born to Run*, 296, 297.

76 **"I was getting back into":** Guitar Center interview with Max Weinberg, YouTube video, September 7, 2017, 3:18, https://www.youtube.com/watch?v=E5I8M6xM DV0.

77 **Over the eight years:** Stephen L. Schwartz, *Atomic Audit: The Cost and Consequences of US Nuclear Weapons* (Brookings Institution Press, 1998), 318.

78 **"You know, my music":** Dave Marsh, "Bruce Springsteen," *Musician*, February 1981.

79 **"most complete and probably":** Greil Marcus, "Real Life Rock," *New West*, November 1982.

79 **"You sent me the":** Brian Hiatt, *Bruce Springsteen: The Stories Behind the Songs* (Abrams, 2019).

80 **"I had just finished a rough":** David Michael Kennedy interview with Snap Galleries, accessed February 2023, https://www.snapgalleries.com/product/david-michael-kennedy-bruce-springsteen-nebraska-album-cover-photograph/.

80 **"fear that they are":** Charles Alexander, "Gathering Gloom for Workers," *Time*, December 14, 1981.

82 **"I see it all around me":** Gary Graff and Bruce Britt, "Recession Rockets Passion Back Into Pop," *Daily Press*, April 17, 1983.

83 **"If you get too close":** Bill Holdship, "Bob Seger: Big Victories," *Creem*, May 1983.

86 **"We simply didn't want":** Holdship, "Bob Seger: Big Victories."

86 **"He said he liked it!":** Steve Pond, "Bob Seger: Nice Guy in the Nasty Lane," *Rolling Stone*, February 3, 1983.

CHAPTER 4: 1983

88 **"Is this a picture of Cleveland?":** Dick Clark, *American Bandstand*, accessed via archive.org, December 10, 1983, 13:44.

90 **"I don't go to PTA meetings":** Christopher Connelly, "Hey John Cougar, What's Your Problem," *Rolling Stone*, December 9, 1982.

90 **"I'm not gonna hang":** Connelly, "Hey John Cougar, What's Your Problem."

90 **"I find out that before I got on":** Holdship, "John Cougar: Pink Houses in the Midwest."

90 **"It was inaccurate reporting":** Holdship, "John Cougar: Pink Houses in the Midwest."

91 **"It was the woman not accepting":** Holdship, "John Cougar: Pink Houses in the Midwest."

92 **According to drummer Kenny Aronoff:** Kenny Aronoff, *Sex, Drums, Rock 'n' Roll! The Hardest Hitting Man in Show Business* (Backbeat Books, 2016).

93 **"I loved it," Aronoff said:** Steve Newton, "Drum Great Kenny Aronoff Was Never Afraid to Go for It," November 25, 1999, reposted on Ear of Newt.

94 **"real contented look":** Bob Batz, "John Cougar Mellencamp Is Back Home in Indiana," *Dayton Daily News*, March 11, 1984.

94 **"there is racism physically built":** April Ryan interview with Pete Buttigieg for the Grio, April 6, 2021.

94 **"The majority of the public":** Holdship, "John Cougar: Pink Houses in the Midwest."

95 **"the message of hope":** Ronald Reagan, "Remarks at Reagan-Bush Rally in Hammonton, New Jersey," American Presidency Project, September 19, 1984, https://www.presidency.ucsb.edu/documents/remarks-reagan-bush-rally-hammonton-new-jersey.

95 **"White House officials called us":** Peter Holt, "Rocking for Reagan," *London Evening Standard*, February 15, 1984.

95 **"I don't know anything":** Sandra Vaugh, "Name May Change but Mellencamp Image Stays Rock Solid," *Commercial Appeal*, March 9, 1984.

95 **"Reagan doesn't know nothin'":** Timothy White, "John Mellencamp's Heartland," *Penthouse*, August 1985.

96 **"Mr. Mellencamp's views"**: "John Mellencamp: No 'Pink Houses' for NOM," Prop 8 Trial Tracker, October 4, 2010, https://web.archive.org/web/20101006185433 /http://prop8trialtracker.com/2010/10/04/john-mellencamp-no-pink-houses-for -nom/.

96 **"has always been country"**: Tim Roland, "Scrappy John Mellencamp Is Everywhere in Country Music: 'There's a Part of Us That All Want to Be Like Him,'" *Billboard*, August 21, 2018.

97 **"I looked onstage and thought"**: Erin Osmon, "John Mellencamp Shows No Signs of Cheering Up," *Los Angeles Times*, June 12, 2023.

97 **"It's about everything in between"**: Roland, "Scrappy John Mellencamp Is Everywhere in Country Music."

103 **"If we'd remained independent"**: Robbin Eggar, "X: Guitars Against the Golden State," *The Face*, April 1984.

104 **"There's all the politics"**: Blake Gumprecht, "Rank and File," *Alternative America*, Winter 1983.

104 **"I just always felt"**: Erin Osmon original interview with Dave Alvin.

105 **"There was this jingoistic"**: Erin Osmon original interview with Dave Alvin.

105 **"I'd refer to us"**: Bob Andelman, "X Marks the Spot Where Exene Cervenka Is Happiest," *Tampa Bay Times*, December 2, 1983.

106 **"For us it was the Ramones"**: Eggar, "X: Guitars Against the Golden State."

108 **"to a stripper beat"**: Miles Giles, "The Strange Saga of Dylan's First Letterman Gig," *Vulture*, May 19, 2015.

109 **"Because of music videos"**: Mary Anna Feczo, "A Legendary Ad Man Makes Rock Vid with Substance," *Musician*, September 1984.

109 **"This is Bobby saying"**: Feczo, "A Legendary Ad Man Makes Rock Vid with Substance."

110 **"We had to be in the new wave"**: *Tom Petty and the Heartbreakers: Runnin' Down a Dream*, directed by Peter Bogdanavich (2007; Warner Bros.), DVD.

CHAPTER 5: 1984

111 **"Just the opposite"**: "Johnson Conquers the Eleventh Event," *Boston Globe*, July 30, 1984.

114 **"It could be one of"**: Sam Sutherland, "Yetnikoff 'Reasonably Optimistic,'" *Billboard*, March 19, 1983.

114 **Separately, the head of:** Richard Harrington, "The Vinyl Days," *Washington Post*, October 25, 1986.

117 **"The Japanese may have"**: Erin Osmon original interview with John Mutz.

117 **"The 'blue collar worker'"**: "Push for High Tech Industry in Indiana's Future," *Daily Reporter*, May 18, 1983.

119 **"I remember people who were"**: Erin Osmon original interview with John MacDonald.

119 **"The people that I run into"**: Erin Osmon original interview with Mike Mitchell.

124 **"Some wild things"**: "Open Air Festival Loreley," produced by Rockpalast on August 25, 1984, https://www.youtube.com/watch?v=-uUbfDR5jPk.

125 **"accessible metaphor"**: Nancy Mitchess, "Vigilance as Metaphor: The Foreign Policy of Ronald Reagan," *SAIS Review* 5, no. 2 (Summer–Fall 1985).

125 **"Little Steven shared concerns"**: Maureen Minter, "'Little Steven' Sings Out His Conscience in Rock and Roll at Arts Center," *Bernardsville News*, July 26, 1984.

125 **"I don't think you should take"**: Minter, "'Little Steven' Sings Out His Conscience in Rock and Roll at Arts Center."

126 **"I deeply respect"**: Robert Cristgau, "Voice of America," *Village Voice*, 1984.

126 **"In the 1980s," he told:** Jeffrey Goldberg, "The Way We Live Now: 12–26–99: Encounter; The Coolest Guy in All of Jersey," *New York Times*, December 26, 1999.

126 **"Guitar solos, to me":** Michael Fremer, "Don Henley Finds His Thrill at The Sunset Grill," interview from 1984, reposted on Analog Planet, April 30, 2009.

127 **"I remember sitting at":** Paul Zollo, *Conversations with Tom Petty* (Omnibus Press, 2020), 105.

127 **"working in bulk":** Zanes, *Petty: The Biography*, 190.

127 **"Jimmy called me":** Dirt Floor Recording & Production, "Why We Love the Linn-Drum!" Facebook video, February 24, 2024, 7:00, https://www.facebook.com/watch /?v=924880079098049.

129 **Henley was taken into custody:** "Names & Faces," *Detroit Free Press*, November 26, 1980.

129 **"just flat-out lied' ":** Christopher Connelly, "The Second Life of Don Henley," *GQ*, August 1991.

129 **"clobbered in the press":** Connelly, "The Second Life of Don Henley."

131 **"We go out to the car":** Brian Koppelman, "Mike Campbell," *The Moment with Brian Koppelman*, podcast published by Gemini XIII, October 27, 2020.

131 **"Are you somebody?":** Fremer, "Don Henley Finds His Thrill at The Sunset Grill."

132 **"The way people relate":** Fremer, "Don Henley Finds His Thrill at The Sunset Grill."

133 **"completely incorrigible":** Daina Darzin, "Bryan Adams Reached Limelight from the Gutter," *Sacramento Bee*, August 4, 1985.

135 **"for if ever a glass of shandy":** David Quantick, "Canada Bry on the Rocks!" *New Musical Express*, May 4, 1985.

135 **"Bryan Adams could be":** Darzin, "Bryan Adams Reached Limelight from the Gutter."

135 **"The U.S.A. may have":** Craig MacInnis, "45,000 Fans Carry a Flag for Bryan Adams," *Toronto Star*, September 23, 1985.

135 **"And after more than a decade":** Jon Pareles, "Bryan Adams, More Mr. Nice Guy," *New York Times*, March 8, 1994.

136 **"smidgen of androgyny":** George F. Will, "Bruce Springsteen's U.S.A.," *Washington Post*, September 12, 1984.

137 **"Like Springsteen, Adams brings":** MacInnis, "45,000 Fans Carry a Flag for Bryan Adams."

137 **"It was an evening":** MacInnis, "45,000 Fans Carry a Flag for Bryan Adams."

138 **"Well, I was going":** Lauren Sarner, "Bryan Adams Confirms 'Provocative' Meaning of the Song 'Summer of '69': Fans Are 'Thick,' " *New York Post*, December 11, 2023.

CHAPTER 6: 1985

141 **"It makes no sense whatsoever":** Bill Holdship, "John Cougar Mellencamp: Working Class Hero in the Rumble Seat," *Creem*, February 1986.

142 **"I mouthed back to him":** Erin Osmon original interview with Maria McKee.

143 **"I mean, we know in the end":** Edwin Pouncey, "The Replacements Drink and Drive," *Sounds*, November 9, 1985.

144 **"It's a really weird":** Bill Holdship, "R.E.M. Rock Reconstruction Getting There," *Creem*, September 1985.

144 **"You also see a lot of people":** Bill Holdship, "John Cougar Mellencamp: Growing Up in Public," *Creem*, December 1987.

147 **"I think I was trying":** Zanes, *Petty: The Biography*, 182.

148 **"When I hear that one":** Zanes, *Petty: The Biography*, 188.

148 **"We used to have dogs"**: Tom Petty interview with John Tobler, Rock's Backpages audio, 1989.

150 **"A lot of the people that"**: Stereo Williams, "Tom Petty's Remarkable Stand Against the Confederate Flag," *Daily Beast*, October 7, 2017.

150 **"I wish I had given it"**: Andy Greene, "Tom Petty on Past Confederate Flag Use: 'It Was Downright Stupid,'" *Rolling Stone*, July 14, 2015.

151 **More than nine hundred male farmers**: "Farmer Suicide Rate Swells in the 1980s, Study Says," Associated Press, republished in *New York Times*, October 14, 1991.

151 **By the end of the decade**: Bernt Nelson, "Echoes of '80s Farm Crisis in Current Economy," Market Intel report, American Farm Bureau Federation website, October 4, 2024.

153 **"I hope for a moment"**: "John Cougar Mellencamp in Chillicothe, MO 1986," YouTube video, published by Adammas Productions, original video shot by F. R. Bailey, posted December 2, 2019, https://www.youtube.com/watch?v=DD0gmTs43aE.

153 **"I believe we need"**: Matt Glidden, "A Look Back: John Mellencamp Rallies with Missouri Farmers," Farm Aid website, May 2018, updated January 13, 2020.

155 **"I don't have a smooth voice"**: "John Mellencamp—1985 Scarecrow Tour Feature," YouTube video, published by the account Vintage Mellencamp, December 16, 2015, https://www.youtube.com/watch?v=DD0gmTs43aE.

156 **"He pushes people to their limit"**: Aronoff, *Sex, Drums, Rock 'n' Roll!*, 119.

157 **"There was one kid"**: David Fricke, "John Cougar Mellencamp: The Comeback Kid," *Rolling Stone*, January 31, 1986.

158 **"Our songs always came about"**: Andy Greene, "John Mellencamp: My Life in 15 Songs," *Rolling Stone*, December 23, 2013.

158 **"With this record"**: "John Mellencamp Discusses the 'Scarecrow' Album and Tour in 1985," YouTube video, MTV interview published by the account Vintage Mellencamp, posted July 7, 2018, https://www.youtube.com/watch?v=6bug-sZPPuU.

158 **"At its best"**: Jimmy Gutterman, "Scarecrow," *Rolling Stone*, September 26, 1985.

160 **"Agriculture must mediate"**: Wendell Berry, *Bringing It to the Table: On Farming and Food* (Counterpoint, 2009), 175.

161 **"You never see a show"**: Robert Hilburn, "Rock, Country Played as One," *Los Angeles Times*, September 28, 1985.

162 **"For those people that need it"**: Neil Young interview with Adam Sweeting, Rock's Backpages Audio, August 1985.

165 **A 2004 report**: Peter Dreier, "Reagan's Legacy: Homelessness in America," *Shelterforce*, May 1, 2004.

165 **"eliminated general revenue"**: Dreier, "Reagan's Legacy: Homelessness in America."

167 **"Willie and I both"**: Neil Young, interview by Adam Sweeting, Rock's Backpages audio, August 1985, mp3, https://www.rocksbackpages.com/Library/Article/neil-young-1985.

168 **"I spoke to a lot"**: Margaret Trimer, "Seeds of Concern Are Sown, but Will They Take Root?" *Detroit Free Press*, September 24, 1985.

169 **"Our emphasis—and this is something"**: David Zimmerman, "The Country and Rock Worlds Reach Out to Solve the Crisis," *USA Today*, September 20, 1985.

169 **"Do not give the money to politicians"**: Zimmerman, "The Country and Rock Worlds Reach Out to Solve the Crisis."

170 **"I guess they stole our idea"**: Gary Graff, "Concert Had Them Talking," *Detroit Free Press*, September 24, 1985.

172 **"I learned so much from Bob Dylan"**: Neil McCormick, "Tom Petty: A Rock Star for the Ages," *Telegraph*, June 16, 2012.

CHAPTER 7: 1986

175 **"I'm really glad I did it now":** Martin Kielty, "Bob Seger's Proud That 'Like a Rock' Sold a Lot of Trucks," *Ultimate Classic Rock*, July 28, 2019.

175 **"Never before in 25 years":** "From the Archives: 1986 Space Shuttle Challenger Explosion," CBS Evening News with Dan Rather, January 28, 1986, https://www.youtube.com/watch?v=hgA4HUfpyF4.

176 **"all part of the process":** Ronald Reagan, "Address to the Nation on the Explosion of the Space Shuttle Challenger," Ronald Reagan Presidential Library and Museum, January 28, 1986.

181 **"a campaign to communicate":** "Chevy's Most Enduring Campaigns: How the Ideas Took Roots," *Ad Age*, October 31, 2011.

181 **"Detroit's down right now":** Talbert, "Seger's Song Revs Chevy's Heartbeat."

182 **"came to hate Bob Seger":** George Vecsey, "Sports of The Times; 3-Point Shot Has Caused Blitz of Ads," *New York Times*, March 29, 1992.

183 **"go into the witness protection program":** "Chevy: Too Many Truck Ads?" *Newsweek*, October 27, 2007, https://www.newsweek.com/chevy-too-many-truck-ads-103009.

183 **Jeep subsequently pulled:** Clemence Michallon, "Bruce Springsteen Reflects on DWI Arrest for First Time as He Returns to Broadway, 'I Was Thrown in Jail,'" *Independent*, June 28, 2021.

185 **"I just felt like we should":** "Bob Seger Talks about His Greatest Hits, Family, Touring, and More," radio interview on Kaedy's Classics on October 13, 1994, YouTube video published by 97.1 River, posted May 6, 2024, https://www.youtube.com/watch?v=rIVfRs1kvfI.

188 **"It's autobiographical in the sense":** Ralph Traitor, "Steve Earle: Highway Patrolman," *Sounds*, June 20, 1987.

188 **"I consider myself to be a straggler":** Traitor, "Steve Earle: Highway Patrolman."

189 **"In the end, you either":** Robert Hulburn, "Steve Earle: Working-Class Songs from the Texas Soil," *Los Angeles Times*, July 20, 1986.

190 **"one of the young Turks":** "Farm Aid: The Line Up," *Austin-American Statesman*, July 3, 1986.

190 **"Well, I'm old":** Andy Greene, "Bruce Springsteen Breaks Down His R&B Covers LP—and Responds to Fan Outrage Over Ticket Prices," *Rolling Stone*, November 18, 2022.

192 **"I didn't just record things":** Annie Zaleski, "How R.E.M. Took a Big Step Forward with 'Lifes Rich Pageant,'" *Diffuser*, July 28, 2016.

193 **"place is very important":** Stuart Tomlinson, "R.E.M.: Songs with Stories," *The Oregonian*, October 3, 1986.

193 **"I think it's a little more topical":** "R.E.M.," *Austin-American Statesman*, September 18, 1986.

193 **"This is a song which":** "R.E.M. 'Underneath the Bunker' @ Pinkpop 1989," YouTube video published by heidigretel, posted June 9, 2009, https://www.youtube.com/watch?v=Nm3-BRM1Zk8.

194 **"This band is like talking to one guy":** Michael Goldberg, "Tom Petty: Back on the Road," *Rolling Stone*, January 16, 1986.

196 **"a Heartbreakers' fave rave":** John Swenson, "Tom Petty Puts Egos Aside and Lets the Music Happen," *Knoxville News-Sentinel*, May 22, 1987.

197 **"dark and loud and dirty":** Richard Cromelin, "The BoDeans: Odd Match, Hot Harmony," *Los Angeles Times*, January 4, 1987.

200 **"Tom Petty basically says":** Erin Osmon original interview with Maria McKee.

200 **"a male Rickie Lee Jones":** Joel Selvin, "Huey Pauses from Album to Visit the Country," *San Francisco Examiner*, April 13, 1986.

201 **"I decided for the first time ever":** Brennan Matthews, "A Conversation with Bruce Hornsby," *Route Magazine*, November 2022.

201 **A star is signed:** "Limelight," *Virginia Gazette*, September 18, 1985.

202 **"In my town he was":** Andy Gill, "Bruce Hornsby: The Virginian," *New Musical Express*, October 25, 1986.

203 **"All of those writers":** "Bruce Hornsby: The Way It Is," YouTube Video published by Top 2000 A Go Go (Dutch Public Television), original video published in 2014, posted to YouTube February 16, 2018, https://www.youtube.com/watch?v=kKZw1ur2CsM.

203 **"It was totally unexpected":** "Bruce Hornsby: The Way It Is."

204 **"I was sort of floored":** Ben Westhoff, "Bruce Hornsby on TuPac: The Original 'Changes' Was a Lot Dirtier," *LA Weekly*, September 12, 2011.

205 **"He wanted to come down":** Helen Brown, "My Entire Class Cheered When Kennedy Was Assassinated: I Felt Awful," *Independent*, August 28, 2020.

205 **"I'd like to know":** Tim Grierson, "How 'The Way It Is' Became an Unlikely Soundtrack to the Black Lives Matter Movement," *MEL Magazine*, 2020.

CHAPTER 8: 1987

206 **"It's horrible to think":** Holdship, "John Cougar Mellencamp: Growing Up in Public."

206 **Never mind that Reagan's:** Timothy Noah, "Ronald Reagan's Family Values: What the Diaries Show," *Slate*, May 3, 2007.

208 **"Everything in my secure little world":** Holdship, "John Cougar Mellencamp: Growing Up in Public."

210 **"I began to think, 'Who in the hell' ":** Robert Hilburn, "The Growing Up of Mr. Mellencamp," *Los Angeles Times*, February 28, 1988.

211 **"This is the first record":** " 'Lonesome Jubilee': A Glimpse of Rural America," *Times*, November 19, 1987.

213 **"Not comfortable at all":** Robert Byrd, "Oprah Winfrey Brings Her Show to Forsyth County," Associated Press, February 9, 1987.

215 **"What's really disgusting":** Greg Kot, "Mellencamp Grew Up but Has Yet to Give In," *Chicago Tribune*, November 29, 1987.

215 **"The title refers to ordinary victories":** "Mellencamp Sings Song of Underdogs, Tries to Help Out," *Palm Beach Post*, October 6, 1987.

216 **"an oddly paced":** Jon Pareles, "Bob Dylan and Tom Petty," *New York Times*, July 17, 1986.

216 **A reviewer for *The Globe and Mail*:** Charles Bermant, "Glitches Add Spontaneity to Bob Dylan and Tom Petty Show," *Globe and Mail*, 1986.

217 **"The rules of the session":** John Swenson, "Tom Petty Puts Egos Aside and Lets the Music Happen," *Knoxville News-Sentinel*, May 22, 1987.

218 **"the most turbulent":** Les Brown, "Five Tumultuous Years," Field Guide '87, *Channels: The Business of Communications* (1987): 8.

219 **"Being a songwriter now in 1986":** Swenson, "Tom Petty Puts Egos Aside and Lets the Music Happen."

220 **In 1983, the League of United Latin American Citizens:** "Reagan Policies Criticized for Hurting US Hispanics," *Christian Science Monitor*, August 25, 1983.

222 **"We love this stuff":** Gazette News Services, " 'La Bamba' Score Handled Lovingly," *Billings Gazette*, August 1, 1987.

222 **"We decided to take":** "100 Best Albums of the '80s," *Rolling Stone*, November 16, 1989.

223 **"the group that vaulted"**: Augustin Gurza, "Partying with the Homeboys," *Los Angeles Times*, May 6, 1985.

226 **"It never worked for me"**: Wayne Bledsoe, "Perfectly Good Career," *Chapel Hill Herald*, December 26, 1993.

226 **"The real artists, like Ry"**: *John Hiatt: Professional Musician*, music documentary from 1987, posted to Vimeo in 2017, https://vimeo.com/203121417.

228 **"I love the lyrics"**: Natalie Weiner, "30 Years of 'Nick of Time,'" *Billboard*, March 21, 2019.

229 **"Songwriting for me"**: *John Hiatt: Professional Musician*.

230 **"You take a kid from driving a truck"**: Tom Schnabel and Marion Hodges, "Robbie Robertson on Fame, God, and American Mythology," KCRW, interview conducted in 1987, transcribed and posted on KCRW.com, September 14, 2023.

231 **"It smelled different"**: Nicholas Jennings, "Robbie Robertson: Songs of a Native Son," *McClean's*, November 1987.

231 **"He jumped over about 20 people"**: "Rick Danko on His Interaction with Bruce Springsteen and a Performance of the Band Playing 'Atlantic City' at the Nightjazz Festival Bergen, Norway, 1994," Facebook video posted by The Band: A History on February 8, 2024, https://www.facebook.com/watch/?v=916532263449139.

232 **"I can't just make a record"**: Michael Goldberg, "The Second Coming of Robbie Robertson," *Rolling Stone*, November 19, 1987.

232 **"You end up creating"**: James Henke, "Bruce Springsteen Leaves E Street: The Rolling Stone Interview," *Rolling Stone*, August 6, 1992.

232 **"the angels and devils"**: Springsteen, *Born to Run*, 349.

232 **"didn't feel right imposing"**: Chris Willman, "Robbie Robertson Rides Again," *Los Angeles Times*, November 1, 1987.

233 **"Native Americans' assistance"**: Ronald Reagan, "Proclamation 5745—American Indian Week, 1987" (speech), November 9, 1987, Ronald Reagan Presidential Library & Museum.

233 **"how they evolve amid"**: "Bernie Speaks 14: American Indian Movement, Vernon Bellecourt," YouTube video published by Town Meeting TV, video originally produced March 27, 1987, https://www.youtube.com/watch?v=Vtm2ePzsVB0.

234 **"All these years later"**: Karen Bliss, "Robbie Robertson on Why He Kept Quiet for Years About His Heritage," *Samaritan Mag*, February 1, 2017.

235 **"That was really hard to do"**: "Bruce Springsteen Inside Tunnel of Love on VH1," YouTube video published by Pointeblanc91, VH1 video originally aired in 1988, https://www.youtube.com/watch?v=Ms1q_1m69ng.

236 **"It's not a total coincidence"**: Rob Tannenbaum, "Daniel Lanois: The Producer as Conscience," *Musician*, December 1986.

237 **"I'm like, 'What the fuck'"**: David Remnick, "We Are Alive," *New Yorker*, July 30, 2012.

238 **"keep playing roulette"**: Geoffrey Himes, "Tougher Than Most: Bruce Springsteen's 'Tunnel of Love' Tour," *Baltimore Sun*, March 1988.

239 **"I wanted for him to go"**: A. D. Amorosi, "Martin Scorsese on Working with Robbie Robertson on 'Flower Moon' Music as the Culmination of a 47-Year Friendship," *Variety*, January 16, 2024.

CHAPTER 9: 1988

240 **"Well, who's making the rules?"**: Arion Berger, "Music," *LA Weekly*, November 10, 1988.

242 **According to the CDC**: "Current Trends Mortality Attributable to HIV Infection/

AIDS—United States, 1981–1990," report by the Centers for Disease Control, January 25, 1991.

245 **"As a child, I always had a sense"**: Steve Pond, "Tracy Chapman: On Her Own Terms," *Rolling Stone*, September 22, 1988.

245 **"I want to reach beyond that"**: Lucy O'Brien, "She's Gotta Ticket: Tracy Chapman," *City Limits*, May 5, 1998.

245 **"It was exactly the same feeling"**: Pond, "Tracy Chapman: On Her Own Terms."

247 **"It's time to stop thinking"**: Kristine McKenna, "The Resilience of Bonnie Raitt," *Los Angeles Times*, April 30, 1989.

249 **"The Federal Penitentiary had a dome"**: Melissa Etheridge, *The Truth Is* (Villard, 2001), 7.

250 **The US prison population:** ACLU, "Race and the War on Drugs," position paper published October 17, 2003.

250 **"This bill helps us"**: Ronald Reagan, "Remarks on Signing the Anti-Drug Abuse Act of 1988" (speech), November 18, 1988, Ronald Reagan Presidential Library & Museum.

250 **"I thought, 'Prisons must be a place'"**: "Johnny Cash's Historic Visit to Leavenworth: A Legendary Prison Concert," kcyesterday.com, https://kcyesterday.com/articles/johnny-cash-leavenworth?srsltid=AfmBOop227hGoKCgeXl8vBttb-ca1V0aPUCm3PECVJQLOtfe9B1Fy9RNc.

250 **"This is the same"**: Dave Steinfeld, "Unbreakable: A Chat with Melissa Etheridge," *Rock and Roll Globe*, July 31, 2024.

252 **"moment of acceptance"**: Arlene M. Schneider, "Melissa Etheridge: Debut Disc Wins Grammy Nod," *Asbury Park Press*, February 12, 1989.

253 **"I think this will be the year"**: Craig MacInnis, "Melissa Etheridge: A Thinking Woman's Singer," *Toronto Star*, September 4, 1988.

254 **"I remember standing on stage"**: Etheridge, *The Truth Is*, 20.

254 **"I'm trying to get something together"**: Neil Strauss, "Melissa Etheridge—She's Everywhere," *New York Times News Service*, December 15, 1994.

257 **"Rough Trade caught me"**: Sean O'Hagan, "Lucinda Williams: Walking the Line," *New Musical Express*, May 20, 1989.

258 **"At the heart of what I do"**: Dave Simpson, "Lucinda Williams: I Hated the Way Major Labels Made My Music Sound," *Guardian*, June 1, 2023.

259 **"so at home in blues and country"**: Robert Christgau, "Lucinda Williams," *Village Voice*, November 8, 1988.

259 **"lets you hear plenty"**: Steve Pond, "Lucinda Williams," *Rolling Stone*, January 26, 1989.

259 **"They make such a big deal"**: "Lucinda Williams: Hard-Living, Hard-Loving Tunes," *Atlanta Journal and Constitution*, March 17, 1989.

260 **"It just blew my mind"**: Peter Larsen, "How Lucinda Williams' Friendship with Tom Petty Led to Touring with Mike Campbell," *Orange County Register*, September 23, 2024.

260 **"And thank God"**: John Bream, "Mellencamp Not Down Singing Blues," *Daily Oklahoman*, June 13, 2003.

261 **"Prince called me up"**: "Bonnie Raitt Quit Drinking and Lost 20 Pounds for Prince Collab," *Kelly Clarkson Show*, video posted to YouTube in 2022, https://www.youtube.com/watch?v=tcQL5xsWfJg.

261 **"For a long time"**: Mark Bego, *Bonnie Raitt: Just in the Nick of Time* (Birch Lane Press, 1995), 125.

CHAPTER 10: 1989

265 **"There are those who use"**: DeNeen L. Brown, "Willie Horton–Style Campaigning? Here's Where It First Came From," *Washington Post*, November 4, 2022.

265 **"naked cruelty"**: "Gravely Ill, Atwater Offers Apology," Associated Press, January 13, 1991.

272 **"I'm not convinced"**: Stephen Holden, "Mellencamp's Empty Success," *New York Times*, May 12, 1989.

273 **"Vicky looks sad"**: Anthony DeCurtis, "John Mellencamp's Void in the Heartland," *Rolling Stone*, June 29, 1989.

273 **"it may be interesting"**: "Mellencamp's No Different," Associated Press, November 1, 1989.

273 **"I don't have anything against corporations"**: "Endorsements," *Fort Worth Star-Telegram*, September 11, 1988.

274 **"I just can't believe"**: DeCurtis, "John Mellencamp's Void in the Heartland."

276 **"It sounds like it was produced"**: Bill Forman, "James McMurtry on Lou Reed, Gun Control and Why Leonard Cohen Must Die," *Colorado Springs Independent*, February 13, 2013.

277 **"I'm here to champion"**: Mark Cooper, "Bonnie Raitt: Raitt's Progress," *Daily Telegraph*, May 26, 1990.

277 **"I was virtually"**: "Grammy Award with Bonnie Raitt for Album of the Year," YouTube video published by the Grammy Museum, original video published in 1989, posted to YouTube March 16, 2016, https://www.youtube.com/watch?v=6FbPxp0me7Y.

279 **"rhythm and grief"**: Bego, *Bonnie Raitt: Just in the Nick of Time*, 133.

AFTERWORD

283 **"This is the key to the engine"**: "The Gaslight Anthem Discuss Bruce Springsteen—Hangin' Out on E Street," YouTube video posted by Bruce Springsteen's official account, published in 2009, https://www.youtube.com/watch?v=fle652O3caw.

284 **"You know, I have become"**: Richard Cromelin, "10 Questions: John Mellencamp," *Los Angeles Times*, November 10, 1991.

285 **"We need ya!"**: Mark Binelli, "Bruce Springsteen's American Gospel," *Rolling Stone*, August 22, 2002.

287 **"Meeting your heroes"**: "The Hold Steady on Springsteen," YouTube video published by MOGvideos, posted in 2009, https://www.youtube.com/watch?v=2yzWyRKWts0.

INDEX

Page numbers in *italics* refer to illustrations.